THE CHRISTIA

Edith
with love from Bell

THE CHRISTIAN GOD

W.S. RHODES

I.S.P.C.K.
1998

THE CHRISTIAN GOD—Published by the Indian Society for Promoting Christian Knowledge (ISPCK), Post Box 1585, Kashmere Gate, Delhi-110006.

Laser typeset by : ISPCK, Post Box 1585, 1654, Madarsa Road, Kashmere Gate, Delhi-110006.
Tel. : 2966323 *Fax :* 011-2965490

Printed at : Cambridge Press, Kashmere Gate, Delhi-110006.

Contents

Preface

The book is on the nature and reality of God. These are topics which have been discussed for hundreds of years by philosophers and theologians. But contributions to the discussion are still being made. And the issues can be set out plainly so that they can be readily grasped by people without specialized knowledge.

In writing the book a great deal of help was received by many people. The first draft was read with great care by Professor Friedrich Huber of Wuppertal. He made numerous suggestions all of which I adopted. Dr Agnes Huber also made valuable comments. Since then the book has changed a great deal; a lot of what they read has been removed and a lot they did not read has been added. But the value of their comment remains. The late Dr. H.J. Taylor very carefully went over Chapter III and saved me from a number of errors.

Some of the issues discussed have come up in a different form in lectures and discussions at Serampore College. Both staff and students have put their fingers on points which were unclear or confused.

I owe a special debt to members of the Overseas Missionary Fellowship who were at the London headquarters some years ago. They made me very welcome and gave me every facility during the months I worked on the historical material in their archives.

I am also indebted to my own family. My daughter Margaret Burnett, herself a writer, went through the book in great detail and made numerous suggestions for improvement. My daughter Carol, an artist, prepared the map and also made suggestions about the writing. But my greatest debt is to my wife Helen for her interest and patience and encouragement through the long gestation period as well as for perceptive criticisms.

I am very grateful to Mrs Valeria Chuter who typed the book. She incorporated a great many amendments and was always ready to type another draft.

I am most grateful to the Drummond Trust, 3 Pitt Terrace, Stirling, for a grant.

Especially I would like to thank Mr Ashish Amos, General Secretary of the ISPCK, for this graciousness and kindness. I also greatly appreciate his efficiency; few books must have been ready for publication in so short a time.

W.S. Rhodes

Chapter I
The Basic Concept of God

All world religions believe that there is more to reality than the world of space and time. It is not simply that there is more than material objects; the world itself contains other things. We ourselves have spiritual characteristics as well as bodily ones. The religious belief is something else. It is that the world, with its spiritual characteristics as well as its material ones, constitutes one order of reality. Connected with it but distinct from it is another. Attempts have been made to retain religion while denying that there is any further order of reality. Whether it is possible to found a religious way of life on that basis is an open question and this is not the place to discuss it. But with that proviso it can be said that all religions, in one way or another, believe that the world, by which is meant the entire spatio-temporal process in all its aspects, is not all there is.

For most religions this further order of reality is the Divine. Having said that the question at once arises as to how the Divine is to be thought of. In the early stages of religion the predominant view is anthropomorphic. The gods, or God, are represented in human form. Sometimes the representation is in animal form. In the Bible there is a remarkable development. There is no development in a philosophical direction. But in serious thought and worship anthropomorphic representations are discarded. The Ten Commandments permit no image of God. And in the tabernacle and the temple there is no image in the most holy place, the sanctum of the Divine presence. In practical religious life the anthropomorphic features of early religion are retained.

The prophets, for example, in their preaching make use of anthropomorphic images such as God's eyes or his hand. But in worship God is imageless.

The Old Testament tradition has two important things to say in this connection. First, God is incomprehensible. Comprehension of the sort we have to do with here depends on comparison; to understand something we want to know what it is like. If we can get a model which has some significant likeness to what we are concerned with we feel that we have some understanding of it. But there is nothing with which God can be compared. As it is put in the book of Isaiah (40.18), "To whom then will you liken God, or what likeness compare with him?" It is not only that God cannot be pictured; he cannot be understood. We have no idea, and can have no idea, of God's essential nature. This fundamental insight is brought out by allowing no images in worship. The Christian Church has often not kept to this prohibition and it has generally allowed mental images of what God is in himself. Perhaps in consequence many people have been misled. They have thought, and do still think, of God as an almighty and everlasting person, who is pure spirit, somewhere beyond the world. That is taken to be God in his essential being. It is far from the orthodox Christian view. But many people suppose that it is and do not find it credible.

The second thing that the Old Testament tradition has to say is that in practical religious life we have to make use of symbols. In devotion and practical obedience we need to use images and words which draw their meaning from human life. There can be no objection to their use once the main point is grasped: God's essential nature is incomprehensible to us and cannot be represented in any way. Yet while we do not know what God is in himself there are things we know about him in his relationship with the world and with ourselves. That means that there are characteristics which we do know. And this is the kind of knowledge which really concerns us: whether God knows about us and cares about us, for example, and whether he has power over events in the world. Knowledge of this sort is possible and can be expressed in images and in words whose meaning comes from human life.

To have such knowledge and to be able to express it in images and words is important for religious life. Without it a command like, "You shall love the Lord your God with all your heart, and with all your soul, and with all your might" (Deuteronomy 6.5) cannot be obeyed in the way intended. The object of love must be something with a definite content and one which can be grasped. Symbols, for example, Lord and Father enable us to do that. And they carry with them the sense that they are not being used in the ordinary way. They do not have the full meaning of their ordinary usage, and they point, as all religious symbols do, to something more than the words themselves express.

Most of the symbols used to enable us to relate to the Divine are anthropomorphic. There is nothing wrong with the use of anthropomorphic symbols so long as it is clear that they are symbols and not descriptions. In one way the cruder the anthropomorphic symbols are the better. It is the more abstract and sophisticated ones that are liable to deceive us into thinking that they are descriptions. If we say, "Underneath are the everlasting arms", there is no temptation to take the phrase literally. If we speak, as we do, of the mind of God, there is. The appropriateness of the term disguises the fact that God's mentality must be utterly different from ours. He does not begin with material supplied by the sense organs; he does not have to weigh up one thing against another and then decide; his feelings cannot be the same as ours. Images and words which get their meaning from life in this world have to be used if we are to say anything about God. But we have to be careful to remember that both are symbols and not to be taken literally.

The knowledge that we have about God has to be brought into relation with other knowledge. Unless this is done religion becomes a more or less separate compartment of life. Sometimes religious knowledge is kept apart from secular knowledge because it is felt to be threatening. The need to relate them is far from being only a modern issue. As soon as the Christian message was taken from Palestine into the Greek speaking world the question arose as to how it was to be related to the ideas of an independent and highly developed culture. Appropriately enough the first example of an attempt to do so is the sermon Paul is reported to have preached at Athens (Acts 17.16-34). The endeavour continued in the early Church. The converts were people of their time and some, anyway, felt the need to relate their Christian beliefs to the ideas they shared with other people.

In the early period Platonism in one or another of its forms was the dominant philosophy. In the thirteenth century it was the task especially of Aquinas to relate Christianity to the rediscovered philosophy of Aristotle. Without the confident handling of the leading ideas of the time in both periods it is doubtful whether Christianity would have survived and become the largest and most influential world religion. Relating the message to these ideas did not mean accommodating it to them; Christian belief was taken as primary and generally was not attenuated. To go on and refer to the efforts made to do the same kind of work in recent centuries and in other cultures is not necessary. But there is an important point to note: a philosophical element is not alien to Christianity. It is not only that Christian belief has had to be related to philosophical ideas; they have been made use of in clarifying its own ideas and beliefs.

In the idea of God there are three main elements. The one we begin with is the one in which the philosophical contribution is strongest. To many people this will be unfamiliar and strange. But it may also be liberating.

1. Ultimate Being

The religious claim is not only that there is a further order of being but that it is ultimate. It is what accounts for our own existence and that of the world we live in. Ultimate being is what everything else depends on and which itself does not depend on anything. Beyond it there is nothing. We are speaking of an altogether different order of being. It is not in space and time but it is what everything in space and time depends on. That means that ultimate being is wholly different from the limited and changeable character of all that is ordinarily known to us. The claim is that beyond all that can be observed and conceptualized there is an order of being which cannot be fully conceptualized. It is necessarily mysterious because it is of another order.

This mysterious ultimate order of being is what we call God. Ultimacy is not the only quality which makes it appropriate to use the word God; other things have to be said also. But ultimacy is the primary one. More than anything else it is what makes God God. That God is ultimate being is not specifically stated in the Bible but it is suggested by the words with which the Bible opens, "In the beginning God created the heavens and the earth". Ultimacy is an important aspect of the way in which Aquinas thought of God and he believed that everyone thought the same.

Ultimate being is not a being. While we recognise that God is different from everything in the world we tend to think of him as an individual being above or alongside the world. We do this partly because we belong to a culture in which people, believers and unbelievers alike, for the most part do think of God in this kind of way. We carry on, in a more sophisticated form, a rather primitive way of thinking about God. We do it the more readily because we can stand over against God and can enter into a relationship with him analogous to the relationships we have with other people. But even so it is not necessary to think of God as an individual being. In India, for example, although images of different gods are to be seen everywhere, they are regarded, by educated people, as representations of ultimate being which underlies and pervades the world. The point here is simply that it is possible to think of God in a way quite different from the one we are used to. It is true that in thinking of God we make him an object in the logical sense of an object of thought. But this does not mean that he is an individual object as finite beings are. Nothing requires us to think of God as an individual being.

Being is the most general statement that can be made about anything: simply that it is; it exists. It stands against non-existence or non-being and it does not characterise in any way whatever. It does not even limit existence to the kind of way finite beings exist, one thing among various other things. In speaking of God as a being we are leaving it open to saying anything else at all. It expresses his existence without making any statement about his nature. By adding to being the term ultimate something more is being said: the being of God is wholly different from that of the finite beings which make up the universe and is their source.

To think of God as ultimate being rather than as an individual being is not in any way to reduce the Christian concept. Nor, in fact have by any means all Christians thought of God as a being. Augustine, for example, thought of God as Being itself. In his *Expositions of the Psalms* (134.4) Augustine says that the things which God has made all have being. Yet when compared with the unchangeable being of God it seems as though he alone has being. He refers to the verse in Exodus (3.14) where Moses asks God his name and gets the reply "I am who I am". Moses has to say to the people of Israel, as Augustine has it, "He Who Is has sent me to you". "He did not say, The Almighty Lord God, the merciful, the just, though he would have said what was quite true, had he so spoken. Everything being taken away by which God might be named and called, he answered that he is called Very Being *ipsum esse,* as though this were his name". Augustine's point is that when all the particular things that can be said about God are set aside what is basic remains: unchanging being. The Exodus passage is referred to again in *Homilies on St John* (38.9f.). Again Augustine says that we have being and that everything which God has made has being. But there is something which God has retained and which makes him different from anything else. The being of God is being itself *ipsum   esse.* Our being is changeable; we are always moving from the past to the future. The being of God—being itself—is unchangeable and does not move through time; God simply is.

2. Providential Power

On the basis of a comparative study of religion E.O. James maintains that the primary feature in the concept of the Divine is providence. Providence, taken in a wide sense, rather than ideas about the origin of the world, is the basic element. Under providence James includes not only guiding and providing for the individual and the community amid the hazards of life but also extraordinary and arresting events in the natural world. There is understood to be providential power or powers permeating the world which control both human destinies and natural processes.

In primal religion this generalised notion of providence gives rise to the idea of a series of spiritual beings who exercise it, notably nature spirits and gods, ancestor spirits and the Supreme God. In other types of religion other elements enter into the concept of the Divine and may dominate it. But providence does not disappear; it remains a fundamental feature of the concept at all levels of culture.[1] This is certainly true of practical religious life. For instance, in Theravada Buddhism providence has an important place in actual life. This is so even though it is recognised to be difficult to fit the idea into the general conceptual framework of the religion. There is, in fact, no type of religion in which providence is not in some way an element in the concept of the Divine or of the Transcendent.

Providence is the fundamental element in the Old Testament's understanding of God. There are other elements, of course, but it is this which does most to shape the religion of the Old Testament. It might have been thought that what was fundamental was the oneness of God as against the polytheism of the neighbouring nations. Certainly this is important; Israel in the early period was often tempted in the direction of polytheism. Again, it might have been thought that what was fundamental in the understanding of God was righteousness. The prophetic emphasis on the righteousness of God and his demand for righteousness among the people is something quite distinctive. The religion of Israel has often been described as ethical monotheism and for good reason. But there is something more fundamental. The God of the Old Testament is the God who called Abraham, delivered his descendents from Egypt, led them through the Sea, provided for them in the desert and gave them the land.

In the religion of Israel there is a very great deal more than the remembering of key events and the recognition of the action of God in them. There are ideas and practices both inherited from the past and adapted to meet the new situations. The Old Testament tradition as it develops embodies moral, social and cultic laws. It includes accounts of the prophets and the writings of some of them and poetic and wisdom literature. But the recognition of the activity of God in the events of history and of individual life is fundamental. God is present and cares and acts. These are the essential features of the concept of providence.

This basic understanding of God is taken over by the New Testament. Compared with the Old Testament it covers a very short period of time. It was written in the years between about 50 A.D. and the end of the century. There is variety in the New Testament. But it has been shown that underlying it all, and present from the start, is one essential message. This is what the Apostolic Church preached to those outside as against what is taught about the new life to those who had become Christians.[2]

The Apostolic preaching began with the fact that certain of the prophets had looked forward to the coming of the Messiah. The idea had developed in the Old Testament of an individual raised up by God to be the bringer of final salvation. There was to be a decisive act of judgment and salvation which would usher in a new era. The Apostles claimed that the prophecy had been fulfilled in the very recent events; they identified Jesus with the Messiah. This carried with it ideas associated with the coming of the Messiah, although they were understood in a way different from the current political interpretation. As in the Old Testament so in the New, God is seen as acting in history and in individual life to bring about his purposes. Throughout the Bible providence remains basic in the understanding of God.

The providential understanding of God continued to be held in the subsequent theology of the Church. If formed an important aspect of Augustine's thinking about God. Providence is important also in the theology of Aquinas. Of the four books of *Summa Contra Gentiles* one is devoted to Providence. The world is seen as a providential order.[3] In developing the idea Aquinas makes use of the distinction between primary and secondary causes. God is the primary cause of all things. He brings them into being and directs them to their own perfection and the perfection of the whole. But he does not control everything that happens. The world has a life of its own and works by the forces inherent in it. These are the secondary causes. They are the ordinary cause and effect relationships that we recognise in daily life and which are investigated by natural science. Secondary causes are real and effective and give the world a relative independence. There is no contradiction, Aquinas maintains, between the primary cause which directs things to their perfection and the relative independence of things working by secondary causes; the primary cause works through the normal action of the secondary causes. The relative independence of things coupled with an overall Divine direction is how Aquinas understood the providential order.

Because of the success of natural science the providential view of the world has come to be virtually replaced by the scientific view. But there is no necessary conflict between them. We can accept the scientific understanding of nature and think of it in terms of cause and effect. At the same time we can agree with Aquinas that the world remains in relationship with providential power by which its course is directed. Aquinas maintained that the world had a life of its own and we may understand it as having even more independence than he allowed. But in a culture dominated by natural science and technology it is still reasonable to think of the world, not only as a network of causes and effects but also a providential order.

It is in connection with the lives of individual people that the idea of God as providential power is most familiar. In the section of the *Summa Theologiae* where Aquinas deals directly with the meaning of the word God he writes, "For the word is derived from his universal providence: everyone who uses the word God has in mind one who cares for all things".[4] That remains true. People sometimes speak of God simply as Providence.

The idea of providence includes not only God's care but also his activity in the world. It means that he has power to act so that things take a course different from what they otherwise would. We are not at present dealing with the justification of this belief; what we are concerned with now is a descriptive analysis of the concept of the Divine. People have thought, and still do think, that God has power to act in the world and that on some occasions feel sure that he does so. This has important consequences.

In the first place a question immediately arises. Does it make sense to speak of God acting in the world? The idea of action in the world comes from our own experience. We have material bodies which produce effects in the material world. There is no reason to think that God is embodied in any way. On the contrary, while there have been ideas about God's embodiment in the world, the main tradition is that God is pure spirit. We have no experience of pure spirit acting in the world. It is suggested that only material forces can do so. Accordingly, the idea of God's providential action is incoherent and can be dismissed. But is it incoherent to speak of action when there is no material means to carry it out? It is argued by Basil Mitchell and others that it is perfectly coherent. The concept of action is complex and is quite different from that of movement. It involves a conscious agent with intentions and purposes which he attempts to realise in his environment. None of this makes reference to a body. Mitchell goes on to speak about the alleged phenomenon of telekinesis. Some people, it is claimed, have the power to alter events, not by means of their body, but simply by willing. For example, the way in which a dice falls may be affected. Whether or not the claim can be justified is not the point here. It is that we can make sense of the claim and know the kind of way in which it could be investigated.[5] So likewise we can make sense of the claim that God acts in the world and we will discuss later how it can be investigated.

Another consequence of God's acting in the world is that he cannot be thought of as remote. If God can affect any process, whether mental or physical, then he must have a relationship with them all. The way in which God is related to things and how he acts in events we cannot say. It has been pointed out that to hold that God acts in the world we do not have to specify how he acts. Given God's uniqueness that must remain a mystery. What is necessary is only that it should be conceptually possible to affirm God's active relatedness to the world.[6] This, as we have just seen, is possible. God's active relatedness to the world is traditionally expressed by saying that God is immanent in the world. Immanence is a spatial symbol. It does not mean that God is only in the world and not also above and beyond the world. Immanence means, in Macquarrie's phrase, "his presence and agency within the things and events of the world".[7] While the world has a large measure of independence, it remains in relationship with the ever present providential power.

Providential power is normally hidden. But in what we call acts of providence it is revealed. Providential action takes many forms and varies greatly in what may be called acuteness. Sometimes we are not sure whether an event was a chance one or whether it was providential. Sometimes the event is so striking as to leave no doubt. Such events, especially when they follow a prayer, we speak of as miracles. Events of this kind are rare in any one person's experience. They occur in situations of critical importance in life. A person may be in acute danger or may be faced with a decision that will determine the course of his whole future life or that of the community for which he is in some way responsible. They do not usually occur even in these situations. Normally life is carried on by using the powers given in creation. In conditions of perplexity we cannot generally expect providential guidance. We have to try to grasp the complexities of the situation and to see what the will of God in it is. We have to accept the consequences of our decisions even when the full consequences could not have been foreseen. This is part of what it means to be a responsible human being. But sometimes there is a response to urgent prayer. Something happens which so precisely meets the particular situation that the individual concerned has no doubt that it is an act of God. The hidden providential power is revealed. When this happens there is awakened a sense of wonder and awe because God has revealed himself. The hidden divine power, present everywhere, is revealed in the event.

God's action in events allows some positive knowledge about him to be had. It is not the only way knowledge about God may be arrived at; reflection on the created world is another source. But it is through his revelation of himself in providential actions that some of the most important affirmations about him may be made. It is through these that we can speak of God's knowledge of us and his love. Without the recognition of God's action in the world it is doubtful whether there would be much ground for making affirmations of this kind.

3. Transcendent Spirit

The third main component in the concept of the Divine is transcendent spirit. Both words are important. Transcendent is used in more than one way. The primary meaning is what is beyond our capacity to experience. When we speak of transcendence in a religious context we mean first something which is beyond the grasp of sense experience and of natural science. We believe that there is a further order of reality which is transcendent. This further order of reality is not necessarily understood as divine. In Theravada Buddhism a further order of reality is believed in but it is understood not as divinity but primarily as law: the law of Karma. The word transcendence does not itself specify the nature of the further order.

When the further order of reality is understood as the Divine something is added to the meaning of transcendence; it comes to mean otherness. God is other than the natural and created order of reality. That is where we belong, spiritual capacities as well as bodily structures. With all other living beings we share a common material basis of life. Here Christianity differs from Platonism. In Platonism, while our bodies belong to the material realm our spirits belong to the divine and spiritual realm. Christianity, with its doctrine of creation out of nothing, puts the divide in a different place. It is between the natural and the transcendent, which in our case is between the human and Divine. While there may be some likeness between our spirits and the Divine, so far from there being any kinship, God is wholly other.

During the present century this point was insisted on especially by Karl Barth. Barth took his stand in opposition to the prevailing liberal theology. His attack went far beyond the issue we are immediately concerned with to the whole outlook of which it formed a part. Barth had been educated in and accepted the Ritschlian theology which flourished in the latter part of the nineteenth century. Ritschl, he said later, stood as the very epitome of the national-liberal German bourgeois of the age of Bismark.[8] The great divide in Ritschlian theology was not so much between the human and the Divine as between the human and the natural. God was looked on as a friendly power who gave help in the struggle to subdue nature both outside and inside human life.

Barth had as one of his teachers Harnack, a leading Ritschlian, who made a deep impression on him. Harnack was professor of Church History in the University of Berlin. He was also Director General of the Royal Library, the largest and most important in Germany. Harnack was widely recognised as a leading representative of the culture of the time. In his academic work his approach to Christianity was largely historical. By means of careful research and critical reflection he could cut away what he regarded as metaphysical and dogmatic accretions and lay bare the essence of the Gospel. This he found in the teaching and personality of Jesus. In a lecture given to students of all facilities he said, "the whole of Jesus' message may be reduced to these two heads—God as the Father, and the human soul so ennobled that it can and does unite with him".[9] A view of God and of Christianity was produced that fitted smoothly into contemporary culture. Barth, who was now a pastor and preacher, was becoming increasingly uneasy about this kind of theology. In the Bible, and particularly in the Pauline epistles he found something quite different. It was a message that could not be readily assimilated to contemporary culture; rather it stood in judgment on that culture.

There was something else which led Barth to reject the liberal theology of the time. One day early in August 1914 he read a statement by ninety three German intellectuals in support of the war policy of Wilhelm II and his advisers. Among the names he was shocked to find almost all the theological teachers he had greatly revered. He then realised that he could no longer follow them in ethics and dogmatics, in the understanding of the Bible and of history.[10] But that was not all. The war itself affected his thinking as it did that of many others. There was something wrong and not only with the theologians' attitude at the outbreak of war but also with the whole prevailing optimistic view of humanity. The nineteenth century view was clearly falsified.

More fundamentally Barth thought, liberal theology was wrong about God. In open correspondence with Harnack in 1923 Barth was asked, "Whether God is simply unlike anything said about him on the basis of the development of culture, on the basis of the knowledge gathered by culture and on the basis of

ethics". He began his reply by saying, "No, God is absolutely
not at all that".[11] For liberal theologians to speak about God was
to speak about human beings in an elevated way. What was
needed was to speak of God's unique being and power and of
his initiative in his relationship with human beings. God must be
God in all his otherness and awesomeness.

God is other than human beings; there is an unlikeness
between his essential being and ours. Yet from what we know
of God in his relationship with the world and with ourselves we
can say that there is also a certain likeness. The points of likeness
may be summed up in the word spirit. Only while our spirituality
is created and dependent on a body God's spirituality is
immaterial and transcendent.

The word spirit, when speaking of human beings, is used
to refer to a particular group of characteristics. It is now being
applied analogically to God. Divine being is thought of as having
qualities which bear some likeness to those we are familiar with
in human life and which can be grouped together as spiritual.
The most important of these are probably self-consciousness,
free will, moral responsibility, aesthetic sensibility and love. On
the basis of our experience of nature, of moral life and of
providence we find that we have to attribute to God qualities
which have some likeness to them.

The first characteristic of Divine spirituality is consciousness. Consciousness may be possessed by an animal. A cat is
aware of its environment and notices and remembers what is in
it. It can form concepts, at least in the sense of recognitional
capacities. It recognises a person whom it has not met before as
a person and will come up to him. It can reason a little. In order
to get to the next garden it may look at the wall and then if it
is too high may go round another way. But an animal is not
conscious of itself to the extent that we are. It cannot form a
concept of itself or reason about itself. Human beings, although
dependent on the natural processes which constitute their bodies,
can distinguish themselves from themselves as well as from the
world. We can be aware of ourselves and make ourselves the
objects of knowledge and judgement and direction. We know

what we are doing and what we are thinking. We know that our attitude to something is and what our motives are—although it is easy to deceive ourselves. We can make judgements on what we think and what we do. We can control ourselves and make ourselves do what we are not inclined to do. In all cases a distinction is made between the self as a subject who knows and judges and the self which is made an object of knowledge and judgement.

Self-consciousness is involved in much of our experience. The ability to separate ourselves, as it were, both from the world and from ourselves opens up a way of viewing the world and human life that would not otherwise be possible. We are not limited to the present time; we can understand the present as it is connected both with the past and with the future. Looking back we can see the history, large and small, which has moulded our culture. Looking ahead we can see various possibilities opening up with choices to make that we may greatly affect the future. This ability to separate ourselves means also that we are not limited to the immediate situation; we can rise above it in imagination and plan and take action to change it. We can have aspirations and can direct our lives towards ideals. We can ask questions about the world and about human life. These and other distinctive features of human life are dependent on self-consciousness.

God's consciousness cannot be the same as ours. It is not limited in extent as ours is. It will be argued in Chapter V that God is not aware of one state of affairs and then of another. That does not mean that he is unaware of the temporal relationship of before and after but that everything is open to him. He does not get to know by slow degrees nor is there any ignorance or uncertainty in his knowledge. Again, it is not only outward situations and events that God is aware of; he is aware also of our thoughts and intentions. This is expressed at the beginning of Psalm 139,

O Lord, thou hast searched me, and known me!
Thou knowest when I sit down and when I rise up;
thou discernest my thoughts from afar.

Thou searchest out my path and my lying down,
   and art acquainted with all my ways.
Even before a word is on my tongue,
   lo, O Lord, thou knowest it altogether.
Thou dost beset me behind and before,
   and layest thy hand upon me.
Such knowledge is too wonderful for me;
   it is high, I cannot attain it.

The second characteristic of Divine spirituality, as of human, we may call free will. The term will does not have a single precise meaning and is used in different ways. When we speak of an effort of will we mean that some task is being carried out even though it is difficult or disagreeable. When we speak of someone as strong willed what we mean is that when he has a purpose to achieve he does not easily give up. We use the expression free will when referring to a person engaged in such things as deliberating, deciding, choosing and acting. The question that arises in this connection is whether a person in choosing and acting is free in what he does or whether he is in some way caused to do it. No doubt we are influenced by causal factors such as health and circumstances and perhaps by psychological forces of which we are unaware. But the view of commonsense it that within certain limits we are free in what we choose and how we act. Especially when we are deliberating and deciding we seem to be free to choose and to do what we choose. This is not the place to discuss whether or not the commonsense view can be justified. For here we are concerned not with human beings but with God.

While we have a limited area of freedom of choice God is completely free. There is no state of affairs which could make God act in a way contrary to how he has chosen to act. In creation, in providence and in redemption there is nothing which can limit God's freedom of action except as he has chosen to be limited. The evil purposes and actions of human beings, for example, cannot do so. As a Psalmist puts it, "Surely the wrath of man shall praise thee" (76.10 AV). God may respond to our prayers. That means he may bring about something that would not otherwise have occurred. It does not mean acting contrary to his will for the world has a large measure of autonomy. When we pray for someone who is critically ill what we are praying is that nature should not be left to take its course; we are not asking God to change his mind and to do something different from what he intended. God may make the achievement of his purposes for the world dependent on human action; he seems constantly to do this. But that is not a constraint imposed from the outside; it is what he has himself chosen.

When we speak of God's will we are referring, very often, not to his power of unrestricted choice but to his wishes. It is the content of his will which concerns us in practical life. This is what he wants for the world and for human life. We are well aware that God's will is not being done in the world and in the lives of people. In much of life the question of God's will hardly arises; we do what the situation requires and no moral element is involved. But there are occasions when there is a right or a good thing to do and so a question of doing or not doing God's will. In addition there may be something particular asked of an individual, a special task, large or small, or a particular vocation to follow.

God calls us to carry out his will. He does not force us to do so; we are free to respond or not to respond. Paul was not disobedient to the heavenly vision (Acts 26.19). But the words imply that he could have been. God's will does not necessarily require very much of us but it can be difficult and costly to follow. And so there may be a tension between what God wants of us and what we want. A living relationship with God depends on faith and love and a willingness to seek out God's will and to obey it. But we are in no way bound to do so. God, who is himself free, respects our freedom of choice.

The third characteristic of Divine spirituality is moral goodness. When we speak of the goodness of God we mean that God has qualities analogous to those which constitute moral goodness in human beings. Part of human goodness consists in doing right. Correspondingly one of the strongest affirmations in the Bible is the rightness or righteousness of God. In a famous phrase Abraham asks God, "Shall not the Judge of all the earth do right?" (Genesis 18.25 AV). God does right because it is his nature to do so. And, on our side, we recognize what is right because we have been created with the capacity of moral awareness. There is more to human goodness than doing right and there is more to the goodness of God than righteousness: loving kindness, mercy, forgiveness, for example. But righteousness is fundamental to what we mean by God's moral goodness.

It is our awareness of what is right and of the claim which this has upon us that is the main reason for affirming the moral goodness of God. If we believe in the reality of God we are bound to take the demands of conscience as the demands of God. It has been pointed out that we can hardly imagine someone in a sincerely religious state of mind at the same time deciding to do what he believed to be wrong.[12] It is not that what is right is always immediately obvious. Moral situations are often complex and what is right may become clear only after careful thought and prayer. But when it is clear we feel sure that this is what God wants of us. And God who requires right must himself be righteous.

The prophets of the Old Testament saw the wrongs of their time and declared that God required right conduct. If the people did not amend their ways and do what was right God would surely act in judgement. For if God requires right he must uphold it by condemning what is wrong. The prophet Micah in a well known passage brings out both God's requirement and the judgement that will result from failure to do it.

> He has told you, O mortal, what is good;
> and what does the Lord require of you
> but to do justice, and to love kindness,
> and to walk humbly with your God?...
> Can I forget the treasures of wickedness
> in the house of the wicked,
> and the scant measure that is accursed?

Can I tolerate wicked scales
　　and a bag of dishonest weights?
Your wealthy are full of violence;
　　your inhabitants speak lies,
　　with tongues of deceit in their mouths.
Therefore I have begun to strike you down,
　　making you desolate because of your sins (6.8-13)

The fourth characteristic of the Divine Spirit is aesthetic creativity. This needs little explanation. The natural world, the creation of God, is full of amazing beauty. It leads us to think of God as being like a creative artist who produces one beautiful thing after another in amazing profusion. What has come to be must represent the kind of thing that God intends. We can say in the opening words of Psalm 19,

The heavens are telling the glory of God;
　　and the firmament proclaims his handiwork.

In trying to formulate what natural beauty implies about the being of God, theologians have been drawn to Plato's account of Beauty in the *Symposium*. Plato speaks of ascending by a ladder of love. Starting with the beauties near at hand a person may end by seeing Beauty that exists for ever and does not change. This is Beauty itself, not God. But the tendency has been to identify Beauty itself with God. Augustine does something like this in a celebrated passage in the *Confessions* (10.38), "Belatedly I loved thee, O Beauty old yet ever new, belatedly I loved thee. For see, thou wast within and I was without and I sought thee out there. Unlovely, I rushed heedlessly among the lovely things thou hast made. Thou wast with me but I was not with thee". God, of course, cannot literally be beauty which is a highly abstract concept. But he is the source both of natural beauty and of our appreciation of beauty.

The fifth characteristic is love. In the New Testament the principal word used is *agape*. This is self-giving love. It is a love that does not desire anything for itself. God has no need which requires something for its satisfaction. Nor is God's love one that is awakened by something in the object of love. There does not have to be any special quality of goodness or beauty about it. In the Old Testament this is brought out in one of the addresses in Deuteronomy (7.7), "It was not because you were more numerous than any other people that the Lord set his heart on you and chose you—for you were the fewest of all peoples". The New Testament is similar. "But God, who is rich in mercy, out of the great love with which he loved us even when we were dead through our trespasses, made us alive together with Christ" (Ephesians 2.4f.). That is how the love of God is understood in the Bible: it does not want to get anything and it is not because of anything; it is a pure self-giving love.

God loves both communities and individuals. A number of the prophets speak of love of God for their people: Hosea, Jeremiah, Ezekiel, the later Isaiah and Malachi all do so. With Hosea the love of God forms the main theme of his preaching. His message is vividly symbolized in his marriage. He was called to marry a prostitute and to give symbolic names to the three children. And for his wife he had to pay a price and to re-educate her. Not much information is given about what actually happened for the interest is in the symbolic significance of the marriage. What does come out is Hosea's patient love for his faithless wife; that is how it is between God and Israel.

It is sometimes said that Hosea is a prophet of mercy while Amos is prophet of judgement. But Hosea is a prophet of judgement also. God has to act in judgement both to condemn sin and to bring the people back to himself. But although God has to judge he is also compassionate,

How can I give you up, Ephraim?
How can I hand you over, O Israel? (11.8)

Love is shown both in care and in mercy; forgiveness is one aspect of God's mercy. That God forgives and restores to fellowship is brought out, among other places, in the passages on the symbolic names given to the children. In the first chapter the second child is to be called Not pitied because God would not have pity on Israel and forgive her. And the third child is to be called Not my people. In the second chapter a warning is given of coming judgement but it looks forward to a time of restoration,

> And I will have pity on Not pitied,
> And I will say to Not my people,
> "You are my people";
> and he shall say, "Thou art my God" (2.23).

Where did Hosea learn about God's love for Israel that he proclaims so vividly? The eminent Old Testament scholar von Rad is quite clear: from God's dealing with the people in the course of their history.[13] Looking back over the past and seeing God's care, his judgement and his mercy, Hosea is sure of the steadfast love of God. He refers to how God called Israel out of Egypt, how he guided the people, provided for them and sent them prophets. It is that providential care which forms the basis of Hosea's message of the love of God.

That is one way we also may know the love of God. It is in personal life that we are most clearly aware of God's providential care. The individual is sure on certain occasions that a particular event did not happen purely by chance. It may not be what he wanted to happen but he has no doubt that it was God's doing. God knows and cares about him.

We know the love of God also in another way: from the life, teaching and especially the death of Jesus Christ. That is what the Apostolic Church declared. Paul, for example writes, "But God proves his love for us in that while we were still sinners Christ died for us" (Romans 5.8). But it must not be thought that this was the only way they knew about the love of God; they knew about it before they became Christians. If Paul, for example, did not already know a good deal about God he could not confidently have written "God was in Christ reconciling the world to himself" (2 Corinthians 5.19 REB). The life and death of Jesus had to be consistent with what he knew independently about God if he was to make such a statement. Paul had that knowledge from God's dealing with the people of Israel as it is recorded in and reflected on in the Old Testament. In particular he was able to learn it from the book of Hosea. He

refers in Romans 9.25f. to the passage quoted above. The book
was a source of knowledge for him as it is for us. And like him
we find the love of God shown afresh in Jesus Christ.

In the New Testament Jesus is never thought of simply as
a man of outstanding goodness. As far back as it is possible for
New Testament research to take us, Jesus is always regarded as
having a special relationship with God. From the very beginning
it was held, as Paul puts it, that God was in him. Just what that
means has been the subject of enormous controversy. But the
controversy has not been over whether God was in Jesus; only
over how that is to be understood. It is the basic claim of
Christianity that in some sense God was in Christ. And that
means that his life and death is a manifestation of the being and
especially of the love of God. The love of Jesus is shown in
persevering to the end and accepting all that he saw was to
happen for the sake of human beings. This love is a reflection,
under the conditions of human life, of the love of God.

It is the person and work of Jesus Christ which leads to
such emphasis on the love of God in the Johannine writings.
People sometimes seem to suggest that John takes love as pretty
well the sole characteristic of God. In fact John makes three
cardinal affirmations about God. They may be taken in the order
in which they are made. First, God is spirit (John 4.24). Spirit
in the Biblical writings does not have the sense in which we use
the word today; it does not get its meaning from human life.
John uses the word to mean principally live-giving, creative
power.[14] The second affirmation is God is light (1 John 1.5). The
principal meaning here, as the context makes clear, is perfect
moral goodness. The third affirmation is God is love (1 John
4.8). And love, as the Greek word indicates, is the generous,
self-giving love that was manifested in Jesus Christ.

A final question remains: can God be described as personal?
Although implied in the Bible, classical theology did not speak
of God as personal. The term person was used for the three
constituents of the Trinity. It was not generally applied to God
until the nineteenth century. The word used was spirit. Apart
from the idea of being immaterial, spirit has largely, although

not entirely, the same content as person. The question is, are there features about God and his relationship with human beings that are better brought out by supplementing the term spirit with personal?

Certainly God is not a person. In ordinary life the word person contains the idea of being an individual; the words may be used interchangeably. It is because of this that many people find the idea of God being personal difficult to accept. But when used of God the idea of an individual is not intended. As was maintained earlier, God is not a being. He is the ultimate being, the ground of all that is. Nevertheless, God has the attributes of self-consciousness and will. It can be said that this makes him personal by definition. There are different views as to what constitutes the idea of a person. But the commonest one centres òn possessing these attributes. And the term personal applied to God has the further connotation of caring for people and being responsive to them. For both these reasons God may properly be spoken of as personal. The term is used analogically. It gets its meaning from human life and God is very different. What is being claimed is that there is enough likeness between what we know of the consciousness, will and love of God, and that of human beings, to make it possible to use the term personal of God.

Is it necessary to do so? The Jewish philosopher Martin Buber maintains that it is. We have to use the term personal of God who enters into a direct relation with us and makes it possible for us to enter into a direct relation with him.[15] Earlier in his book Buber describes what is involved in a personal relationship between two people. It is something which we enter into with our whole being and which has a definite structure. There are two main features. First, independence. The two selves are set over against one another. Each accepts the other as he is and as a whole. I value him as a person in his own right, with his own interests and purposes. There is no attempt to force my will on him; he has a will of his own which is not directly accessible to me. Any attempt to influence it except as the outcome of his own insight and choice means that the relationship is no longer a fully personal one. Nor can there be any attempt to dominate him. He is accepted as a person with his own independent being.

The second feature of a personal relationship is mutuality. There is an unreserved mutual responsiveness. The two people listen to one another and respond to one another in the give and take of talk. Responsiveness may be shown in other ways: with the eyes, by a touch, or in an action. Response to the other may include sympathetically entering into his whole situation. But instead I may withhold myself and fail to take the action which responsiveness requires. There are situations which do not allow the full mutuality of a personal relationship to develop. The teacher must meet the pupil in a bi-polar relation. He must not regard him merely as the sum of his qualities, strivings and inhibitions. He must enter without reserve into a relationship with him as a whole person. Nevertheless, for the work of teaching to go on full mutuality is limited on the side of the pupil. Much the same applies to the relationship between a psychiatrist and his patient. But a full personal relationship requires an unreserved mutual responsiveness.

The relationship with God is of a similar kind. He does not over-rule our wills but waits for a response to what he gives and to what he asks. Nor is there any merging with God as some forms of mysticism have claimed; on the contrary we stand our ground. But mutuality is of the more limited sort like that of pupil and teacher or patient and psychiatrist. Nevertheless, the relationship is personal on both sides. Our response is described in the personal categories of trust and love and willing obedience. On God's side responsiveness is shown in events in the world which we recognize to be acts of providence and of answered prayer. Unless something takes place corresponding with what we have asked we cannot be sure that there is a response.

References

1. E.O. James, *The Concept of Deity,* London, 1950, Ch.I.
2. C.H. Dodd, *The Apostolic Preaching and its Developments,* London, 1936.
3. *Summa contra Gentiles,* III, ch. 64ff.

4. *Summa Theologiae,* Ia. 13, 8.
5. B. Mitchell, *The Justification of Religious Belief,* London, 1973, paperback ed. pp, 7f.
6. T.F. Tracy, *God, Action and Embodiment,* Grand Rapids, 1984, p. 62.
7. J. Macquarrie, *In Search of Deity,* London 1984, p. 177.
8. K. Barth, *From Rousseau to Ritschl,* E.T. London, 1959, p. 392.
9. A. Harnack, *What is Christianity?* E.T. London, 1901, p. 63.
10. K. Barth, *The Humanity of God,* E.T. London, 1960, paperback ed. pp. 12f.
11. H.M. Rumscheidt, *Revelation and Theology,* Cambridge, 1972, p. 50.
12. A.C. Ewing, *Value and Reality,* London, 1973, p. 188.
13. *Old Testament Theology,* Vol. II, E.T. 1965, p. 140.
14. C.K. Barrett, *The Gospel According to St. John,* London, 1955, p. 199.
15. M. Buber, *I and Thou,* 2nd ed. Edinburgh, 1958, p. 135.

Chapter II
Reasons for Belief in God

Someone may be asked how he or she came to believe in God. There can be many answers. It may have come through being brought up in a religious home or through attending a certain church. A particular person may have had a profound influence or it may be a group of people. A young man in China, for example, brought up as an atheist, was invited by a neighbour to visit a group of believers. He joined them and for twelve years they met in complete secrecy; now he is a pastor. These are answers to one sort of question about belief: what are its sources? But there is another sort of question that may be asked about belief: what are its grounds? Most people think that this is a question that needs asking. It may be put by a sceptic. Or a believer may want to be sure that there are adequate reasons for belief.

Many different reasons have been put forward for belief in God. Nevertheless what is appealed to, or the way in which the appeal is made, may not be generally familiar. So adequate description is needed in each case before an assessment can properly be made.

1. Can God be Directly Evident?

By directly evident in this connection what is meant is independently of the senses. Can there be an awareness of God that is not mediated by sense experience? The claim is that there are special kinds of direct awareness. Certainly interpretation is involved in saying that they are the awareness of God and this is of great importance as will be seen. This makes the expression directly evident not strictly accurate. But it can be used because the emphasis is on having the special awareness rather than on the interpretation. The expression is useful also in order to distinguish the experiences to be described now from one of a very different sort that will be discussed later. The claim that there is such awareness may take two quite different forms.

(a) The Holy

The importance in religion of the experience of the Holy was brought out especially by Rudolf Otto.[1] He was not the first theologian to draw attention to it. And Old Testament scholars had been investigating the meaning of the Hebrew *qodesh* since about the middle of the nineteenth century. But Otto was able to bring out in a fresh way just what the experience of holiness was. One of his principal points was that it was something quite specific and distinct from everything else.

Ordinarily we use the word holy to mean the completely moral or the good. That was Kant's usage: the will which unwaveringly obeys the moral law from the motive of duty alone he called a holy will. In the same kind of way when we hear the word holy used of a person we think of an individual of outstanding goodness—someone like St Francis, perhaps. Otto holds that this is misleading. Certainly in all developed religions the idea of the holy does have in it a most important moral element. But originally this was not so; the holy had nothing to do with the moral.

In order to focus attention on the element which is specific in the awareness of the holy, Otto introduced a special term: the numinous. It is taken from the Latin word *numen* meaning divinity. It stands for the holy minus the moral and rational elements which subsequently came to be associated with it. The numinous is a religious category and cannot be reduced to any other. Nor can it be described in terms of anything else. All that can be done is to suggest other states of mind which resemble it or which may be contrasted with it. Then it is hoped that, when experienced, the feeling will be recognised.

The experience of the numinous, according to Otto, is the consciousness of the presence of a *mysterium tremendum et fascinans*. Each of these terms needs some explanation.

We start with *tremendum*. It means first awesome. It is something to be feared. But fear is not specifically religious emotion. There is in it the feeling of standing before something not only all-powerful but of an altogether different nature from anything in the world. It is related to the feeling of eeriness in a place reputed to be haunted. But again the religious feeling is not exactly this. It is expressed in primal religion by making the images of the gods grotesque and horrible. In the Hinduism of Bengal it is represented by Kali, the frightening mother goddess who wears a garland of human skulls. In popular liberal Christianity, with its easy-going friendliness with the Heavenly Father, the feeling has been lost. But it is there in the New Testament. "Let us offer to God acceptable worship, with reverence and awe", says the Writer to the Hebrews, "for our God is a consuming fire" (12.28f.). The Old Testament symbol is directly affirmed as having its place in the new religion. This is all the more significant because it comes from a writer whose main purpose is to get his readers to go forward, leaving behind all that is outmoded and arguing in particular that the sacrificial worship of the Old Testament has been completely superseded.[2] The feeling referred to is best described as awe. It has in it the sense of unapproachability. At the burning bush Moses heard the command to take off his shoes because he was standing on holy ground. At temples and mosques we do the same.

Tremendum has in it two other components. There is a sense of overpowering majesty. We feel that we are in the presence of absolute power. This produces in us what Otto calls creature-feeling. He draws attention to some words of Abraham as he pleaded with God for mercy on Sodom, "Behold, I have taken upon myself to speak to the Lord, I who am but dust and ashes" (Genesis 18.27). Abraham felt himself as nothing in the presence of an overwhelming power. The third component is dynamism. It is represented in various ways by taking analogies from human life to bring out something of the living, feeling, active power with which we have to do. There is a feeling not only of awesomeness and majesty but of something compelling and alive.

What it is that is *tremendum* is described as *mysterium*. The word signifies the radical otherness of the numinous. We have the consciousness of something completely different from ourselves and from the world. This again may be illustrated from the Old Testament. At the beginning of the religious development it records holiness was understood as a mysterious other than human power. For example, at the giving of the law Mount Sinai was regarded as filled with mysterious power. Anyone who touched the mountain would be charged with holiness and dangerous. He was to be put to death by stoning or shooting with an arrow; no one was to touch him (Exodus 19.12f.). They were in the presence of a power altogether other than that of the ordinary familiar world.

Lastly there is the word *fascinans*. The *mysterium* is not only awesome and overpowering and dynamic; it also attracts and captivates. It is the object of longing and searching for its own sake as well as for the benefit it brings. The pilgrim to a Himalayan shrine does not only go for the completion of a vow or the remission of sins or for the meeting of some particular need; he goes also because he is drawn to seek a fuller grasp of the *mysterium*. In all such endeavours an intimate relationship is sought which cannot adequately be described but which satisfies and exalts the spirit.

So far no reference has been made to moral value. This is following Otto in his contention that the holy does not necessarily have anything moral about it. But he recognises that in all, except the most primitive religions the experience of the numinous is shot through with the moral. The holy as we normally experience it is therefore complex. There is the numinous but combined with it are rational and moral elements. To suggest how this could come about Otto gives an example from another sphere of life where such a combination certainly occurs. Personal affection is a universal human feeling. It may be interpenetrated by a separate and non-rational element, sex. From the instinctive life which we share with animals impulses come which combine with the specifically human feelings of liking, friendship and companionship. Sexual love is a combination of the two quite different feelings. Likewise the holy is a combination of the numinous and the moral.[3]

In the Old Testament, although there was some appreciation of the moral element earlier, it is particularly with the four prophets of the eighth century BC, beginning with Amos, that holiness came to include righteousness as a main element of its content. God by his nature is righteous and demands righteousness from his worshippers. In especial, they are to care for the poor and the weak. The meaning of holiness was now otherness and awesomeness, together with moral goodness.

Isaiah, the last of the eighth century prophets, gives a wonderful account of his vision in the temple (6.1-8). In it are mingled the elements of awesomeness and majesty, together with the moral goodness which judges us. He saw the Lord enthroned on high, heard the chant holy, holy, holy and felt the shaking of the foundations of the temple. There came to him the mortifying consciousness of his own sin and of the sin of the people among whom he lived. A burning coal, brought from the altar, touched his lips and he was told that his guilt was taken away and his sin forgiven. Then he heard the voice of the Lord asking, "Whom shall I send, and who will go for us?" The response he made to his vision of the holy set him apart as a prophet.

How is the holy experienced today by people influenced by Christianity? And what, in particular, of the numinous aspect? It is commonly experienced in two different kinds of situation. One is that of nature. We sometimes come upon a beauty and a vastness and a tranquility, or it may be a power, which is overwhelming. From the middle hills of the Himalayas one looks out over the trees on range after range of mountains leading up to the great snow clad peaks rising majestically above them. All this is natural. But through the natural the idea may form of something present that is more than natural. And with it may come the feeling of mystery and of awe. That is how Wordsworth felt at Tintern Abbey. The language in which he describes his feeling comes close to what Otto was later to say.

The other kind of situation in which we may have an awareness of the numinous is the specifically religious. It may be in private prayer. It may be a small group meeting together. It may be public prayer; it was said of Spurgeon that he would lift the whole great congregation into the presence of God. The feeling may come in the solemnity of the ordered ritual of public worship or in religious music. It may come in preaching. Oman, who had the same sort of view as Otto, suggests that the preacher whom people flock to hear is not the one who influences by his teaching; it is the one who makes people feel that surely God is in this place.[4]

The feeling of the numinous may be awakened, Otto maintains, by the church or temple itself. Tillich was one who was influenced by such an experience. He grew up in a small mediaeval town in Germany where his father was the Lutheran pastor. They lived in the parish house, with the confessional school on one side and the beautiful Gothic church on the other. Here Tillich had the experience of the holy. When he came to read Otto he recognised at once the feeling described. This was one of the factors which determined his approach to theology. He began with the experience of the holy and moved to the idea of God.[5]

So far the exposition has been limited to the special feeling that Otto describes. But he goes beyond description. His claim is that the experience of the holy makes us aware of something actually there: a numinous Presence. There is a problem in understanding Otto at this point. He refers to the awareness of the holy as *a priori*. The term is used in a special way and has been taken to mean different things by different people. Some have thought he meant an indefinable idea, others a kind of sensation. In spite of this uncertainty it seems clear that Otto maintains that in the experience of the holy we are directly aware of a special aspect of reality. His claim is that the experience is cognitive; it tells us something of the way things are. There is something beyond the self, not apprehended by the senses, but nonetheless real. The experience of the holy is the awareness of the Divine presence.

Now the question has to be put: is it certain that the experience of the holy is the direct awareness of a spiritual presence and therefore the basis on which the reality of the Divine can be affirmed? There are two points anyway at which doubts may arise.

First, it has not been demonstrated that Divine presence is involved. It is possible that the experience is entirely natural. For example, when looking at a scene of outstanding grandeur and beauty we may have a feeling of awe and of majesty. We may have also the feeling, as Wordsworth had, of a presence pervading it all. Yet an interpretive element can be present in an apparently spontaneous response. We bring to the scene certain presuppositions. It may be that someone else coming to the scene with different presuppositions would feel differently. He might have the feeling of awe and mystery but not the feeling of a numinous presence which is basic to Otto's account. Of course he might be blinded by his presuppositions and miss what is actually there. But it is at least a possibility that the conscious- ness of the Divine presence in an immediate interpretation and is not a direct awareness.

Second, while Divine presence may be involved there may not be a direct awareness of it. Rather, the experience may be a response to the Divine believed on other grounds to be present. Suppose, for example, we receive a remarkable answer to a specific prayer—perhaps the complete recovery of someone given up by the doctors. We have a feeling of mystery and awe. This is because God has heard the prayer of ordinary human beings and has acted. But the first step in our response is a judgment: this is the action of God. The feeling of mystery and awe is secondary. It is not that by which we recognise the Divine presence in the situation. It is because we recognise the Divine presence that we have the feeling. In the same kind of way we may have the feeling of mystery and awe in a church. This is because the building is associated with the Divine presence; it is set apart for worship. The feeling of the holy is a proper part of our response to the Divine. But it is not a way in which the Divine is directly evident to us.

(b) Mysticism

Mystical experience is the other main way in which direct awareness of the Divine is claimed. Mystics aim at more than this; they seek union with the Divine. But direct awareness is part of the experience they describe and that is why it is of interest here. Again before any assessment can be made as to whether or not there really is a direct awareness some account of the experience may be needed.

The term mysticism is commonly used today to mean a sense of union or even identity with something other than oneself.[6] It is this sense of union running through the descriptions of the experience given at many different times and in many different cultures which justifies the use of the same word to refer to them all. But the sense may be of two different kinds. Today they are usually called extrovertive and introvertive. The terms have nothing to do with Jung's classification of personality; they are simply ways of characterising the experience. Because of their differences separate descriptions are required.

(i) Extrovertive Mysticism

This type of experience may not be less common but it is much less commonly written about. It is not necessarily given a religious interpretation and is sometimes called natural mystical experience. But generally those who have it do regard it as being of religious significance.

Extrovertive mystical experience is usually spontaneous. There is no attempt to isolate the mind from what is outside. Unexpectedly, there comes to the individual the sense that everything belongs together and he is himself a part of it. It is not the various things perceived are no longer present. But they are perceived transfigured because they are seen as part of a unity which embraces them all. What was to ordinary sense experience a number of individual things, more or less separate from one another, now looks quite different. Everything is there with no barriers, as it were, keeping them apart. Yet there is no merging; while everything belongs together nothing has lost its distinctiveness and individuality. The experience is accompanied by an exaltation of spirit and a feeling of great peace and joy.

To some degree the feeling may continue after the mystical experience has passed. And it may return when the experience is relived in memory.

The experience carries with it a sense of reality; this is how things really are in the world. Our ordinary commonsense view of the world works perfectly well for ordinary purposes. But finally it is unreal. Although we do not often see it so, on those rare occasions when we do we know quite well that the world which appears transfigured is not only a more beautiful one, it is the real one. However strange to commonsense, the mystic is convinced that his experience reveals to him the way things really are.

Although extrovertive mystical experience usually comes spontaneously, it is possible to induce it. What seems to be the same kind of experience may be brought on by Yoga techniques[7] and by certain drugs, of which the best known is mescalin. The drug in its natural form, peyotl, is used by some American Indians for religious purposes. It is important to be clear about one thing in this connection: whatever may be the significance of the experience it is not affected by the fact that it can be induced by drugs. It may be that drugs facilitate that view of what the world really is which comes to us occasionally without the use of drugs.

In most cases, as just mentioned, the experience is regarded as a religious one. The religious understanding that most readily suggests itself is pantheism. This is the view that the universe is one and is divine; there is no distinction between Creator and creature. Such a position is sometimes taken. But if the individual already has a religious outlook the experience is usually interpreted in conformity with that outlook. For the Hindu the experienced unity is Brahman. For the Christian it is God, immanent in the whole created order. The experience comes to people in the present day world and may have a great effect on their lives; it gives them, rightly or wrongly, a conviction of the reality and closeness of the Divine.

(ii) Introvertive Mysticism

In contrast with the extrovertive type the natural setting of this form of mysticism is the convent or monastery. But that does not mean that mystics may not be active in the world in obedience to what is seen as the will of God.

Mystical prayer is generally regarded as falling into a number of stages. Often four are described. It has been noted that the stages seem much the same in Hindu, Muslim and Christian mystics; they are also similar to the stages of absorption described in Buddhism.[8] A clear and detailed account of the different stages is given by St Teresa of Avila who lived from 1515 to 1582. In her autobiography there are four stages,[9] although in the *Interior Castle* she makes it seven. The former account will be followed.

The first stage is one of concentration on God. The beginner has to learn to pay no attention to what he sees and hears and learn to keep his mind from distracting thoughts. He has to be alone and must think over his past life. He must try to meditate on the life of Christ and this fatigues the mind. For many days there may be a distaste for the whole thing. But he must persist in spite of it and think of Christ and his Cross. There may be a feeling of aridity and evil thoughts may come but he has to be determined and carry on. Once the state is reached when he desires to be alone and commune with God the greater part of the work is done. The person who goes on resolutely and does not set too much store by consolations and feelings of tenderness in devotion has begun building on a firm foundation.

The second stage is called by St Teresa, and by others, the prayer of quiet. The strain on the attention disappears. The understanding and memory are more or less at rest and must be kept so. Only the will is occupied. The individual offers himself wholly to God, so there is a union of the will. A feeling of profound satisfaction is experienced and he is filled with peace and joy. Covetousness for the things of the world begins to disappear. There is a sense of security which is combined with humility and there begins to develop a love of God which is free from self-interest. Many people reach this stage but few pass beyond it.

The third stage may be called contemplation. It is a
deepening of the preceding state of prayer. The faculties are
dormant and retain only the power of occupying themselves
with God. It seems like a death to everything in the world and
the profound enjoyment of God. It is a glad folly in which the
soul does not know whether to speak or be silent, whether to
laugh or to cry. All it wants is to please God who now possesses
it wholly. This kind of prayer is a union of the entire soul with
God. Yet it retains sufficient sense to realise that it is in the
world and is not a complete union of all the faculties although
it is approaching this.

The fourth stage is the prayer of union. Here the union of
all the faculties is complete. There is no feeling but only rejoicing
which is not accompanied by an understanding of what it is
rejoicing in. The joy cannot be expressed because there is no
power left in body or soul to communicate it. The eyes close
involuntarily, or if they remain open, can barely see. The person
can hear but cannot understand what he hears. He cannot speak
and all bodily sense disappears. The time in which the faculties
are suspended is short—less than half an hour. But it is some
hours before normal mental life is resumed. Of this fourth stage
St Teresa writes, "I can only say that the soul feels close to God
and that there abides within it such a certainty that it cannot
possibly do other than believe".[10]

In this state of prayer St Teresa sometimes experienced a
rapture or ecstasy and this she felt to be of the greatest importance.
An ecstasy cannot be resisted. It comes like a swift strong impulse
that seems to lift the spirit away and carry it above all created
things. The spirit appears no longer to animate the body which
becomes colder and is unable to move. It remains in the position
it was in when the ecstasy began. Consciousness is rarely lost;
the person can still hear and understand but as though from a
long way off. But when the ecstasy is at its height all the faculties
are lost. After it is over some hours elapse before the body is
able to move again and the understanding and memory may not
be themselves for a day or two. The ecstasy makes a person
afraid and he needs to be courageous. He has to risk everything
and resign himself into the hands of God and willingly go

wherever he is carried. It brings great delight and arouses the deepest love and this continues. The spirit is engulfed in God. There may be revelations and visions which are humbling and strengthening. But ecstasy gives nothing to the understanding.

Another Christian mystic to whom reference must be made is Eckhart, a German Dominican friar, who lived from about 1260 to 1328.

Eckhart's characteristic teaching comes out in two sermons on the Eternal Birth. This is the name he sometimes gave to coming to oneness with the Divine. To reach it moved by love, we must enter into the innermost depth of our being. This requires a total emptying of the self so that we are left like a desert void of all that was peculiarly our own.[11] Memory, understanding and will must all be left behind. So must sense perception, imagination and everything in which we find ourselves and have ourselves in view. What of ideas of God, for example that he is good, wise and compassionate? They too must be left behind for, divine as they are, they are introduced from the outside through the senses. Nor is reasoning of any avail here. It may be asked, "What is the use of my intellect if it has to be inert and altogether idle? Is it my best plan to raise my mind to the unknowing knowing which obviously cannot be anything? Must I remain in total darkness?" Aye, surely! Thou canst do no better than take up thy abode in total darkness and ignorance.[12] Again it is asked, "For a person in such downright nothingness would it not be better to be doing something to beguile the gloom and desolation; to pray or read or go to church or else to make shift by working at some useful occupation?" The answer is No, be sure of this: absolute stillness, absolute idleness is the best of all.[13] Then when we are completely empty God will overflow into us, as it were.

It must not be thought that Eckhart maintained that life was to be spent in contemplation. There is a life of action also. During contemplation, of course, even the thought of good works that needed doing must be avoided. But afterwards we should get busy, for no one can or should engage in contemplation all the time.[14]

Eckhart was a committed Christian. Nevertheless it has been shown by Suzuki how close in some respects he is to

Mahayana Buddhism. Eckhart speaks of unknowing knowing.
Correspondingly Suzuki, a Zen Buddhist, remarks that the Zen
teachers are all unknowing knowers or knowing unknowners.[15]
But it is especially over the insistence on emptiness that the
similarity is so close. Eckhart says that for the Eternal Birth to
take place the mind must be empty. In Mahayana Buddhism
Sunyata, the Void or Emptiness is basic. The idea is metaphysical;
it is a void full of infinite possibilities. But the source of the idea
lies in mystical experience. "Pure experience is the mind seeing
itself as reflected in itself... This is possible only when the mind
is *Sunyata* itself, that is, when the mind is devoid of all its
possible contents except itself.[16] The last sentence is not very
different from some of Eckhart's.

St Teresa even if she did not use the expression, had things
to say about the emptiness of the mind in achieving mystical
experience. She writes of the third stage of prayer, "This state
is a sleep of the faculties, which are neither wholly lost nor yet
can understand how they work".[17] And closely associated with
St Teresa, and for a time her spiritual director, was the other
great Spanish mystic of the period, St John of the Cross. He does
speak directly about emptiness. It is proper at the beginning of
the spiritual life to practice meditation in which ideas and images
are made use of. But there comes a stage at which meditation
and reasoning have to be left behind. He writes of "the emptiness
and detachment to which in this night, we have to abandon the
faculties of the soul".[18] This is not very far from the emptiness
of the mind described by Suzuki as necessary for mystical
experience. Yet he as a Zen Buddhist is a monist and does not
believe in God in the kind of way Christians do. The point being
made is that the insistence on emptiness found in Zen Buddhism
is not only shared by a mystic like Eckhart who regarded the
experience as one of union with the Godhead beyond the three
persons of the Trinity into which it is eternally differentiated; it
is shared by a more orthodox mystic like St Teresa.

It would appear that part of what the introvertive mystic
does is to turn inwards to basic consciousness. To reach it he
rids his mind of everything else: sensations, desires, images,
thoughts. The basic undifferentiated consciousness he is left with

is immediately interpreted in accordance with what he believes. For Suzuki it is seen as the Void; for Eckhart as the Divine essence, for Teresa as the living God.

But is that kind of interpretation the right one? Is this emptiness of consciousness, insisted on by many mystics, in itself the awareness of the Divine? This was strongly denied by the important fourteenth century Flemish mystic Ruusbroec. His criticism was directed against a heretical movement of the time known as the Free Spirit. They experienced what Ruusbroec calls a false emptiness.[19] The empty consciousness was interpreted as a direct awareness of and union with God. The experience was felt to be so great a thing that it was not to be disturbed by any works however good. So those who had the experience lived in a stage of passivity without performing any activity directed either to God or to neighbour. For Ruusbroec this meant that there must be something radically wrong. A life of active goodness in accordance with the commands of God was the essential basis for the spiritual life. So also was following the practices of the Church. But these people did not know, love, will, pray or desire, for they thought that they already possessed all that the practices of the Church are intended to give. Today it may be that there is no group to which such criticisms apply. But Ruusbroec's main point remains: an empty consciousness is something perfectly natural and is open to anyone, no matter what kind of life he is living, who can free his mind from all its particular contents.

It must not be thought that Ruusbroec was against having the consciousness free from all particular contents. Quite the reverse; it was a necessary part of what he regarded as genuine mystical experience. He was himself a thorough going mystic and sometimes used expressions that led to his being criticised by a leading mystical theologian of the time for holding heretical views. He spoke, for example, of losing ourselves and flowing forth into the wild darkness of the Godhead.[20] He seemed to be saying that the mystic could reach a union of being with God rather than remaining distinct. But he went on to explain in a later work that when he wrote that we are one with God this was to be understood as a oneness in love and not in being.[21]

Can this other aspect of mystical experience, of which Ruusbroec is a notable example, be counted as direct awareness of God? Ruusbroec, like Teresa, was a mystic of love and love does not in itself give an awareness of its object. Knowledge about God, for Ruusbroec, comes from nature and from Scripture. He accepted fully the doctrines of the Church and his mysticism was built on that basis. Neither a mysticism of love, nor the experience of complete tranquility which results from the emptying of consciousness, is taken as making God directly evident.

A similar denial of the claim that in the basic introvertive mystical experience we are directly aware of and united with the Divine, comes from Martin Buber. Writing six hundred years later than Ruusbroec he makes much the same criticism. He had himself reached the experience of undifferentiated unity: consciousness free from all particular contents. He had felt that this was union with the primal being or the Godhead. And he thinks that anyone who has the experience is bound to feel this. But later he came to the conclusion that the unity he had reached was only the basic unity of his own soul.[22]

Neither of these criticisms directly refutes the mystic's claim to an immediate awareness of the Divine. And many people, after careful examination, think that the claim holds up. Franks Davis, for example, in a recent study writes that "these fragmentary and context-laden experiences can still be apprehensions of the living God, the holy 'other' of numinous experiences and the unitive 'ground of being' of mystical experiences".[23] What the criticisms of Ruusbroec and Buber do is to provide an alternative explanation of the basic mystical experience. Because this alternative explanation is perfectly feasible introvertive mystical experience, while a proper part of religious life, cannot be taken with any certainty to be a direct awareness of the Divine. And if this is so it would be hazardous to rely on extrovertive mystical experience.

2. Indirectly Evident or Inferred?

If not directly evident to us, can the Divine be indirectly evident? Can there be an awareness of God which is mediated by sense experience but which is not inferential? This is a topic on which the philosophical theologian John Hick has written extensively. And while other people also have done so it will be sufficient to restrict consideration to what Hick has to say.

It should be mentioned first that the paradigm case of the indirectly evident is the perception of a material object. This is quite different from the awareness of God since God cannot be sensed. Nevertheless a connection can be found in the idea of recognition. We tend to think that when we perceive a material object it is directly evident to us. But this is not the case. Quite apart from intermediate stages, what is received from the sensory organs has to be recognised as something. If it is something familiar recognition is very quick. We do not as a rule simply hear a sound; we hear a baby cry, or a dog bark, or a rifle shot. We do not usually see a complex coloured shape; we see a tree, or a house, or a person. What we see is seen as a certain kind of thing.

It is not only objects that can be seen as being of a certain kind. Hick points out that the same is true of situations and events. We can recognise different kinds of situations, for example a birthday party or a political meeting. These situations are seen as a whole and recognised as what they are. In doing this more than one sense may be employed so the term "seeing-as" is expanded into the wider "experiencing-as".[24]

Now comes a further point: certain situations are experienced as making a moral demand. Hick gives as an illustration seeing someone caught at the bottom of a cliff with the tide coming in fast; we are aware that we have to do something about it. The situation has a significance beyond the purely natural disposition of objects and forces that on one level make it up; we recognise in it a moral claim. Hick suggests that there is an analogous awareness of the presence of God in situations and events. We may experience a situation or event as mediating the presence and activity of God. The situation or event comes about as a result of ordinary natural and human causes. But in and through them, on another level as it were, we recognise the presence and action of God.

This action of God in events in the world was referred to
in the preceding chapter in connection with God as providential
power. While such action is not the only way in which belief in
the reality of God may be justified Hick holds that it is of
primary importance. He refers to the prophets of the Old
Testament. In the experience of Amos it was God who was
threatening selfish and complacent Israel with Assyrain conquest
and calling for repentance. For Jeremiah it was God who was
bringing up the Babylonian army against Jerusalem and
summoning the people to turn to God from their greed and
wickedness. Humanly explicable events were experienced also
as acts of God.

This recognition of the presence and action of God in the
events of their time, according to Hick, was in no way inferential.
Hosea did not *infer* God's mercy, nor Isaiah his universal
sovereignty, nor Jeremiah his righteousness. Rather they knew
that they lived in the presence of God and were conscious of his
acting towards them, and towards their nation, in his mercy, in
his righteousness and in his absolute sovereignty. Again Hick
writes, "God was not, for Amos or Jeremiah or Jesus of Nazareth,
an inferred entity but an experienced personal presence".[25]

This is an impressive idea of how it is possible to recognise
the action of God. And while from the records that we have it
is difficult to be certain, it is at least a probable account of the
way in which the prophets thought. They belonged to a tradition
which believed that God was active in controlling events and
they understood themselves to be living in the presence of God.
It is reasonable to think that the prophets did not make inferences
as to whether God was active in a particular event; they simply
saw it in that way.

But that is not our position today. Most religious people
think that the world has a relative independence. When there is
a famine we do not think that God brought it. The question is
the other way round: why did he not act to prevent it? Certainly
there are people who claim to see the action of God in all events
including many of the small events of everyday life. We think
they are mistaken and see what is not there. That means that if

it is the case that God does act in certain events we have to distinguish them from those in which we think that there is no Divine action. There has to be something special about an event in which we think that God is actively involved. Certainly there are events, notably miracles, about which we feel that without question God is at work. In some other cases the interpretation does have the feeling of being spontaneous. But often the interpretation needs careful weighing up. We have to ask ourselves: is this chance or is it providence? In such cases we do not simply experience the event as the action of God. On the contrary, we go over the reasons for thinking that providence is at work in these events. We may think that the likelihood of the event happening by chance is exceedingly remote. Or it may follow, perhaps very quickly, a specific prayer for that very thing. Whether the reasons are good or bad they are evidence produced in support of a conclusion. This is inference, not seeing-as. If that is how it is in these cases it is probably so in all. Inference can be made very rapidly and it is likely that when recognition seems spontaneous it is in fact done by quick inference.

That recognition of the presence and action of God in events is probably done by inference does not mean that there is anything doubtful about it. Hick writes disparagingly of inferred entities; he makes a contrast between an inferred entity and an experienced presence. But it is by inference that the presence of certain things is known. They are met with in various connections. Natural science is one. For example, in the early years of this century Hopkins carried out a series of nutritional experiments with young rats. He fed them with diets containing only the five nutritional factors then known: water, protein, carbohydrate, fat and minerals. The rats ceased to grow and became ill. When a small amount of milk was added to the diet health was restored and growth resumed. Hopkins inferred that there were hitherto unknown accessory factors in the milk. These accessory food factors were subsequently called vitamins and they have been isolated. But their presence was known first by inference. Another connection in which the presence of something is known by inference is detective work. After investigating the circumstances of someone who is missing the police may issue a warning of the presence of a dangerous killer in the area. They go on inference. But they do not doubt the reality of what they infer. So it is with God; the reality of his action in events is not made doubtful because it is known by inference.

Hick is surely right, when discussing our belief in the reality of God, to put his emphasis on the recognition of God in the events of life. As his examples show this is Biblical religion. My only criticism of his account is about the way in which the recognition is done. It appears that, today at least, it is not done in a way analogous to the recognition that is a part of sense perception. It is done by inference. The events of life provide evidence from which the reality of God may be inferred.

But it is not the only evidence. There is also the natural world. The evidence for the reality of God has long been divided into these two sorts. Hume, for example, although he was discussing chiefly origins of religious belief and not the evidence for its truth, adopted the division in *The Natural History of Religion,* published in 1757. He referred to the works of nature and the events of life. He allowed that the works of nature may also provide evidence for the reality of God. The events of life, he thought, could show only how the belief may have originated. But it may be that Hume was wrong. In any case both lines of evidence require careful assessment.

3. What kind of Inference?

If it is granted that the justification of religious belief has to be inferential a further question arises: what kind of inference can be used?

In arguing from the works of nature one kind of argument used has been deductive. Deductive arguments have a special value: they give proof. In the simplest form there are two premisses and a conclusion. For example, a doctor looking at a sick child might argue:

If he has Koplik's spots in his mouth he has measles.
I see that there are Koplik's spots.
Therefore, he has measles.

Provided that the premisses are known to be true and the form of argument is valid the conclusion is proved. That is because it was implicit in the premisses although that may not have been so obvious as in this simple example. Deductive arguments for the reality of God have been extensively criticised. It now seems doubtful whether a purely deductive argument is possible.

Non-deductive arguments do not prove their conclusion; they confirm or provide evidence for it. The conclusion is not implicit in the premisses and goes beyond the information they contain. For example, the doctor might argue: the child has a temperature, a running nose, red eyes and a barking cough. Although there are no Koplik's spots to be seen he probably has measles. The doctor has good reason for his conclusion but it is not certain.

The doctor's argument is to the best explanation. He thinks of a diagnosis that best explains all the symptoms and signs. Arguments to the best explanation are used in all sorts of connections. Scientific arguments are of this kind. So are the arguments of investigators of an air crash. They look for all the clues they can find. Then they give an account of what went wrong that best explains all the evidence. Gardeners may argue in the same kind of way. In some places the plants are not doing well. Does lack of water, or of sunshine or of some nutrient or attack by a fungus give the best explanation of all the findings?

The question now arises as to how good the explanation is. Or to put it the other way round, in each of the arguments to be presented, how can we assess the amount of support the evidence gives to the conclusion? This may be done by a formal method of reasoning. Probability theory can be used in much the same way as in scientific theories to assess the degree of support the evidence gives.[26] But this is not the only way the amount of support provided by the evidence can be assessed. There are informal ways of reasoning which depend on personal judgement.[27] For example historians, who use informal reasoning in assessing their evidence, are often able to arrive at quite definite conclusions. Again, it is the business of courts of law to assess evidence and come to a decision. This they do by the exercise of personal judgement and not by the use of probability theory. In the present connection also it may be held that personal judgement, consistently applied, can properly be used to assess the evidence.

There is one further characteristic of the arguments to be mentioned; they are cumulative. In a cumulative argument while each piece of evidence, or each constituent argument, taken by itself, gives limited support to the conclusion, taken together the support may be strong. The theory of evolution is supported by a cumulative argument. It draws on a large number of quite different pieces of evidence: material buried in the rocks in a certain sequence, comparative anatomy, the possession by some species of structures useless for their way of life, geographical distribution and others. Each of these pieces of evidence taken separately gives some support to the theory. Taken together the support is extremely strong. The question of the reality of God must be taken in the same way. The strength of each of the arguments has to be assessed. Account has to be taken of the contrary evidence presented by the fact of evil; is it compatible with the kind of God being argued for? Finally a judgement has to be made on the cumulative weight of all the arguments.

References

1. *The Idea of the Holy,* 1917.

2. W. Manson, *The Epistle to the Hebrews,* London, 1951, pp. 23f.

3. *Op. cit.,* paperback ed. pp. 61f.

4. J. Oman, *The Natural and the Supernatural,* Cambridge, 1931, p. 65.

5. Autobiographical Reflections in *The Theology of Paul Tillich,* ed. C.W. Kegley and R.W. Bretall, New York, 1952, p. 6.

6. R.C. Zaehner, *Mysticism: Sacred and Profane,* Oxford, 1957, paperback ed., p. 32.

7. *Ibid.,* pp. 97f.

8. F. Heiler, *Prayer,* Oxford, 1937 ed., p. 194.

9. *Life,* chs. XI to XXI in *Complete Works of St Teresa,* Vol. I, London, 1946.

10. *Ibid.,* p. 110.

11. *Meister Eckhart,* E.T. C de B. Evans, Vol. I, London, 1924, pp. 18ff.

12. *Ibid.,* p. 21.

13. *Ibid.,* p. 22.

14. Fragment: Love Cannot be Lazy, in *Late Medieval Mysticism,* ed. R.C. Petry, Philadelphia, 1957, p. 207.

15. D.T. Suzuki, *Mysticism: Christian and Buddhist,* London, 1957, paperback ed., p. 15.

16. *Ibid.,* p. 19.

17. *Op. cit.,* p. 96.

18. *Ascent of Mount Carmel,* Bk. II, ch. VII. 1 in *Complete Works of Saint John of the Cross,* London, 1964, p. 82.

19. John Ruusbroec, *The Spiritual Espousals and Other Works,* ed. J.A. Wiseman, New York, 1985, pp. 136ff.

20. *Ibid.,* p. 132.

21. *A Mirror of Eternal Blessedness,* in *The Spiritual Espousals and Other Works,* p. 247.

22. *Between Man and Man,* London, 1947, paperback ed., p. 43.

23. C. Franks Davis, *The Evidential Force of Religious Experience,* Oxford, 1989, p. 227.

24. J.H. Hick, Religious Faith as Experiencing-As, in *Talk of God,* ed. G.N.A. Vesey, London, 1969, pp. 20-32.

25. J.H. Hick, *Arguments for the Existence of God,* London, 1970, p. 116.

26. R. Swinburne, *The Existence of God,* Oxford, 1977, Revised ed., 1991, pp. 15ff.

27. R. Prevost, *Probability and Theistic Explanation,* Oxford, 1990, pp. 58ff.

Chapter III
Arguments from the World

The world has always suggested to people that there must be some unseen reality on which it depends. It is not only unsophisticated people who think like this. And while the belief of an individual depends to a large extent on the culture to which he belongs, a person may come to believe in the reality of the Divine independently of his culture. At a time when Communism still dominated Russian life a young priest described how he had come to believe in God. He belonged to an atheist family living in an atheist society. He was a pupil at a special school for advanced children and concentrated on chemistry and mathematics. He felt that there must be some higher powers and became interested in religion. When he was about fifteen he began to believe in God. That is natural religion. It is a response to the mystery and the order and the beauty of the world.

In natural religion the response is unstudied. Yet there is implicit reasoning in it. I remember the reaction of an uneducated woman in India when she heard that some people did not believe in God. At once she pointed to the flowering trees outside and asked, "How do they think all that got here?" This represents the outlook of many people. Butler remarks that there is no need of abstruse reasonings and distinctions to convince an unprejudiced understanding that there is a God. But they may be necessary to answer abstruse difficulties once such are raised.[1] Because abstruse difficulties have in fact been raised abstruse reasonings and distinctions are necessary. They make up a large part of natural theology. It is concerned with other topics also. But its main business is to put into clear logical form the implicit reasoning of natural religion and to reply to objections.

This is done in the form of a number of arguments. They are generally taken together as a group. In order to avoid confusion it should be mentioned that one of the group is of a different kind from the others. This is the ontological argument. It does not start with facts about the world; it starts from a definition of God and moves by deduction to his existence. Given this concept of God, it is claimed, his existence necessarily follows. There are distinguished present-day philosophers who consider the argument valid. But the general opinion is that it is not valid. It will not be discussed here.

1. The Argument from the Existence of the World

The argument is not, like others to be discussed later, from particular features of the world; it is from the fact that there is a world. Why should there be a world at all? A sense of wonder and awe at the existence of the world lies behind this type of argument, generally called cosmological. The existence of the world must be accounted for in some way; something must have brought it into existence. The first three of Aquinas' five ways are arguments from the existence of the world to the existence of God as its explanation. They will not be followed here. Instead the argument is based on the version put forward by the philosopher and theologian Samuel Clarke in 1704.[2] It is perhaps the most forceful presentation of the argument. But while Clarke's argument is strictly deductive the form of it given here is not.

(a) The best explanation of the world's existence is ultimate self-existing being

Clarke argued that the whole of existing things could not consist of an infinite succession of dependent beings. It required for its explanation the existence of an independent being and one that was self-existent.

As in all deductive versions of the argument Clarke uses as one premise the principle of sufficient reason. It cannot be proved to be true but we all commonly assume it. The statement of the

principle here is: whatever exists must have a cause or reason of
its existence. Something cannot exist for no reason at all. To
find the reason of anything's existence we have to start with the
thing in question and go back to what it depends on for its
coming into existence. People owe their existence to their parents,
for example, and they to theirs. In following the chain of
dependency there could be either of two outcomes. One is that
we go on tracing an infinite succession of dependent beings
without any ultimate reason for their existence; the other is that
we do reach an ultimate reason.

The first alternative is said to be absurd. In an infinite
succession of dependent beings each depends for its existence
on the power and efficacy of that being which immediately
precedes it. This again depends on the one beyond and so on in
the infinite succession. But the whole infinite chain or succession
of dependent beings has itself nothing to depend on. Yet it requires
something as much as any particular object which begins to
exist in time. It is reasonable to ask what it was that determined
something to exist rather than nothing and bestowed being on
the particular succession which constitutes the universe. We have
to go to the second alternative and postulate a necessarily existent
being who carries the reason of his existence in himself or, as
I shall put it, ultimate self-existing being.

In Part IX of his *Dialogues Concerning Natural Religion*
Hume made several criticisms of the argument. One has been
especially influential and is widely judged to be fatal to it. Once
an explanation has been given of each of the objects in a chain
or succession there is no need to look for an explanation of the
whole. The uniting of the various parts into a whole is the work
of the mind and has no influence on the nature of things. "Did
I show you the particular causes of each individual in a collection
of twenty particles of matter, I should think it very unreasonable,
should you afterwards ask me, what was the cause of the whole
twenty. This is sufficiently explained in explaining the cause of
the parts".

Is Hume right in thinking that when each member of a
collection has been explained the whole has been explained?

Gale maintains that this is not necessarily the case and it can be shown by counter examples.[3] Suppose there is a group of five people sitting in the lounge of a hotel in Delhi. Each gives an explanation of why he or she is there. One is from a school in England where she teaches geography. A man was in India as a child and wants to see it again. Another likes to travel and had never been to India. A woman got interested in India by reading stories about it. Another had just lost her husband and was advised to go to India for a complete change. Each has a reason for being there. But may not the conjunctive fact that they are all there together also require explanation? When we learn that they are on a Cook's tour and are waiting for the courier, the full explanation is provided. Clarke's argument, then, holds up against Hume's most important criticism of it.

As already mentioned the argument depends on the principle of sufficient reason. In place of this an argument to the best explanation is adequate for our purpose. The conclusion of the first part of the argument then becomes: the best explanation of the existence of the world is ultimate self-existing being of some sort.

This conclusion is very important. But there is no need to go into detailed discussion of further objections to the argument and replies to them. For the naturalist or materialist has no difficulty in accepting this part of the argument. It is the second part that he cannot agree with.

(b) The nature of ultimate self-existing being

That this was the most controversial part of the argument was quite clear to Clarke. The heart of the matter is whether self-existent being has intelligence. Clarke put the point forcibly in his proposition VIII. *"The self-existent and original cause of all things must be an intelligent being.* In this proposition lies the main question between us and the atheists. For, that something must be self-existent; and that which is self-existent must necessarily be eternal and infinite and the original cause of all things; will not have much dispute. But all atheists, whether they hold the world to be *of itself* eternal both as to matter and form, or whether they hold the matter only to be necessary and the form to be contingent, or whatever hypothesis they frame; have always asserted and must maintain, either directly or indirectly, that the self-existent being is not an *intelligent* being...." The question of the existence of God becomes the question of the nature of self-existent being.

In recent years materialists have suggested that self-existing being is energy with matter forming from it. Self-existing being of this sort, it is claimed, would allow the whole vast process of the development of the world and of living things to be explained. As is well-known, very plausible accounts can be given along these lines.

There is no need to deny that energy may be basic in the development of the universe or that it may be eternal and infinite. What is denied is that it is ultimate. Clarke notes that something might exist eternally and yet depend on something else. He gives as an illustration the light from the sun. If the sun were eternal, light, which is dependent on it, would eternally proceed from it (p. 35). Eternity does not in itself imply ultimacy; other considerations have to be taken into account. Something beyond energy is required to explain how this actual world came into being. It is this world with its intricacy and its beauty that has to be explained. And human beings with self-consciousness and moral sensitivity are part of it. Only after the arguments based on particular features of the world have been set out can a judgement properly be made on the nature of ultimate self-existing being.

2. The Argument from Ordered Complexity

The argument is that the complex order we find in the world cannot have been arrived at purely of its own accord. There must be Divine direction. This corresponds with Aquinas' fifth way: all bodies obeying natural laws, even when they lack awareness, tend to a goal; that implies direction by someone with awareness.[4] The argument is given the name teleological from *telos* meaning end or goal. It is often called the argument to design. This is misleading. It is too suggestive of a human activity. Design involves making plans, choosing carefully between alternatives and fitting means to ends. This is anthropomorphic and it is no part of the argument in its strongest form.

The most celebrated statement of the argument in the English speaking world was made by William Paley in 1802. His book, *Natural Theology,* starts with an illustration. Suppose I was walking across a heath and happened to kick a stone. I might ask myself how the stone came to be there. The answer might be that possibly it had always been there. But supposing I found a watch on the ground and asked the same question? I could not answer that perhaps it had always been there. This is because on inspecting it I see the complex arrangement of cog-wheels and balance and spring. But there is more than that. They are arranged for a purpose; they enable someone to tell the time. Such an instrument cannot have got together by chance. There must have been a watch maker.

The book is a long cumulative argument drawing on much of the science of the day. But it is especially to human anatomy that Paley turns for evidence. Almost half the book is anatomy. In the body there are numbers of structures with an astonishing fitness for particular functions and all make for the well-being of the whole. Paley refers, for example, to the tendon of the superior oblique (trochlear) muscle which is one of six that move the eyeball. It goes, suitably lubricated, through a fibro—cartilaginous ring which changes the direction of the pull by more than a right angle. This is rather like a rope on a ship going over a block. But Paley's primary argument is not from analogy although he does also argue in that way. The chief point about the comparisons is that they bring out the extreme improbability that the structures of the body have come into being purely by chance. He says a little earlier, "I desire no greater certainty in reasoning than that by which chance is excluded from the present disposition of the natural world".[5] The current assumption was that each structure was specially designed. But the argument is not dependent on this. It is that they could not have come into being simply by chance; intelligence must be at work.

Paley's was far from being the first presentation of the argument. In the eighteenth century it was generally regarded as very strong and as the primary ground for belief in God.

There are two classical examinations of the argument which have influenced all subsequent discussion. One is by Hume who subjected the argument to detailed criticism in his *Dialogues Concerning Natural Religion,* published in 1779. The other is by Kant. He had read a German translation of Hume's work in manuscript a year before publishing his *Critique of Pure Reason.* He does not add a great deal to the points made by Hume although he may have arrived at his own position independently. However that may be the *Dialogues* bring out all that is required and may be taken as the basis for discussion of the argument. One of Hume's points has to do with the problem of evil. This will be discussed in Chapter VIII. What has to be discussed here are three other issues which Hume brings up.

(a) The argument from analogy is weak

After some preliminary discussion in Part I Cleanthes, generally taken to represent the kind of view held by Butler, states his case. The world resembles a great machine. It is subdivided into an infinite number of smaller machines. All the machines, even in their minutest parts, are adjusted to one another with great accuracy. And that is what we see throughout nature: means are adapted to ends in a way exactly resembling, although greatly exceeding, what is found in things made by human intelligence. Since the effects in the two cases exactly resemble one another we are led to infer, by the rules of analogy, that the causes also resemble one another. There must be an Author of nature who is somewhat similar to the mind of human beings. The argument demonstrates both the reality of the Divine and his similarity to human mind and intelligence (Part II).

Philo, usually taken to represent Hume's position, replies that the natural world is not very like the products of human intelligence. It is not, for example, like a house or a watch. In point of fact, it is more like an animal or vegetable body. In these organisms there is the closest sympathy between their constituent parts and each part operates towards its own preservation and that of the whole. The products of human design are not like that. And why should mind be taken as the model of what it is that makes the world? There may be unknown principles at work. In any case we know some that produce order. The generation of one living being from another is an example. It is possible that the world has arisen from a seed thrown off by another world and accordingly is like an animal or vegetable.

Both characters argue as far as they can by analogy. Cleanthes says that the world resembles a machine, therefore it is a machine, therefore it arose from design. Philo says that the world resembles an animal, therefore it is an animal, therefore it arose by generation or something like it. Each reaches his position by arguing from analogy.

This first criticism, that the argument from analogy is weak, is easily answered. The teleological argument in its strongest form is not from analogy but from probability. How like the world is to the products of human intelligence and whether it is more like something else is irrelevant; the logic of the argument is not analogy. Of course it was reasonable for Hume to take it as analogy; that is how it was mostly taken in his day—and how it is often taken today. Paley, who is later and had read the *Dialogues,* argues primarily on the basis of probability. If the argument is to have any value this is the way it has to be taken.

It is true that analogy cannot altogether be avoided in attempting to understand how the world came into being. Analogy is used in the same kind of way in science. Harré puts the point clearly. "Building a theory is a matter of developing an appropriate concept by analogy. This is the essential heart of science because it is the basis of explanation".[6] In the religious case the analogy taken is human intelligence. Nevertheless the argument itself is not based on analogy but on probability: that the things in the world should have got their complex forms with no intelligent direction is highly improbable.

It is sometimes suggested that this is not an issue to which the idea of probability is applicable. One reason is the require- ments of a probability theory. When using an argument from inverse probability to support a hypothesis it must possess some initial probability. An argument from inverse probability has the form, "if a given outcome is more probable on hypothesis A than on hypothesis B, then it is more probable that A rather than B is correct." Hypothesis A is that the world has had been formed under Divine direction. It must have some probability before the argument from inverse probability is brought in. This, Ewing suggests, is given by the conviction a great many people have about the reality of God.[7] No doubt that does not give much prior probability but it gives at least some. And this is all that is needed to allow the argument to proceed. In addition some probability is supplied by the other arguments for the reality of God; there is no reason why this one should be taken before the others.

Another objection to the use of probability is that the world is unique and probability has no application when only one entity is being considered. But that is a confusion. The argument is not, in the first place, about the one world; it is about the many particular things in the world. What is being maintained is that it is highly improbable that the immensely complex things in the world could have come into being without any direction by intelligence.

(b) Little can be drawn from the argument

The point Hume is making is that people who wrote on natural religion tried to get more from the argument than it warranted. Hume is perfectly right. They did think that a good deal of knowledge about God could be derived from the teleological argument. Both natural attributes like knowledge and power, and moral attributes like goodness, could properly be inferred. Hume denies all this. The argument is from effect to cause. But from a given effect we can only infer a cause sufficient to produce the effect. He illustrates the point with a pair of scales. Suppose we can only see one side. Then if it goes up all we can say is that the weight on the other side is greater. We cannot say by how much or even whether there is one or several weights. So from the works of nature we may perhaps infer mind but not one resembling the human. Nor can we infer infinity or perfection or even unity—there may be several deities working together for all we can say (Part V).

The conclusion so far reached is that it is very improbable that the ordered complexity of the things which make up the world is due simply to chance. Now it can be added that there must be some principle of order at work. And unless another source of order can be suggested as a serious possibility we are bound to think of it as analogous to the human mind. That leaves us with the question: could there be another principle which will account for the complex order of the world. This is discussed in Part VIII.

(c) Complex order may have other sources

The source suggested is taken from one line of Greek thought. The theory is that everything is made up of atoms. The atoms vary in size, weight and shape and are infinite in number. In the beginning they rain obliquely down in empty space. The atoms collide and get entangled. In this sort of way innumerable worlds may be formed; no intelligent direction is necessary.

Hume takes matter to be in constant movement. As against the Greeks, he suggests that the number of particles is finite. But he does require infinite time. In infinite time every possible arrangement of the particles must occur an infinite number of times. This is due to the power of infinity and presents no problem. The problem is for matter to be in continual motion and yet to maintain the constancy of the forms it produces. It is suggested that this will happen eventually. New forms will continually be tried until a form comes into being which can maintain itself in spite of the movement of its constituent parts.

In the case of living things maintenance of their forms will depend on the various parts being adjusted to one another and to the well-being of the whole organism. There has also to be an adjustment to the environment. An defect in these adjustments and the organism will be destroyed. All this can come about from the action of blind unguided force. Yet when matter is so arranged that the forms which have come into being are preserved the appearance will be that everything is designed.

Hume simply wanted to show that alternatives to intelligent direction could be suggested to account for the complex order of the world. His conjecture was not meant to be taken very seriously nor was it at the time. It was purely speculative with no evidence offered in support. But things changed dramatically in the middle of the nineteenth century. Darwin and Wallace independently and simultaneously put forward the theory of evolution by variation and natural selection. And with the publication of the *Origin of Species* a year later, in 1859, the idea of special creation, hitherto generally accepted, had to be abandoned. The teleological argument does not necessarily maintain the special creation of each species, although that was assumed. What it does maintain is that a directing intelligence is in some way involved. Evolution by chance variation and natural selection seemed to make even that unnecessary.

Darwin produced a mass of evidence in support of the theory. And it explained things which could not be accounted for on the supposition of special creation. The distribution of the cranial nerves in human beings is an example. There are two tiny muscles in the middle ear which work together. Why should one be supplied by the fifth nerve and the other by the seventh? The answer lies in the distribution of nerves to the gills of primitive fish. A sequence of far reaching changes in structure can be traced from fish through reptiles up to mammals. Through it all the distribution of the nerves remains constant.

Darwin's theory postulated two factors at work. There was both variation and natural selection. His views on variation have required amendment. Like almost everyone else he did not know of Mendel's work on heredity begun about 1856. It only became widely known after a Dutch biologist came upon it in 1900. Even then it was not quickly recognised as supplementing Darwin's theory and in no way an alternative. Mendel showed that characteristics were passed on, not by any process of blending, but as distinct units of inheritance. These units were subsequently called genes. They are not effected by changes in the body but do themselves occasionally undergo change— mutation. These changes takes place by chance. Chance may work in two ways. There may be independent and extraneous factors influencing the gene. And in the presence of causative influences the gene may respond in more than one way.

It has been maintained that because mutations take place by chance there cannot be any purposive direction in the evolutionary process. This does not follow. As the statistician D.J. Bartholomew points out, chance can be used in carrying out a purpose.[8] If, for example, some dangerous or unwelcome task has to be done by one person out of a group they may draw lots for it. In the case of evolution Bartholomew suggests that the fact that mutations are chance events may serve a purpose. By giving rise to a great variety of types chance mutation ensures that there will be at least some which are capable of carrying on under difficult conditions.[9] The nuclear physicist and theologian W.G. Pollard, on the other hand takes a different view. Just because mutations are chance events it is possible that there may be a Divine direction. It is chance events, Pollard holds, that are open to such influence.[10] This is discussed further in Chapter V. Pollard believes that God is active in all events, a view that has already been rejected. But it may be that God acts in mutations occasionally in order to bring about some especially significant step in the evolutionary process. Either way, the fact that mutations are chance events does not it inself rule out direction.

The other factor in Darwin's theory is natural selection. It is this which ordinarily gives direction to evolution. Change can be progressive, directed along particular lines of development by selection. It grasps and gives permanence to those changes in structure and behaviour which fit an organism for its evnironment. Fitness means more than is suggested by the phrase struggle for existence. It covers the whole life of the organism. In the case of many animals and birds fitness includes courtship and mating, rearing of offspring and group relationships as well as the ability to find food and escape predators. One of the things which favours changes taking place in a certain direction may be a new environment. An example is the fish that came to live on land— there are existing fish which sometimes come to land. In this case it is the ability to breathe which is important. In other cases it may be feeding habits. Those animals with most ability to adapt to the environment are likely to be selected for survival and reproduction. So instead of direction in the formation of structure and behaviour by intelligence there is direction by natural selection.

Darwin's theory applies to the development of living things. Already in the nineteenth century people saw that it would not apply to the physical and chemical conditions which allowed living things to emerge. In recent years scientific investigation has shown how very precise the conditions must be for life and consciousness to develop. A whole series of conditions had to be pretty well exactly as they in fact were for that to be possible. In many cases it appears very improbable that such conditions should appear autonomously. It is these considerations which now supply the main weight of the argument from ordered complexity. Yet it was not theologians but scientists who drew attention to them. The examples given here are taken from the very large book on the subject by Barrow and Tipler[11] and from the well known popular books by Stephen Hawking[12] and Paul Davies especially.[13]

Barrow and Tipler give an explanation of the facts they record by what is called the anthropic principle. This has two forms. The weak form was put forward by Brandon Carter in 1974 and states, "What we can expect to observe must be restricted by the conditions necessary for our existence as observers". It alludes is the first place to something important although well known. The observations we make are limited by our position and our capacities; there may be a great deal we cannot observe. The principle is sometimes interpreted as saying: there is nothing surprising in our observing the remarkable conditions which produced us; if they had not been what they were we would not be here to observe them. But the problem is not how it is that we are able to observe the conditions; it is how they came to be. Barrow and Tipler face this and interpret the principle in a much more far reaching way. They use it to explain the conditions in the natural world on which our existence depends. They write "Many observations of the natural world, although remarkable *a priori,* can be seen in this light as the inevitable consequence of our own existence".[14] There is surely some confusion here. We can hardly affect the course of things before we exist. Rather it is because things were as they were that it was possible for observers to come into being.

A strong form of the anthropic principle was also put forward by Carter, "The universe must have those properties which allow life to develop within it at some stage in its history". The word must is ambiguous and the principle has been taken in several ways. One way is that somehow intelligent life must come into existence at some stage in the history of the universe.[15] For such ideas there is no clear justification. It has to be said that while what have been called anthropic coincidences are striking, they are not explained by the anthropic principles that have been propounded.

We will now look at a number of the conditions in the development of the universe which had to be precisely as they were for life and consciousness to be possible.

(i) Beginnings

In 1929 the American astronomer Edwin Hubble reported his discovery that the universe was expanding. This is exceedingly important for our understanding of the universe. One corollary is that it is likely to have had a beginning rather than always existing. If the expansion rate is extended backwards a stage is reached at which the universe will have begun. This is about fifteen thousand million years ago. The figure is confirmed by independent dating of the oldest stars. The beginning is generally referred to as the big bang. It is the course of events in which space, time and matter came into being and the universe so begun started expanding. An immense amount of heat and light would be produced. Shortly afterwards a large amount of cosmic gases, mostly hydrogen and helium, would be formed.

The rate of expansion of the universe is of critical impor- tance. It had to be such that it would keep the universe expanding against the force of gravity. This operates between every particle and every object in the universe; the bigger they are and the closer together the stronger the force. Gravity pulls the cosmic material together; expansion scatters it apart. If the expansion rate were too small the universe would collapse in on itself. If it were too great nothing could be formed as the material is driven apart. The very existence of the universe depends on the precise values of the two figures. Had either the rate of expansion or the force of gravity been slightly different from what they were the universe would not have formed.

(ii) Galaxies

These are very large assemblages of stars. Besides stars there is gas and dust. The galaxy we belong to, the Milky Way, is similar to many others. It is disc-like with a centre made up of a lot of stars and spiral arms also containing many stars. The whole structure slowly rotates. A galaxy contains about a hundred thousand million stars. The size also is enormous; ours is about a hundred thousand light-years across. The universe has some hundred thousand million galaxies.

Galaxies would form as the universe cooled and expanded. The material from which they were made would be masses of gas, mostly hydrogen and helium. It is thought that some regions would be a little denser than others. That is where a galaxy would form. In these regions there would be more gravitational attraction, the cosmic material would come together and more material would be drawn in from the surroundings making the region denser still. As that happened the gravitational pull from material outside might start it rotating. In the dense region itself there would be areas in which there was further separating out by contraction and here stars would begin to form in the galaxy.

But there must be more to it than this. It has been calculated that the dense regions referred to would not grow fast enough to overcome the expansion which reduces the density of the cosmic gasses. While very little can be said about it there must have been something special about the initial conditions of the universe. They would have to be such that there were irregularities in the density of the gasses. The irregularities would have to be sufficient to allow galaxies to form yet not so great as to bring about gravitational collapse to black holes. If it was the initial conditions that were responsible for the irregularities then here again things had to be just right.

(iii) Stars

As just mentioned a star is formed in a galaxy as a mass of gas, mostly hydrogen, contracts in on itself under the influence of gravity. The contraction leads to heating. The temperature at the centre becomes high enough for nuclear reactions and hydrogen is converted to helium. The additional heat produced raises the pressure until it balances the gravitational force and the gas stops contracting. Big stars need to be hotter to balance the gravitational attraction and so burn up their hydrogen more quickly. But eventually this will happen to every star and it will come to an end.

This takes place in more than one way. Of special significance is what may happen to a big star. When it is no longer able to generate sufficient heat to keep up its internal pressure the centre part may collapse inwards. Then it sometimes happens that the outer parts are blown off in a great explosion. Brilliant light is produced for a few days in what is called a supernova. This has an important part to play in making life possible. The original cosmic material in a galaxy is mostly hydrogen and helium. But inside a big star which becomes very hot large amounts of heavier elements are made. It is the supernova eruption which scatters this material in the galaxy. When later generations of stars and planets are formed they incorporate some of this material. It is in this way that important elements like carbon and iron become available.

Our sun is an average sized star. It is located in one of the spiral arms of the galaxy. The heat and light it radiates come from the burning of hydrogen into helium by a nuclear process. The rate of energy production and energy loss are balanced so the sun remains in a stable state. It is important for steady conditions on earth that this should be the case.

The lifetime of the sun depends on the rate at which heat energy is produced and lost. It is produced at the centre and lost at the surface. The ease with which it gets to the surface is partly dependent on the opacity of the material it passes through and this is affected by the electromagnetic force. Very big stars transport heat energy to the surface mainly by radiation. These are blue giants; they rapidly use up their nuclear fuel. Small stars transport heat energy to the surface largely by convection. These are red dwarfs; they have a lower surface temperature and give out less energy. The sun, like most stars, falls between the two. Its functioning depends on the precise values of two of the four fundamental forces in the universe. If gravity were very slightly stronger or the electromagnetic force slightly weaker all the stars would behave like blue giants. If the changes were the other way round they would all be like red dwarfs. Either way there could not be life as we know it.

(iv) Atoms

We all know that at bottom matter is far from being the solid, inert stuff we ordinarily think of. What we do not always realise is how precise is the structure of its minute constituents and how active they are. Atoms, the basic building block of everything, have a nucleus of varying size and electrons which can be understood as orbiting around it. All the rest is space. The force needed to keep the electrons in place comes from the electromagnetic attraction between the positively charged nucleus and the negatively charged electrons. This force also holds atoms together to form molecules, the next level in the structure of matter.

The simplest atom is that of the very important element hydrogen. It has a nucleus made of one proton with one electron in orbit. The charge on the proton and the electron, the same value for each positive or negative, is a universal constant; it is the same strength in all protons and electrons. In heavy hydrogen, or deuterium, the nucleus has another particle in it, the neutron. This is almost the same size as the proton but is electrically neutral. The two particles are held together by the strong nuclear force, the third fundamental force. There is still only one electron.

Another element that has been mentioned is helium. This has double the mass of deuterium. It has two protons, two neutrons and two electrons in orbit. An element that will be referred to shortly, as of the greatest significance for living beings, is carbon. It has six protons, six neutrons and six electrons. The strong nuclear force binds together all the particles in the nucleus against the mutual repulsion of the protons.

The strong nuclear force has a limited range and only works between particles which are close together. By contrast the electric force of repulsion works between all protons in the nucleus. So a very big nucleus, with many protons, tends to be unstable. For while a proton in a nucleus is kept there by the nuclear force of those nearby, it tends to be pushed out by the accumulated electric field of all the protons. Accordingly, elements with a very big nucleus, above that of uranium, have relatively short lifetimes. Now suppose that the strong nuclear force was a little less strong. Then other nuclei, such as that of iron, would be unstable and not likely to last.

Suppose, on the other hand, that the strong nuclear force was a little stronger. It would then be able to hold together two protons in a nucleus to form a di-proton. But because of the mutual repulsion of the protons the nucleus would be less stable than deuteron, the nucleus of deuterium, which has one proton and one neutron. Under the influence of the weak nuclear force, one of whose effects is to change one particle into another, the di-proton would readily change to a deuteron. Deuterium is formed as a first stage in the burning of hydrogen to helium in the sun. The process is normally a slow one. But if deuteron was formed from a di-proton the process would be very much faster. The hydrogen would quickly be used up and the sun would shine no more. So the existence of living beings is dependent on the exact value of the strong nuclear force.

(v) Carbon

The element carbon has special powers of combination; it forms far more compounds than any other element. So much is this so that carbon compounds form a special branch of chemistry; organic chemistry is by definition the chemistry of carbon. It is the basic element in living things; life is often said to be carbon based. It is sometimes suggested that silicon, which is in some ways similar to carbon, could also be a basis for life. But silicon compounds do not have the stability of carbon compounds. Nor has any such life been found. It seems that for life carbon is required.

As already mentioned carbon is made in the stars. Barrow and Tipler give a clear account of how this is done.[16] When the hydrogen of a star is used up the pressure support of the star, which came from converting hydrogen to helium, is lost and the star begins to contract under gravity. This raises the temperature and another reaction takes place: helium is converted to carbon.

$$3 \text{ He}^4 \rightarrow C^{12}$$

In point of fact there is an intermediate step in which beryllium is formed. So the whole reaction is:

$$2 \text{ He}^4 \rightarrow Be^8$$
$$Be^8 + He^4 \rightarrow C^{12}$$

But unless the reaction proceeds with maximal efficiency very little carbon would be produced. The efficiency of the reaction depends upon quite precise figures for the energy levels involved. The energy levels of helium and beryllium have to correspond closely with a vital energy level of carbon if the reaction is to proceed rapidly. Measurement has shown that the levels do correspond.

There is a danger in the other direction; the reaction could go too far. If another helium nucleus entered the reaction all the carbon would be converted to oxygen.

$$C^{12} + He^4 \rightarrow O^{16}$$

In this case the active energy level of the oxygen nucleus is below the total energy of carbon and helium. This means that the reaction cannot take place efficiently. So here too the precise values for the energy levels of the nuclei involved ensures that there is enough carbon for living things to exist. In the jargon usually used in this connection, the value of the energy levels appear to be finely tuned.

We now return to living things themselves. Is it probable, as commonly believed, that chance variation and natural selection alone are sufficient to account for the ordered complexity of living things? The answer to questions of this kind can only come from the examination of particular cases. Two cases will therefore be presented for consideration. One is from the beginning and the other from what is often regarded as the culmination of the evolutionary process. In the first case some biochemical terms will be used which may not be familiar to everyone. This is unavoidable since in the consideration of cases it is the detail which counts.

The first case is the origin of life. All life, apart from viruses which are not self-sufficient, is cellular. So the question is, is it probable that cellular life has arisen by natural processes alone? Animal cells are exceedingly complex—chemical factories they have been called. But they will have developed from something simpler. The simplest cell we know of is the bacterial cell. Even this is far from simple, but we have no idea what anything simpler would be like, so we have to begin here. The bacterial cell has no nucleus but it has the same basic features as other cells.

All cells are surrounded by a membrane. It keeps the contents of the cell from being dissipated to the outside. The membrane has the special property of being selectively permeable. Some molecules, which are necessary to the life of the cell can come in, while others are kept out. Both the being and the working of the cell are dependent on the membrane.

Cells have to build up the many chemical compounds necessary for their growth and division. They take in from their environment simple, or relatively simple substances, such as glucose. From them the complex ones which the cells require are constructed. At the temperature of living things these processes would be exceedingly slow. But all cells have certain substances, catalysts, which speed up the reactions. The special catalysts only found in cells are called enzymes. They are highly specific; a particular enzyme is normally required for each of the many chemical reactions in the cell.

Of the substances built up in this way a most important group for the life of the cell is proteins. They form part of the material out of which the cell membrane is made up. And they form the enzymes which are themselves always proteins.

Proteins are usually very large molecules. They are made up of chains of chemical substances called amino acids. Generally there is one long chain but there may be two or more. The chain is folded in a particular way giving the molecule a shape which is important for its function. Amino acids, from which proteins are built up, are relatively simple substances. Only twenty different ones are used in living things. But a protein may have up to three thousand of them. The sequence of amino acids in the chain is irregular and is specific to the particular protein. This gives each protein a precise and complex chemical structure. That means the making of it requires precise information.

This information is held in the genetic material of the cell. It is coded in an immensely long molecule whose overall chemical structure is the same in all living things from bacteria to human beings. This is DNA. The form of the long molecule is spiral in the loose sense—rather like a spiral staircase. The two sides are made of a sugar combined with phosphoric acid. This never varies. The steps which run between the two sides are made up of a purine and a pyramidine base, one from each side joining the other. Both are fairly simple substances whose basic structure is a ring of carbon and nitrogen atoms. Purines have one ring, pyramidines two. The three substances, a sugar, phosphoric acid and either a purine or a pyramidine base, form compounds known as nucleotides. DNA is made up of a vast number of them, one after another, in two connected strands forming a huge coiled molecule.

In the DNA molecule only four different bases are used, two purines and two pyramidines. But there may be many thousands of them. This means that an enormous number of combinations is possible in the order in which they come. In each molecule the order is both irregular and highly specific. It is through this order that the information necessary for the ordering of amino acids in proteins is coded. It is done by the sequence of purines and pyramidines in the molecule. A group of three successive bases corresponds to each of the amino acids and so determines that order in which they come in the protein chain.

Since one of the functions of DNA is a code for directing protein synthesis a means of translation is required. The base sequence of DNA has to be translated into the amino acid sequence of proteins. This is by no means simple. Taking the case of animal cells, DNA is in the nucleus while protein synthesis takes place outside it. This situation is met by transcribing the base sequence of DNA on to a single stranded molecule of the same type. Other intermediaries also are used in the process. In addition, as already mentioned, for the building up of proteins specific enzymes are required. They are themselves coded in DNA.

As well as their ability to code protein making information DNA molecules have another remarkable property. They are able to replicate themselves. The molecule separates into the two strands of which it is composed. These are not identical. But each part is able to make up the complementary half from free nucleotide bases. So two molecules are formed where there was only one before. The process is made possible by the precise structure of the molecule. As just mentioned, of the four bases which are employed in the making of the molecule two are purines and two pyramidines. The key factor is that a particular purine in one strand always links with a particular pyramidine in the other. So if a particular purine comes at a certain place in the one strand a particular pyramidine must come at the corresponding place in the other strand. It is this complementary nature of the molecular structure of the double stranded spiral which enables one half to act as a kind of mould in forming the other half. The two properties of DNA described, the ability to carry information for protein building and the ability to replicate are the most important factors in making possible the emergence of living things. It may well be that DNA was not the original molecule. But something with similar properties would be required for life to be possible.

Not long ago it was thought that the origin of life might not be very difficult to explain. Simple organic molecules might have been produced under conditions which are not improbable. These might come together to form the self-replicating molecules on which life depends. Experimental work has been carried out along these lines. Chemical conditions were created to resemble those thought to prevail in primeval times and powerful electric charges were applied to correspond with electric storms. There were remarkable results. Amino acids, sugars and purines, all necessary for living things, have been produced in this way. But no self-replicating molecules have appeared. DNA has been produced in other experiments but only when the appropriate enzyme, a protein, was added to the other chemical substances. What is wanted is production without this kind of help. Had self-replicating molecules, doubtless simpler than those we are familiar with, been formed, it would be expected that mutation and selection would lead to more complex ones in the course of time. But none so far have been produced, and this is not for want of trying. It may be done eventually for clearly it is chemically possible. But that will be under intelligent direction—setting up all the required conditions.

In the case of the first self-replicating molecules the only natural process available to bring them into being would be chance ones. The odds against these elaborate duplex molecules coming together in this way are great. And if they are to direct the building of proteins they must have the appropriate structure for it. Some translating mechanism seems also to be required. That all this should happen by chance is very improbable. Writing twenty years ago, the eminent molecular biologist Monod described the origin of life as something of a miracle.[17] Others have said much the same. Conditions must have been, anyway once, exactly right for the formation of the elaborate chemical substances on which life depends. Nothing has been discovered during the last twenty years to make the occurrence of all the conditions any less miraculous.

Now we come to the second case. The human central nervous system is the most complex structure in existence. In the cortex of the brain there are ten thousand million active cells each with an elaborate system of connections. And there are supporting cells as well. The brain itself has other important parts with many more cells. One very large mass is the cerebellum. It is responsible for the involuntary control of various kinds of muscular activity. The different parts of the brain are connected with the cortex and with one another by well defined tracts of nerve fibres. Below the brain is the brain stem in which all the cranial nerves, except the first two, have their centres. In it also are the vital centres controlling the heart, breathing and the bore of arteries which depends on muscles in their walls. Below this is the spinal cord with local connections and long tracts of nerve fibres. There are ascending tracts carrying impulses from sensory receptors of different kinds. And there are descending tracts carrying impulses to the muscles. It is likely that it is the extreme complexity of the human central nervous system which makes possible powers that no computer possesses.

It is not only the ordered complexity of the brain and spinal cord which is so remarkable. It is also that it is built afresh in every individual starting from a single cell, the fertilized ovum. It shows first as a groove on one surface of the beginnings of the embryo. This is converted into a tube by the fusion of the outer lips and it becomes depressed beneath the surface. Then steadily the whole immense development takes place. The development is not made any less remarkable because we can now understand something of the way in which it is directed. The astonishing fact remains that generation by generation this most complex of all instruments builds itself up automatically and nearly always with faultless perfection.

The development of the central nervous system in the individual is not made any less remarkable by the fact that we can trace the evolutionary steps by which it was arrived at. The cerebellum and its connections may be taken as an example. Its beginnings are associated with the balancing function of the ear. The ear nerve, VIII, runs into the brain stem. One large group of cells there has to do with balance. From this area an outgrowth develops in a backward direction to form the early cerebellum. From it impulses reach the muscles through the intersegmental nerve tract. This is the most primitive of all the nerve tracts in the spinal cord. Later in evolutionary history a new long descending tract develops from it. Later still other parts of the cerebellum develop which largely overshadow the older part. New connections are made and the input to the cerebellum is no longer all from the ear.

It may be added that the ear has itself a notable evolutionary history. One mechanism involved in hearing is the little air to water transformer in the middle ear. We can trace the way it was formed out of the jaw joint of an old time reptile. There is no question as to whether the structures of the body, including the central nervous system, came into being through an evolutionary process. Nor is there any question as to whether genetic mutation and natural selection were the means.

The question is whether mutation and selection alone will account for so remarkable a development as the human central nervous system and its building in every individual. Dawkins writes that his personal feeling is that once cumulative selection has got started only a relatively small amount of luck has to be postulated for the subsequent evolution of life and intelligence. He says that cumulative selection seems to him powerful enough to make the evolution of intelligence probable if not inevitable.[18] Cumulative selection undoubtedly is a powerful process. The mutations selected for survival are made the base for further mutation and selection. Yet every mutation, it is assumed, comes about simply by chance. Dawkins' statement is a judgment of credibility. In recent years doubts have been expressed as to whether such a judgment is warranted in view of the complexity of the human central nervous system and of the many other systems with which it is co-ordinated.

There is a further point. Biologists usually believe that a certain structure has developed because to have it gave an advantage. That is how natural selection works; it encourages the development of something useful for survival. Dawkins, for example, writes, "Presumably there was no need for our ancestors to cope with sizes and times outside the narrow range of everyday practicality, so our brains never evolved the capacity to imagine them".[19] But there is a strange thing about the brain: it had powers far in excess of what would be needed for survival at the time it reached its present size and complexity. The structures which make possible advanced conceptual thinking came into being at a time when there was no need for it and it would have no selective advantage. As Polkinghorne puts it, "it seems incredible that, say, Einstein's ability to conceive of the General Theory of Relativity was just a spin-off from the struggle for survival".[20]

We are often warned against arguing from the incom-pleteness of a scientific account of some natural process. Gaps get filled in with further research and what was formerly inexplicable is explained. But in the case we are discussing the position is different. What seemed complex turns out to be even more complex than had been supposed. The acquisition of new knowledge tends to make the claim that mutation and selection alone provide a complete explanation of the development of the central nervous system, and the other systems of the body, less and not more probable.

If we judge that chance mutation and natural selection are not in themselves sufficient to explain these developments we have to postulate intelligent direction in some form. Although he does not himself think the facts require it, this is a possibility which Huxley honestly faces. He says that because supernatural intelligence is outside present day science it is not for that reason necessarily inconceivable.[21] To avoid misunderstanding it needs to be said that the postulation of a Divine factor in evolution does not in any way limit scientific investigation. We still want to know exactly how the present state of affairs came into being. If Divine activity were involved, this would not affect the scientific account of the way in which the development of living things took place.

A Divine factor might be thought to operate in one of two ways. One is that the Divine direction takes place at the very beginning. In the originating act of creation the whole subsequent development is foreordained and no further Divine action is required. But if some of the processes of nature are spontaneous foreordination would not be possible. For the only way that certain events occurring at different stages in the development of the world could be foreordained would be by exceedingly complex causal processes. But spontaneous means not causally determined. Complete development according to plan could not be built into a system with an important element of spontaneity. As will be explained in Chapter V, foreknowledge of spontaneous events is possible for God; foreordination is not.

The other way in which Divine direction could be exercised is by some degree of responsiveness to, and influence on, the course of development as it occurred. This is providential action. It must be part of the way in which the Divine intention is realised in the natural world. Perhaps such intervention has not been frequent and the world has had a large degree of independence in its development.

As against the religious view of things the materialist view is that chance events and natural selection alone will give a complete explanation of the ordered complexity of the world. Enough has been said to cast doubt on the adequacy of such a view. The argument from ordered complexity has become stronger in recent years. But it is not, as was once thought, conclusive.

3. The Argument from Morality

The moral argument was brought into prominence by Kant. From his time to the early part of this century moral arguments were widely used. A moral argument of a very different kind from Kant's had been put forward a generation earlier by Hutcheson and is parallel to the Argument from Ordered Complexity. An argument of this sort calls attention to a remarkable feature of human life and asks whether it is credible that it came into being by natural processes alone. Hutcheson's argument is strictly to the goodness of God but it can be taken also as an argument to the reality of God. It comes at the end of his *Inquiry*. "Nay, this very moral sense, implanted in rational agents, to delight in, and admire whatever actions flow from a study of the good of others, is one of the strongest evidences of goodness in the Author of nature".[22]

What has to be asked is whether human moral judgment and moral action can wholly be accounted for by natural processes. Before taking up this question it has to be specified what sort of action is being considered. I am not here concerned with ordinary moral behaviour: being honest and kind and trustworthy and such like which writers on moral philosophy often have in mind. I am concerned with those acts of extreme moral goodness which are not generally asked of people but which people are capable of, notably literal self-sacrifice. For example, while there are limits to human endurance a captured intelligence agent will often not give away secrets under torture and will rather die than betray others in his organisation. What has to be accounted for is that there are things which we value more than life itself.

One way of attempting to account for this kind of action is biological. Animals sometimes behave in a similar way. Of course some similarity in behaviour is to be expected; we are related biologically. The question is whether the similarity in behaviour is very close and whether it can be fully explained on a purely natural basis. Like human acts of self-sacrifice certain animals will forfeit their lives for the sake of other members of the related group. This is explicable because the tendency to act in this way is of mutual benefit and the genes making for it are likely to be selected for survival.

But although the actions are similar the similarity is not so close as appears at first sight. Animals do these things instinctively and it is true that human acts of self-sacrifice are sometimes done on impulse. But not always. An act of self-sacrifice deliberately undertaken out of loyalty to individuals or devotion to a cause is not fully explained by a similarity to what is sometimes done by animals. Human beings understand what is involved in such actions and they understand what death is. They have the ability to weigh up the cost of moral demands and the freedom either to respond or to refuse. To sacrifice one's life on instinct is one thing; to sacrifice it by deliberately choosing to do what is judged to be right is another.

A second way of attempting to explain acts of moral goodness is sociological. As we grow up we learn how to live with other people in society. We pick up its rules and traditions of behaviour and they become internalised and made our own. We grasp such ideas as honesty, respect for other people and justice. And so our whole outlook and way of thinking about life together with other people is formed. It is moulded by the requirements and practices of the society to which we belong.

All this is true and important but it is not what we are talking about. What we want to know is not how reasonable social behaviour comes about. It is how those acts of goodness come about which society does not require and does not expect. There are people, for example, who live very modestly while, without anyone knowing about it, giving away large sums of money to people in need. Acts of this kind are not due to the pressures of society on individual members for society exerts no such pressures. How is it that people do acts of all kinds far beyond anything they have been moulded for by society?

A third explanation of behaviour of this kind is psychological. As is well known Freud described the human personality as having a threefold structure. On the lowest level are the instinctive drives of the id. The central position is occupied by the ego. It is related to external reality and is concerned with the well being of the whole person. Above it is the superego which embodies restrictions imposed by authorities in the external world. It is only partly conscious and its work seems wholly negative. The superego represents parents and other authorities which forbid the ego to satisfy all the instinctive drives. It comes to take the parents' place and itself observe and guide and threaten as they once did. The superego is not open to reason; it is authoritarian. Its business is to repress the instinctive drives that cannot be satisfied in the social environment. It does so with great power. Freud's account is based on clinical experience and does correspond with a great deal that goes on in the name of conscience.

But it does not correspond completely. Conscience is the mind making moral judgements. They are not purely negative. Nor are they all the outcome of internalized and unconscious demands of parents and other authorities. Nor again are they necessarily the consciously accepted rules laid down by society or by groups within it to which we may belong. Conscience can be educated. And it can be open to reason and to the facts of the situation. We can be free to decide what the situation requires; that is something we judge for ourselves, not something caused by various influences. It is evident therefore that explanation along psychological lines is not adequate to account for the kind of action we are concerned with. A psychological explanation can also be given for certain traits of character which might be thought to have a bearing on the matter. But that is not an explanation for what we are thinking about. It is how ordinary normal people, faced with special situations, sometimes come to make free and deliberate acts of moral goodness at great risk or great cost to themselves.

The argument is not that biological, sociological and psychological factors are not involved in forming our moral nature; no doubt they are. It is that neither each individually nor all taken together is a sufficient explanation. They will not fully account for the way in which people sometimes respond to situations with acts of outstanding moral goodness. When people maintain that such actions can readily be accounted for by the factors mentioned one doubts whether they have faced imaginatively what it takes to do them. For example, there were men and women in Nazi Germany who took the risk of being sent to a concentration camp in order to save people they hardly knew from the same fate. When actions of this kind are seriously thought about it does not seem reasonable to believe that our remarkable moral nature developed simply under the influence of the processes referred to. Rather it suggests direction by a power sensitive to moral goodness.

4. The Argument from Beauty

The argument from beauty has two aspects. There is the improbability of natural processes alone leading to the beauty of the world and the improbability of natural processes alone leading to human sensitivity to beauty.

Nothing is more striking about the natural world than its beauty—the splendour of a horse-chestnut tree in full bloom, or the elegance of a fox, for example. Wherever we look in the natural world there is beauty to be found. It is difficult to believe that so many beautiful things came into being without any kind of direction by a power sensitive to beauty.

However, before the beauty of the world can be taken as a serious argument for the reality of God there is a question to be answered: is not what we regard as beautiful entirely subjective? I like or admire certain things and so do many other people. Some things give us a special kind of satisfaction while

others do not. And this is, in part anyway, culturally influenced;
Western classical music, for example, often does not appeal to
Indians. And it is what appeals that counts. We can define the
kind of qualities that appeal to us. We can set up standards of
taste which are accepted within our culture. But, on a subjective
view, what these things finally depend on is the taste of certain
people recognised as authorities.

Against this view it can be pointed out that judgments
made about what is beautiful are not wholly subjective. Beautiful
things are beautiful because they possess certain characteristics.
This was the position taken, for example, by the Greeks. Chamoux
sums it up by saying that they were persuaded that beauty resided
in mathematical relationships whose laws our intelligence can
discover.[23] Put more broadly it may be said that something we
look at, or hear, and judge as beautiful has among other
characteristics, such qualities as proportion, balance, delicacy,
harmony, unity in variety. These qualities are there in the object.
Certainly people differ as to the different values they assign to
different qualities and to the whole. Nevertheless objects which
we judge to be beautiful posses certain specifiable qualities.

It seems clear that both subjective and objective factors are
involved when we judge something to be beautiful. Certainly it
is the case that even when things are not to our taste we can
make judgments of aesthetic value. We may prefer classical
architecture to Gothic. Yet we can recognise the perfect
proportions and the organic unity of a great church in the
perpendicular style. Attempts have been made to delineate the
different parts played by subjective and objective factors in
aesthetic judgment. That need not concern us here. All that is
important for the argument is that beautiful things have qualities
which make them beautiful.

What we now have to ask is whether the qualities that
make things beautiful can be accounted for by natural processes
alone. It might be possible in a number of ways.

Beauty may be produced by chance influences. We often
find natural scenes, mountains and rivers and lakes, for example,
very beautiful. They have developed gradually, over long periods

of time, and are the outcome of various natural forces. Chance happenings may bring into being something of wonderful beauty. A great waterfall is made when a river falls over a precipice; it just happens to flow that way. So it is with mountains; they are thrown up by powerful natural forces which themselves have no tendency to produce anything of beauty. Yet chance influences also produce scenes which are not beautiful: the desolation after a forest fire, for example, or the decaying bodies of animals left by a flood. Chance will account directly for only some of the beauty of the world.

Beautiful forms may be the outcome of inherent mathematical relationships. The beauty of crystals—diamonds for example—is something that can be accounted for in this way. Crystals are a regular arrangement of vast numbers of atoms or molecules of the same kind. Diamonds are pure carbon atoms arranged in a tetrahedral pattern. They can also be arranged in a different geometrical pattern which gives graphite. The forms of the crystals are the consequence of the form of the atoms themselves and this too is a mathematical matter. In the case of living things the mathematical relationships of their forms was already being studied in the nineteenth century. D'Arcy Thompson remarks on the exquisite beauty of the molluscan shell. He goes on to demonstrate the mathematics involved in the formation of shells and horns. If the circular growing edge of the shell producing area has a steady head to tail decrease in growth rate the form of the shell will be a plane spiral. If, as in the snail, the decrease in growth rate is differently graded as between the two sides the form is the more interesting turbinate spiral.[24] This is simply a matter of differential growth rates.

The beauty of living things may also be the outcome of evolutionary processes. It can happen in two ways.

Beauty may be associated with fitness for function. We often admire objects made by human beings which are exactly suited to their use. Economy and precision in design gives one kind of aesthetic satisfaction. So it is with certain living things— sea-gulls, for example. Their form, we assume, has been developed to meet functional needs and we judge it beautiful.

Yet things exactly suited to their function are not necessarily beautiful. We do not find any aesthetic satisfaction in racing cars although in other ways we may think highly of them. It is only in certain cases that fitness for function is sufficient to account for the beauty of an object. And it is only in certain cases that the beauty of living things can be attributed to fitness for function.

Beauty may come also from sexual selection. This is an important factor in evolutionary development. In the case of animals and birds it is the male that does the attracting and the female the choosing. Male characteristics, for instance the plumage of the pheasant, are believed to have developed in response to female preference. Sexual selection will explain the development of certain male characteristics. But it leaves a problem over the female. How is it her taste is so good? Why is it that females rarely like features that are ugly or colours that are garish? This is not easily accounted for; sensitivity to beauty has no survival value either for the individual or for the species.

The position is much the same with flowering plants. In cases where it applies, pollination by insects may be the means by which beautiful forms and colours are selected. We have then to suppose that the remarkable beauty of form and colour has developed because insects are attracted to these characteristics. They can be shown to be attracted to bright colours. But the point here is not the brightness of the colour but its delicacy as compared, often enough, with the crudity of artificial ones. If insects are responsible for the exquisite beauty of form and colour in so many flowers they must have great sensitivity to these qualities.

It is not only the sensitivity to form and colour of birds and insects that requires explanation. As mentioned at the beginning of the section, there is the aesthetic sensitivity of human beings to account for. Our main concern so far has been the beauty of the world. The sense of beauty in human beings also requires explanation. It is one of the most characteristic features of human life and has been present from a very early period as cave drawings show. But it has no obvious survival value.

Human sensitivity to beauty cannot be accounted for on materialist lines and the beauty of the world only partly so. Unless there is an intelligence sensitive to beauty in some way directing the course of things the facts must remain without full explanation. But while not wholly satisfying that is a position which it is perfectly possible to adopt. And so, like the others, the argument from beauty has some force. It is not in itself compelling but contributes to the cumulative argument for the reality of the Divine.

References

1. *The Analogy of Religion,* 1736, ed. J.H. Bernard, London, 1900, p. 268.

2. Samuel Clarke, *A Demonstration of the Being and Attributes of God,* 9th ed. London, 1738.

3. R.M. Gale, *On the Nature and Existence of God,* Cambridge, 1991, pp. 252ff.

4. *Summa Theologiae,* Ia, 2, 3.

5. *Paley's Natural Theology,* ed. H. Brougham and C. Bell, 1836, Vol. I, p. 80.

6. R. Harré, *The Philosophies of Science,* Oxford, 1972, p. 171.

7. A.C. Ewing, Two 'Proofs' of God's Existence, *Religious Studies,* 1, Cambridge, 1965, pp. 42f.

8. D.J. Bartholomew, *God of Chance,* London, 1984, p. 83.

9. *Ibid.,* p. 99.

10. W.G. Pollard, *Chance and Providence,* London, 1959, p. 56.

11. J.D. Barrow and F.W. Tipler, *The Anthropic Cosmological Principle,* Oxford, 1986.

12. S.W. Hawking, *A Brief History of Time,* London, 1988.

13. J.C.W. Davies, *The Accidental Universe,* Cambridge, 1982.

14. *Op. cit.,* p. 219.

15. *Ibid.,* pp. 22f.

16. *Op. cit.,* p. 251ff.

17. J. Monod, *Chance and Necessity,* E.T. London, 1972, pp. 131, 135.

18. R. Dawkins, *The Blind Watchmaker,* London, 1986, paperback ed. p. 146.

19. *Ibid.,* p. 160.

20. J. Polkinghorne, *Science and Creation,* London, 1988, p. 21.

21. A.F. Huxley, How far will Darwin take us? in *Evolution from Molecules to Men,* ed. D.S. Bendall, Cambridge, 1983, paperback ed. p. 9.

22. *An Inquiry concerning the Original of our Ideas of Virtue and Moral Good,* 1725, in *British Moralists,* ed. L.A. Selby-Bigge, Vol. I, Oxford, 1897, p. 176.

23. F. Chamoux, *The Civilisation of Greece,* E.T. London, 1965, p. 369.

24. D'Arcy W. Thompson, *On Growth and Form,* Cambridge, 1917, new edition 1942, pp. 748ff.

Chapter IV

Arguments From Religious Experience

1. The Appeal to Experience

The criticism of the arguments from the world to the existence of God by Hume and Kant was taken as decisive by many Protestant theologians. This was even before the criticisms were reinforced by Darwin's ideas. In place of the arguments more than one line was taken. The one of greatest importance throughout the nineteenth century was the appeal to some form of individual religious experience. And although, as we have seen, the arguments do have some force they are not conclusive. So the appeal to experience remains necessary.

Two important forms of religious experience were described earlier, mysticism and the Holy, and there is no need to consider them further. Both are claims to a direct awareness of God. Other examples of such claims are those made by Schleiermacher and William James and something has first to be said about them. But most of the chapter is not concerned with claims to a direct awareness of God. It is concerned with arguments for the reality of God which are based on religious experience of a different kind.

Schleiermacher was the first important theologian to make religious experience the basis for belief in the reality of God. He was one of the leading figures in the Romantic movement in Germany and shared many of its interests. The movement was a reaction against the cold intellectualism and moralism of the

Enlightenment. In its place it put a new emphasis on feeling. Strong feelings of all kinds were admired. With that went a delight in nature, especially what was great and violent; no one had taken much pleasure in mountains and storms in the preceding century. In society it was individual freedom as against authority of any sort that was valued. The movement made itself felt in many areas of life: in art and architecture, in literature and music, in philosophy and in politics where the main issue was nationalism. Accordingly, as a Romantic, in trying to find a new basis for religion it was to feeling that Schleiermacher turned.

Schleiermacher's early work *On Religion: Speeches to its Cultured Despisers* was published in 1799. The cultured despisers to whom the book is addressed were the young Romantics with whom he associated in Berlin. He wanted, in the first place, to show that religion was not what they thought it was. One reason why religion was despised was its condition at the time. In many quarters it was reduced to belief in the existence of God together with a set of moral rules. Conduct in accordance with them was encouraged by promises and threats about life hereafter. But there was also a very different type of religion that was little noticed in intellectual circles: pietism. An example of this tradition was Moravianism in which love for Jesus was central. Schleiermacher had been sent to a Moravian school. He was deeply influenced by its living faith and warmth of devotion and of fellowship. He broke from it because of its cultural narrowness. But later on he was to say that a revised Moravianism was his ideal of Christian life.

If religion is something different from what the cultured despisers supposed what exactly is it? Schleiermacher begins by saying what it is not. It resigns all claims to anything that belongs either to science or morality.[1] Schleiermacher wants it understood that religion is an autonomous area of life and is independent of ideas derived from science and ethics. He goes on to say what religion is. It is to have life and to know life in the all encompassing presence of the Infinite.

How is awareness of the Infinite reached? Certainly not from science in the form of the teleological argument nor from ethics in Kant's new moral argument. In the common analysis of mental life three elements are distinguished: knowing, doing and feeling. Schleiermacher regards knowing as the sphere of science and doing as the sphere of ethics. That leaves feeling, the element in which the Romantics were especially interested. It is in the inner experience of feeling, Schleiermacher maintains, that the awareness of the Infinite comes.

What Schleiermacher means by feeling is not at once evident. In the first edition of the book he speaks of intuition and feeling. But in the second edition the word intuition, which suggests a form of knowing, is generally dropped, as it is in his later writing. What he seems to mean by feeling is an immediate awareness of things that comes before any ideas have been formed. He writes, "But that only is immediate which has not yet passed through the stage of idea, but has grown up purely in feeling" (p. 54). Schleiermacher thinks that in this primordial feeling we become aware of the world about us. We are aware in the first place of finite things. But in and through the awareness of the finite we can become aware of the Infinite. This is the feeling that is religious. It is therefore natural for him to speak of religion as a feeling of the Infinite and as a sense and taste for the Infinite.

In suggesting that we become aware of things in feeling it looks as if Schleiermacher has been misled by an ambiguity in the word. He does not make a clear distinction between the feeling of some independent thing, which is properly sensing, and the feeling of pleasure and pain or liking and disliking. It is in the latter sense that feeling is distinguished from knowing and doing. But feeling in this sense does not make us aware of anything; it comes into play when we are already aware of things. Feeling as sensing, on the other hand, does make us aware of things. It appears that when Schleiermacher dropped the word intuition he thought that he had retained an element of awareness in the word feeling.

There is no need to go further and discuss his very influential Systematic Theology, *The Christian Faith*, published twenty years later. It need only be said that here the feeling is more closely defined and there is some change of view. It is now the feeling of absolute dependence. This is the consciousness that our whole being and activity is dependent upon a source outside of us.[2] He goes on almost at once to say what this source is. It is not the world in the sense of the totality of temporal existence and still less is it any part of the world. It is what is meant by the word God. And so "to feel oneself absolutely dependent and to be conscious of being in relation with God are one and the same thing" (p. 17).

The word God gets its meaning directly from the feeling of absolute dependence. It stands simply for the source of the feeling. That is the fundamental meaning of the word. Any further content that the word may be given, for example, eternal or omnipotent, must be traceable back to this fundamental meaning. But the consequence of this procedure is to leave the idea of God so reduced as to be no longer an adequate object of religious devotion.

In avoiding knowing and relying on feeling Schleiermacher failed in his enterprise on the two counts mentioned: there is a confusion in his idea of feeling and we are left with an impoverished idea of God. He does not succeed in showing that the basis of religion is to be found purely in feeling.

A position in some respects similar to that of Schleiermacher was taken by William James. He writes "I do believe that feeling is the deeper source of religion".[3] A little further on he says that intellectual operations presuppose immediate experiences as their subject matter. They are interpretations and inferences which are secondary to religious feeling. As with Schleiermacher the real basis of religion is to be found in feeling and not in thought. Religious beliefs are derived from the feeling.

James differs from Schleiermacher in that he sets out a large number of first hand accounts of the religious experience of individual men and women. This makes up the bulk of the book. Then he considers how they can be explained and what arguments can be based on them. In the survey of experiences there is a lecture on the religion of healthy-mindedness "which looks on all things and sees that they are good" (p. 86). He goes on to accounts of the sick soul and the divided self. Then come lectures on conversion. They are followed by those on saintliness which James takes as the collective name for the fruit of religion in character. Then he deals with mystical experience. It is part of James' purpose to provide a compendium of religious experience in all its variety.

But beneath the variety there is something they have in common. This is the sense of an unseen reality. Early in the book James writes, "It is as if there were in the human consciousness a *sense of reality, a feeling of objective presence, a perception* of what we may call 'something there', more deep and more general than any of the special and particular 'senses' by which the current psychology supposes existent realities to be originally revealed" (p. 58). While there is no special sense, James thinks that we can sometimes be aware of an unseen reality in a way that is "more like a sensation than an intellectual operation properly so called" (p. 64). This sense of something or someone being present is not necessarily religious and James gives several examples of such experiences. But he regards the sense of an unseen presence as an essential feature of experiences which are religious. Later he writes "the sense of Presence of a higher and friendly power seems to be the fundamental feature of the spiritual life" (p. 269).

In a later chapter James has something further to say about this unseen reality which is sensed. He has given a great many examples of religious experiences. He believes that their immediate source lies in the subconscious or unconscious mind then beginning to be recognised. Just as there is more to the world than sense perception can grasp so there is more to the self than the conscious mind. James suggests that the subconscious forms the nearer side, as it were, of what he calles the "more" (p. 502). On the further side our being plunges into an altogether other dimension of existence. It is here, he says, that most of our ideals originate. And so we belong to it in a more intimate sense than we belong to the visible world, for we belong wherever our ideals belong. Yet this unseen region is not merely ideal for it produces effects in the world. When we commune with it work is done on our finite personality for we are turned into new people (p. 506). James calls this idea of the "more" an over-belief. It goes beyond the evidence but he regards it as the best explanation of the experiences he has described.

What of the basic experience of the feeling of an unseen presence? James says that it comes by sensing and likens the experience to sense perception. It has been pointed out that an important feature of the likeness is the convincingness of the experience.[4] But convincingness may come in other ways. James himself, as already mentioned, describes non-religious cases of the feeling of an unseen presence and they too are convincing. Such cases are not uncommon. A person may have the sense that there is someone or something in the room. But when he turns round or looks carefully he finds nothing. It seemed like sense perception but was an illusion—an apparent sense perception involving a false belief. The similarity between the non-religious and the religious cases suggests that the latter also could be a matter not of sensing, as James took it to be, but of belief. Whether the firm belief, amounting to conviction, in the presence of an unseen reality is true or false cannot be decided simply by feeling it to be there.

James thought that if religion is worth anything it must be more than a way of looking at the world. The world itself must be different from what a materialist thinks it to be. "It must be such that different events can be expected in it, different conduct must be required" (p. 508). It was not only materialism that James was critical of; he was critical also of a certain type of religion. He considered it an incredible proposition that God should exist and yet make no difference to what happens in the world (p. 512). The difference that James himself chiefly had in mind were the experiences set out earlier in the book. He thought that there were real differences in people's lives which came through the subconscious but which had their origin in prayerful communion with the transcendent "More". And he suggested that there were likely also to be other kinds of difference.

Can it be shown, or made probable, that there are differences not only in people's lives but also in events in the world for which God is in some way responsible? Tillich brings out the importance of events although what he is discussing is not the reality of God but revelation. In revelation there is always a subjective and an objective side to the experience. "If nothing happens objectively, nothing is revealed. If no one receives what happens subjectively, the event fails to reveal anything".[5] The objective element in the experience Tillich refers to as miracle. And in justifying belief in the reality of God it is to miracle, and the related topic of providence, that we must turn for a type of religious experience with more evidential value than other types.

2. Providence and Miracle

Sometimes the term religious experience is used in a way that does not include providence and miracle. Franks Davis, for example writes, "but then it is no longer an argument from religious experience, rather an argument from providence or miracles".[6] But that restriction is not part of ordinary usage. When ordinary people speak about religious experience they may refer to the sense of the holy, mysticism or a feeling of absolute dependence or to some of the experiences that James describes. Again, the reference may be to classical examples: the vision that changed Paul's life, or the experience that changed Pascal's and of which he kept a record sewn in his jacket. But very often the reference is to what are taken as instances of providence and sometimes of miracle. Ward uses the term religious experience in this sense as well as in others. He says that this kind of experience is to be found in personal biography both in the Bible and in the lives of people in subsequent periods. In the disappointments, opportunities and achievements of life elements of purpose are discerned which lead people to say that their lives are being guided or shaped in a specific way. Ward makes the point that belief in such guiding is not an inference from a prior belief in a personal God. It is a basic response to the course of one's own life. The reality of God discloses itself in someone's personal history and enables him or her to speak of God as a providential power.[7] An agnostic friend, who is a very able professional philosopher made exactly the same point in conversation; experiences in his own life made him wonder if there was not some kind of Divine guidance at work.

This kind of experience is an aspect of providence. Providence is a large topic and is discussed in the following chapter. Here we shall deal mainly with miracle. But, as will be seen, the two are closely related.

A miracle is a striking event, in response to prayer, in which the action of God is manifested and a sense of awe and wonder is evoked. Wonder is the root meaning of the word. The event may or may not appear to be contrary to the normal sequences of nature. This twofold possibility divides miracles into two types: those which are contrary to the ordinary course of nature—contranatural—and those which are not. In the one case a miracle is *supra et contra naturam,* and in the other only *supra naturam.*

It has been suggested by some philosophers that in the interests of clarity the term miracle should be restricted to the contranatural type. Certainly this has generally been done not only by philosophers but also by theologians from the early centuries until modern times. But such a restriction does not apply to ordinary religious discussion today. Quite the reverse. If one notes the way the word miracle is used by religious people in serious conversation it will be found that the reference is hardly ever to contranatural events. What the word miracle is used to refer to is certain rare and striking events in a person's life which he or she is sure are the work of God. It is used spontaneously and I do not think that the use can be said to be metaphorical. There is no getting away from the fact that the word miracle is used in a way that covers striking events of both types.

To bring out just what constitutes a miracle it is worth looking carefully at a classical example. We shall examine in some detail the account of the crossing of the Red Sea. This is the most important miracle in the Old Testament and is referred to in every part. The miracle involves both nature and human life. Examination of it should show where the heart of miracle lies.

What we are primarily concerned with here is the meaning of a word and not the historicity of an event. Yet the question has to be asked as to how far the Biblical account of the crossing of the Red Sea is to be taken as historical. It is the more necessary to ask this because the account of the events in the book of Exodus neither is, nor is intended to be, the kind of history that is written today. It is an account of what God was doing for the people of Israel. As Hyatt says in his commentary, it relates how God brought them out of bondage and made a covenant with them. Nevertheless, he goes on to say, the book of Exodus professes to be history and its narrative undoubtedly rests on a solid core of historical happening.[8] Johnstone, on the other hand, takes a quite different view. The book is a confession of faith. What it says is that it is God who directs the course of events. But that is put in the form of a narrative of Israel's origins. It is history only in the minimal sense that it reflects the general movement of events at the time: the loss of Egypt's West Asiatic Empire and the emergence of new nation states in Syria and Canaan.[9] For our purpose it is not of first importance which view is correct. Either there was an actual crossing of a stretch of water or there was an imaginary one; whatever is the case the idea of miracle is expressed and that is what we are after. But I take the more usual view that the account reflects actual historical events. No doubt they can be seen as part of a wider movement involving other peoples. But within it Israel had a particular history which for itself was of unique significance.

What we want to know is the way or ways in which a miracle is thought of in the book of Exodus. To do this it is necessary to say something briefly about the sources from which the account we have is built up. Investigation of this matter has been going on for more than a hundred years. Nothing is beyond question but certain results are very widely accepted. Old Testament scholars have criteria by which they have been able to distinguish three main sources. While reservations have been expressed about the indiscriminate use of such work this is an area in which it appears appropriate.

It is likely that the principal sources were written ones. But they had a long oral tradition behind them. Methods have been worked out for tracing the history of the tradition, although it has to be said that a good deal of speculation may be involved.

The aim is to identify individual traditions, classify them into types and set them in their context of life. In the case of the Exodus narrative this would be a ritual one; narrators would pass on the tradition at specified seasonal gatherings. It is from here that the earliest written sources would probably chiefly come.

The earliest and far the most important source is called J. The symbol is taken from the initial letter of the Divine name used in this source, Jahweh (nowadays spelt Yahweh). J covers the whole period of the book of Exodus and provides the basic narrative. It is itself made up of various traditions that have been brought together by the writer. The J source has been dated in the ninth century BC. But a more recent judgement is that it was produced at the time of Solomon in the tenth century. Even on this earlier date it comes from a period about three hundred years after the events with which it deals. But it is possible for material that is repeated on ritual occasions to be preserved relatively unchanged over very long periods.

The second source in order of date is E. The symbol comes from the initial letter of Elohim, the Divine name often used in this source. It is dated in the eighth century. In the chapters with which we are concerned it is only represented by a few verses (13.7-19; 14.7, 16a, 19a).

Finally there is P, the priestly source. It is usually dated in the fifth century. This puts it some eight hundred years after the events recounted. However P is thought to preserve some very ancient material including narrative.

The J and P accounts each form a continuous narrative of the crossing of the Sea and they can be separated from one another by literary analysis; that given by Hyatt will be followed here. The two extracts given are passages in sequence of the relative parts of the two narratives. They are taken from the Revised Standard Version. The verse numbers of Chapter 14, from which they come, are given in brackets.

First the J account: "And Moses said to the people, 'Fear not, stand firm, and see the salvation of the Lord, which he will work for you today; for the Egyptians whom you see today, you shall never see again (13). The Lord will fight for you, and you have only to be still' (14). And the pillar of cloud moved from before them and stood behind them (19b), coming between the host of Egypt and the host of Israel. And there was the cloud and the darkness; and the night passed without one coming near the other all night (20). And the Lord drove the sea back by a strong east wind all night, and made the sea dry land (21b). And in the morning watch the Lord in the pillar of fire and of cloud looked down upon the host of the Egyptians and discomfited the host of the Egyptians (24), clogging their chariot wheels so that they moved heavily; and the Egyptians said, 'Let us flee from before Israel; for the Lord fights for them against the Egyptians' (25). And the sea returned to its wanted flow when the morning appeared; and the Egyptians fled into it, and the Lord routed the Egyptians in the midst of the sea (27b)".

The P account reads: "Then Moses stretched out his hand over the sea (21a); and the waters were divided (21c). And the people of Israel went into the midst of the sea on dry ground, the waters being a wall to them on their right hand and on their left (22). The Egyptians pursued, and went in after them into the midst of the sea, all Pharoah's horses, his chariots, and his horsemen (23). Then the lord said to Moses, 'Stretch out your hand over the sea, that the waters may come back upon the Egyptians, upon their chariots, and upon their horseman' (26). So Moses stretched forth his hand over the sea (27a). The waters returned and covered the chariots and the horsemen and all the host of Pharaoh that had followed them into the sea; not so much as one remained (28). But the people of Israel walked on dry ground through the sea, the waters being a wall to them on their right hand and on their left (29)".

The separation of the sources does not in itself enable us to distinguish with certainty what is historical from what is legendary. Clearly the J source must be our principal guide in trying to establish just what happened. But even in the J source there may be exaggerations. On the other hand, as already mentioned, the P source may preserve some ancient traditions and cannot simply be set aside. No Egyptian records have been found that mention the events. But then victories are more likely

to be recorded than defeats. Nor was the Egyptian force
necessarily very large—only very dangerous. Again, the number
of Israelites who left Egypt may not have been great enough to
merit recording. So for what happened all that can be done is to
make probable judgements on the basis of the Biblical evidence
and more general knowledge about the area at the time.

The date of the exodus cannot be settled with certainty but
it is commonly put as the thirteenth century. The date is connected
with that of the occupation of Palestine and it too is uncertain.
There is some Egyptian evidence but its significance is far from
clear. A comparison may be made between the conditions
described in the book of Exodus with those known from Egyptian
material. The pharoahs Seti I and Rameses II moved their
principal residence from Thebes (Luxor) in the south to the
eastern Delta. The city of Raamses was rebuilt there as the
capital and extensive other building work was undertaken.
Rameses II is known to have used what are loosely called
Hebrews in labouring work. Corresponding with this we read in
Exodus 1.11 that the Israelites built for Pharoah the store cities
of Pithom and Raamses. It is possible that the Biblical author,
writing at a later date, knew of the building operations and
working conditions in the reign of Rameses II (1305 and 1237)
and incorporated it into his account. But the thirteenth century
does seem the most probable period.

The next point to discuss is where the crossing of the water
took place. In Exodus 14 the stretch of water is precisely defined
by place names, although they cannot now be identified with
certainty. But it is not called the Red Sea. The term is not used
until 15.4 which is poetic and is generally dated late. In the
parallel accounts given in Numbers 33 the sea crossed and the
Red Sea are clearly distinguished; the Red Sea was reached four
stages later on. There the term is used as we use it now and as
it is used elsewhere in the Old Testament, notably in 1 Kings
9.26. Just possibly there is another usage. It has often been
pointed out that the Hebrew word translated "red" normally means
something like "reed" and the word translated "sea" is general
enough to cover any piece of water from a sea to a marsh. All
that we can say with certainty is that the water crossed was not

a part of what we now call the Red Sea. It was too far away and the fleeing Israelites would have been overtaken by the Egyptians before they got there.

It is not obvious why there was any water to cross. Even when there was a lake at El Ballah almost half the border between Egypt and Sinai has no water barrier. But there were a series of fortresses that guarded the eastern border. It is likely to be because of these that the Israelites, after coming south to Succoth and the edge of the wilderness (13.20), turned north again. There was an important fortress near the present El Qantara. Wright suggests that it was to avoid this fortress that the Israelites went further north. What now lay between them and Sinai was an arm of the vast Lake Menzaleh which stretches down from the Mediterranean and this is what had to be crossed.[10]

There are two other main suggestions as to the location of the crossing. One is at the far north on the Mediterranean coast. A narrow sand bar is all that separates the Mediterranean from Lake Sirbonis. Many German scholars believe that this has most to be said for it. The other suggestion is the region of the Bitter Lakes to the south. Davies, who reviews the geographical questions connected with the Exodus, thinks that this is the most probable place.[11] Since the topography of the area has been altered by the digging of the Suez canal not much weight can be put on present day estimations of which of the possible water barriers is the most likely. But, for what it is worth, it may be added that anyone familiar with the region is likely to consider that the shallow waters of the southern extension of Lake Menzaleh best fits the J account. This agrees with the view held by many Old Testament scholars. However, the precise location of the water crossed is not of primary importance.

The Israelites were trapped between the water, a fortress and the Egyptian army. As to what happened the J source gives a perfectly plausible account. A strong east wind drove back the water. This made it possible for the lightly armed Israelites to cross on foot. The Egyptians followed and their chariots stuck in the mud. They panicked and fled as best they could with the water returning to its normal level. So the Israelites were able to make good their escape.

What was the miracle? It was this: the Israelites, trapped and facing imminent disaster, could see no way out. Then, against all probability, a way of escape opened up. This was taken as a miracle as far back in the tradition as we can go. The song of Miriam (15.21) is judged to be one of the oldest poet couplets in the Old Testament; many scholars think that it is contemporary with the events.

Sing to the Lord, for he has triumphed gloriously;
the horse and his rider he has thrown into the sea.

(Probably chariot should be read instead of rider as in RSV margin on 15.21). The miracle was a striking natural event which coincided with the people's need and answered their prayers. Nothing contranatural was required for the event to be recognised as a miracle.

In the very late P passages the Divine action is heightened. The waters move when, at the command of God, Moses stretches out his hand. And they stand like walls as the Israelites pass through. Taken by itself the P narrative would be counted as the report of a contranatural miracle. The J narrative, on the other hand, would be counted as a providential miracle. This is a clear example of how the account of a miracle may pass from the providential to the contranatural type. But we cannot assume that this is the only way accounts of contranatural miracles arise. Perhaps there are such miracles even if they are exceedingly rare. There are many claims that they occur and a discussion of them is necessary.

(a) The Contranatural Type of Miracle

The first question to ask is, can a miracle of this kind occur? Should it simply be ruled out as impossible? A definition of miracle that is often taken as standard is Hume's and it is not very different from Aquinas' idea of one. A miracle is "a transgression of a law of nature by a particular volition of the Deity, or by the interposition of some invisible agent".[12] So the question becomes, can there be a violation of a law of nature?

A law of nature states a generalisation made from observa-tions. An example is Boyle's law, discovered as a result of experiments on the compressibility of air: at a given temperature the pressure and volume of a gas vary inversely. In Hume's view a law of nature describes the way things regularly happen. One event is always followed by another. The law does not say that it is bound to do so, only that it always does. Since natural laws simply describe regularities it might be thought that Hume would expect that variations might sometimes occur. But that is not what he expected. On the contrary, because a regular sequence of events has gone on always and everywhere it could confidentally be expected to continue. So besides describing what does happen under certain conditions the laws allow predictions to be made about what will happen on future occasions under the same conditions. Hume maintains that there are no necessary connections between events. Natural laws state what does happen and what will happen but not what must happen. Many people want to go beyond this minimal account of natural laws and hold that they are statements of necessity. They express what must happen under specific conditions.

In whatever sense a law of nature is taken a miracle of the contranatural type is a violation. This is clearly the case if the laws are necessary. Under certain conditions certain things must happen. But if a miracle occurs something quite different happens. In spite of the law of gravity a man who steps on to the water does not sink into it. And even with the more limited idea of a law of nature Hume could describe a miracle as a violation. For things always behave in a certain way so that in particular circumstances we can count on what will happen. But in a miracle they do not happen that way.

How could a violation take place? A law of nature describes what always happens and perhaps what must happen under given conditions. But the conditions are not generally completely specified. Writing about the laws of nature in a very different connection Waismann refers to, "the vague supposition that 'a normal situation subsists', that 'no disturbing factors are present' or in whatever way we may hint at the possibility of intervention of some unforeseen conditions".[13] But, C.S. Lewis points out, if a miracle occurs the conditions are quite different.[14] Just such a disturbing factor is present. In the ordinary course of events it is perfectly correct to assume that there is no Divine factor at work. For science that is part of its method and for theology it is an aspect of the relative independence of the world. But that is very different from saying that there can never be any special Divine action in the world. And if there is the usual course of nature may be interrupted.

But do miracles in fact occur? That was Hume's question. He denied that we ever got enough evidence to say that a miracle had occurred. Claims about the occurrence of a miracle come to us by testimony. Hume does not consider the case where someone believes that he himself has witnessed a miracle; he is concerned with what other people report. But it is always possible that testimony may not be correct. Someone may be mistaken about what takes place, or he may be credulous, or biased, or he may be lying. Against the testimony of an event occurring contrary to the regular course of nature has to be set the testimony to its invariable regularity over a very long period and in all parts of the world. This is so strong that Hume thinks it is always to be preferred. The probability that the testimony to the occurrence of a miracle is mistaken is much greater than the probability that a law of nature should be transgressed. Hume is not saying that contranatural miracles are impossible; he is saying that testimony will never be strong enough to warrant acceptance.

Against this conclusion it has to be said that there are factors which enhance our estimation of the strength of testimony. The conditions in which observations are made may be very good; the witness may be very reliable; much care may have been taken in ascertaining the facts; and especially a number of independent witnesses may agree on what they report. Very improbable events cannot be ruled out because they have never happened before and appear contrary to the way things work, nor because testimony is often mistaken and sometimes deceitful. There could be conditions of observation and of reporting which give good reason for believing the testimony to an exceedingly improbable event.

Does this apply not merely to very improbable events but to miracles of the contranatural type? As already mentioned

Hume does allow that in theory such miracles could occur. What he does not allow is that they could be the foundation of a system of religion. It has been rightly said that this is the principal point of the whole section.[15] And we have to agree with Hume. Without independent reason to believe in the reality of God the testimony to the occurrence of a miracle which involves the violation of a law of nature would have to be exceedingly strong. For it would have to overcome the overwhelming testimony to the invariable regularity of the laws and hence to the presumption of continued regularity.

But, as Swinburne and others have pointed out, the situation is entirely different if one has already good reason to believe in the reality of God.[16] In that case there is not the same presumption against a miracle occurring. It is not irrational to believe that God, who has a certain character and is always present, might bring about events which are contrary to observed natural laws. Strong testimony would still be required. But it would not have to be of the cast iron strength that would be required if there were no prior belief in God.

It is clear that miracles of this type cannot be used as a main ground for belief in God. But they may be important in other connections. In discussions about miracles what is often in mind is not the reality of God but the resurrection of Jesus. It is worth noting that the resurrection stories are not accounts of bringing a dead man back to life. They are accounts of bringing a dead man into a new and different life; on a number of occasions we are told that Jesus was not immediately recognised by those to whom he appeared. Even so what is being asserted is something contrary to the regular course of nature.

(b) The Providential Type of Miracle

In this type of miracle the events are not contrary to the normal working of nature. The Divine intention is carried out through the ordinary sequences of cause and effect. That means that the events are providential in character. Why then do we speak of miracle at all in this connection? Why not special providence? The reason is that the events we call miracles do have distinguishing features. Events which are purely providential may not be specifically asked for and perhaps not noticed at the time. By contrast the heart of a miracle is a dramatic answer to prayer.

The distinguishing features of miracle require setting out in more detail. Descriptions of them are not drawn from accounts of miracles reported to have taken place centuries ago. To do that would require preliminary historical investigation. They come from present day accounts of miracles given by those who have experienced them. But simply as a matter of convenience the principal features will be illustrated from the Exodus miracle; that will save giving further descriptions of particular miracles at this stage. Three main features may be distinguished in a providential miracle.

First, a specific prayer. The prayer is for something to happen which is otherwise very unlikely to happen. At the Exodus it was exceedingly unlikely that anything would happen to save the people from being caught by the Egyptian army. We are told in the J account that the people cried to the Lord (10). In recent times, too, people have sometimes been in acute danger and have prayed for something to happen that will save them. But while there is always a real need of some kind it is not always an acute one. It may, for example, be the cure of a chronic illness, either of oneself or of someone else. Everything that is humanly possible has been done and there is no cure. That is why people go to places like Lourdes; there is no guarantee that God will heal them but everything else has been tried. The prayer in a miracle is quite precise and is for something that is exceedingly improbable in the ordinary course of things.

The second characteristic feature of a providential miracle is a striking event. Not every event that answers a prayer is striking. To be striking it must be something quite contrary to the normal expectations of the situation. In many cases it is the timing of the event which makes it striking. That was so in the Exodus miracle. Had the waters been driven back a few hours later the Israelites would have been captured or slaughtered. But it is not only the timing of events which may make them striking. It sometimes happens that for a main event to be possible a number of smaller events which are independent of one another each has to take place. A family escaping from the interior of China at the time of the Boxer Rising experienced a series of most improbable events. Had any one of them failed to take place they would all have been killed. Their escape was regarded as literally miraculous.[17]

Events against the probabilities of the situation do happen by chance. They also may be very striking. Because such chance events do occur cases claimed as providential miracles require very careful examination before they are accepted as such. As in much scientific work the question of chance has to be taken very seriously. There statistical methods are used to exclude it. In the case of miracles that is seldom possible and all that can be done is to make an honest assessment of each case. To do so requires not only that the event completely answers a prayer; alternative explanations, including chance, of the event occurring just the way it did must be judged exceedingly unlikely. To make such a judgement requires detailed knowledge of all the factors involved in the situation, including that which can only come from the inside.

The third characteristic of this type of miracle is a sense of awe and wonder. It is not due to the fact that something contrary to nature and amazing has happened, for nothing of that sort has. It comes for two reasons. One is that God has revealed himself. Ordinarily we believe that God is present, we pray to him and try to do his will. But he remains hidden. In a miracle something happens which shows he is actively present. The feeling of awe and wonder comes from this awareness of the presence of God. The other reason for the feeling comes, as Farmer points out, from the awareness that God is dealing with us personally.[18] Knowing all that goes on in the world he nonetheless deals with us as individuals. It is in a miracle especially that this becomes evident. That the Ultimate is responsive to individual people is a matter of wonder and of awe.

If miracles occur, and can clearly be recognised, they provide important evidence for the reality of God. And while miracles are rare in the experience of any one person, enough have been reported to take them seriously. It is their evidential implications that lie at the centre of the debate about miracles. Here we are concerned with providential miracles. It has been questioned, and not only by sceptics, whether this kind of miracle can be of evidential value. A number of points may be raised.

The first question is about the recognition of a miracle. It is suggested that a miracle of this sort can only be recognised by the person who experiences it. This is Farmer's view, for example.[19] He is convinced of the reality of a miracle. But he thinks that a miracle is so intimately related to the individual's concrete situation that he alone can appreciate just how remarkable the event is. I think that Farmer underestimates our ability imaginatively to enter into the situation of others. Good biographers can do it and so can other people. With imaginative understanding we can enter into the concrete situation of the individual well enough to estimate just how precisely the event met the situation and just how improbable. We are not therefore prevented from recognising a miracle simply because we did not ourselves experience it.

To recognise something as a miracle does not mean that demonstration is possible. Farmer speaks of demonstrative proof. But that is not what is being argued for. The question is whether in a particular case there are sufficient grounds for believing that an event was not a chance one but was a miracle. The grounds are the extreme improbability of the event taking place as it did by chance, or for any other reason, together with the fact that it was asked for. It is the combination of these two factors which makes an event recognisable as a miracle. That is how it was in the case of the Exodus miracle: the improbability of any saving event taking place together with the fact it was asked for.

The second objection to the evidential value of a providential miracle is that to interpret an event as a miracle depends on having a prior belief in God. Therefore it cannot be used as evidence for the reality of God; that would be arguing in a circle. Certainly the person who prays for something does as a rule believe fully in the reality of God. But, as Price points out, belief is not an all or nothing affair; it is not necessarily the case that a person either believes or does not believe. It is quite possible, and quite common, to half believe something. Perhaps someone usually avoids walking under a ladder because he believes that it brings bad luck. But when hurrying to catch a train he takes no notice of the ladder and goes under it; he is really only a half believer.[20] In religious matters it may be much the same. Someone may have been brought up in a religious environment and half believe. To make a prayer in a threatening situation requires only half belief. It has happened on many occasions, for example in war, that people who only half believed have cried out to God. They have been dramatically and unexpectedly saved and have regarded the experience as evidential. The event confirmed whatever belief there was initially. Often it has changed the whole subsequent course of a person's life.

For a miracle to be of evidential value to someone who did not himself experience it the position is a little different. He must be ready to entertain the possibility that God is real and be ready to enter imaginatively into the situation of the other person. But no prior belief in the reality of God is necessary.

The third objection is this: the expectation of some event in answer to prayer leads to the interpretation of a chance event as an answer. Because the event is in accordance with a prayer it is taken as the answer to the prayer. Suppose a person is deeply perplexed about what he ought to do. He prays for guidance. He watches out for it. Then something quite unexpected happens which makes things clear. Just because he was looking for guidance he would be likely to interpret the event as the action of God. But while it would be taken as an answer to prayer it would not be thought of as a miracle. To be a miracle requires an event which not only answers the prayer and not only was unexpected; it has to be exceedingly unlikely to have come about by chance.

Finally, the fact that a specific prayer was made and was followed by an event which precisely corresponded with it and which was very unlikely to have come about by chance, does not necessarily mean Divine action. There may be other explanations.

Medical cases are an example. When healing occurs after specific prayer it is seldom that one can say that a miracle has occurred. Very remarkable cures happen. But because there may be powerful psychosomatic influences present the healing is not necessarily due to the action of God. Again, there may be poorly understood natural factors at work. A case came to my notice recently of recovery from microscopically proved disseminated cancer; such things happen from time to time. There has to be something special about a case before it can be said that a miracle has occurred. But while healing miracles, like all miracles, are rare they do seem to happen. Osteomyelitis is a chronic infection of bone, notoriously hard to cure, in which pus discharges from openings in the skin. I heard of a case where, as the patient was being prayed for in a healing service, a piece of dead bone came out of one of the openings and allowed healing to take place.

Parapsychology has been suggested as a possible explanation of apparent miracles. Langford gives a possible, although imaginary, example of how a lot of people praying during a drought might bring rain.[21] But while parapsychology could be an explanation of some cases of an apparent miracle, it often will not do; the answer to the prayer may be too long delayed for parapsychology to be a plausible explanation.

Such explanations have to be borne in mind and excluded. Provided that can be done miracles of the providential type appear to occur and may be recognised by the features described. If they occur they may be evidential. Whether they in fact do occur can only be estimated by examination of particular cases.

(c) Can Providence be Evidential?

If providence can clearly be recognised it may be evidential. The question is whether we can ever have sufficient grounds of claiming that an event is providential. Unlike a miracle there is not necessarily a specific prayer and so no event which precisely corresponds and which was very unlikely to have come about by chance. By providence we mean Divine direction of certain events in life. A person is sometimes struck by the fact that a number of events in his life seem to have worked together as if intended.

He does not have in mind an outcome which is trivial or selfish. He may, for example, have come to be engaged in work which he believes to be of real value to other people and which it was not his original intention to do. He feels that it was not simply his own choosing; rather he was led to it. Again, it may be that something happens which meets a genuine need and which there was no reason to expect. In both cases events appear to have been directed to a purpose.

But is the appearance deceptive? That is what Wiles thinks. He remarks that many particular cases in which communities or individuals speak of God's action appear to others both morally and spiritually unacceptable.[22] That is so and it needs saying. But the important question is not whether there are some events which are wrongly attributed to the action of God. It is whether there are any which are rightly attributed and if so how they may be recognised. As with a miracle that can only be answered by detailed examination of particular cases and this is done in Chapters VI and VII. But Wiles himself refers to two cases. One of them is the way Augustine came to faith. It is worth examining in more detail than Wiles does.[23]

Augustine thought his conversion was guided by providence; Wiles thinks not. Augustine had moved from north Africa to Rome and then to Milan as professor of rhetoric. His hope was eventually to be made governor of a province. As a young man he had joined the Manichean sect and later was attracted to Neoplatonism. Christianity, which he was familiar with as a boy, he regarded as a religion for uneducated people. In Ambrose, Bishop of Milan, he met a highly intelligent and educated man who had himself been a provincial governor. He now became seriously interested in Christianity. He knew that one could be a Christian and live as a married man in the world. But that was not for him; he would want to serve God wholly. So for him to be a Christian meant giving up the ordinary life of the world with its ambitions and in particular giving up sexual activity. That meant a tremendous wrench. He was deeply divided on what to do. Things came to a head one day in the house in Milan after an unexpected visit by a fellow countryman who held high office in the Emperor's court. He told Augustine, and the friend

who was with him, about the conversion of Anthony who gave
up his wealth and went to live in the Egyptian desert as a hermit,
and of two government secret agents who became monks.
Augustine, greatly disturbed, felt that he had to make a decision.
He went into the garden and after a time heard the voice of a
child from a neighbouring house singing over and over *tolle,
lege; tolle lege,* pick up and read. He went at once and picked
up the book of Pauline epistles which he had left on a bench.
The first verses to catch his eye were those at the close of
Romans 13, "... not in reveling and drunkenness, not in debauchery
and licentiousness, not in quarreling and jealousy. But put on the
Lord Jesus Christ and make no provision for the flesh, to gratify
its desires". "I wanted to read no further" he writes "nor did I
need to" *(Confessions VIII. 29)*.

The first thing to ask is whether this is a true account of
what took place. It was written thirteen years later. And Augustine
was an expert in the use of language to make an impression. The
account in the *Confessions* may to some extent be checked from
what is said in the very different books written shortly after the
event. Chadwick writes that the comparison shows that, while
the account is in quasi-poetic form, in essentials it is reliable.[24]

The view that Augustine's conversion was the result of
purely human factors can be supported in more than one way. It
was the outcome of a long period of inner conflict. On the one
hand was sexual desire and ambition; on the other dissatisfaction
and unhappiness. The conflict needed to be resolved by a decision.
Retirement from ordinary life in the world was not uncommon
and not restricted to Christians; pagan Platonists had an ideal of
philosophical retirement which involved the giving up of career
and of sexual relations. It has been suggested also that a main
reason for Augustine's decision was that he had developed chest
trouble which affected his voice. It prevented loud and prolonged
speaking so that he had to give up his work.

These points may be met. On the last, Augustine does not
himself say that the chest trouble was the reason for giving up
his work. It could have been but he could also have taken leave
of absence. And although Augustine was dissatisfied and unhappy

and needed to make a decision, it was by no means inevitable that it was Christianity that he would decide for. Brown points out that pagan Platonism was a real possibility.[25]

Augustine had no doubt that it was providence that led to his conversion and answered his mother's prayers. The events preceding it were guided and in particular his lighting on the text in Romans. Certainly it was extraordinarily relevant to his state of mind. Opening the Bible, or some other book, and reading what first meets the eye does not seem to us today a proper way of seeking Divine guidance. But it was commonly done at the time as it has been subsequently. It may be that the ever present God accommodates to human limitations. In this case all that we have to go on is Augustine's expectation of guidance and the remarkable appropriateness of the text.

It cannot be decided beyond question whether or not there was a providential element in Augustine's conversion. But for that to have any plausibility at all depends on a prior belief in the reality of God. This suggests that in general, providence could not be of evidential value. In the case of a miracle a similar objection was made and could be met. With providence that is more difficult but perhaps not impossible.

In a paper first published in 1952 C.B. Martin challenged the claim that the believer had any way of obtaining knowledge that was not open to the unbeliever. Some leading theologians at the time maintained that the believer could have a direct awareness of God. On this basis they claimed a knowledge of the existence of God. With most of what Martin says I am in entire agreement. But at one point he writes, "Nor is there any increased capacity for prediction produced in the Christian believer which we cannot explain on a secular basis".[26] The implication is that if there were such a capacity it would be good evidence for the basic religious affirmation of the reality of the Divine. This is because, where applicable, the ability to predict is an important test of truth in natural science. Martin thinks that a religious believer has no comparable ability.

Prediction in religion is, of course, different from prediction in a natural science. God is not thought of as an object to be manipulated in order to confirm a hypothesis. Religious prediction is more like predicting how a friend will act under certain circumstances; if he is there we can count on him to act in a particular way. In the Bible predictions are made by the prophets. There was a time when the predictive activity of the prophets was played down. They were preachers of righteousness who denounced the social injustices they saw about them and called for a change of heart and a change of conduct. While this is certainly the case the prophets on some occasions also made predictions. So much is this the case that, according to Deuteronomy, one way, although not the only way, of telling a true prophet from a false one is the ability to predict. If what the prophet predicts is not fulfilled he is to be disregarded (18.22). In actual fact predictions were not always fulfilled but the point here is simply that religious predictions were made.

In the modern world there are people who have made predictions about God's actions in the world. Rightly or wrongly they have predicted that God would providentially supply the material needs of themselves and of their work. And they have made themselves completely dependent on the predictions being fulfilled. They claim that what was predicted came about and that it came about through God's providential actions. To weigh up such claims requires detailed examination of the lives and characters of the people making them; of the circumstances in which predictions were made; and whether the fulfillment could have come about without any Divine action. Such an examination is made in Chapters VI and VII. But first something has to be said about providence.

References

1. F. Schleiermacher, *On Religion : Speeches to its Cultured Despisers*, E.T. London, 1893, p. 35.

2. *The Christian Faith*, 1821, E.T. Edinburgh, 1928, paperback ed. New York, 1963, p. 16.

3. W. James, *The Varieties of Religious Experience*, London, 1902 (1943 ed.), p. 422.

4. Wayne Proudfoot, *Religious Experience*, Berkeley, 1985, p. 162.

5. P. Tillich, *Systematic Theology*, Vol. I, Digswell Place, 1953, p. 124.

6. C. Franks Davis, *The Evidential Force of Religious Experience,* Oxford, 1989, p. 35.

7. K. Ward, *The Concept of God,* Oxford, 1974, paperback ed. p. 163.

8. J.P. Hyatt, *Exodus,* London, 1971, pp. 37f.

9. W. Johnstone, *Exodus,* Sheffield, 1990, pp. 33ff.

10. G.E. Wright, *Biblical Archaeology,* 2nd ed, London, 1962, pp. 61f.

11. G.I. Davies, *The Way of the Wilderness,* Cambridge, 1979, pp. 80ff.

12. D. Hume, *An Enquiry Concerning the Human Understanding,* 1748, ed. L.A. Selby-Bigge, Oxford, 1902, Section X, p. 115n.

13. F. Waismann, Verifiability, 1945, in *The Theory of Meaning,* ed. G H R Parkinson, Oxford, 1968, p 44

14. C.S. Lewis, *Miracles,* London, 1947, pp. 70f.

15. A. Flew, *Hume's Philosophy of Belief,* London, 1961, p. 188.

16. R. Swinburne, *The Concept of Miracle,* London, 1970, pp. 65ff.

17. A.E. Glover, *A Thousand Miles of Miracle in China,* London, 1904.

18. H.H. Farmer, *The World and God,* 2nd ed. London, 1936, p. 127.

19. *Ibid.,* pp. 114f.

20. H.H. Price, *Belief,* London, 1969, pp. 302ff.

21. M.J. Langford, *Providence,* London, 1981, pp. 16f.

22. M. Wiles, *God's Action in the World,* London, 1986, p. 2.

23. *Ibid.,* p. 81.

24. H. Chadwick, *Augustine,* Oxford, 1986, paperback ed. p. 67.

25. P. Brown, *Augustine of Hippo,* London, 1967, paperback ed. p. 104.

26. C.B. Martin, A Religious Way of Knowing in *New Essays in Philosophical Theology,* ed. A. Flew and A. Macintyre, London, 1955, paperback ed. p. 79.

Chapter V

Providence in Human Life

1. The Concept of Providence

It is individual life which is our chief present-day source of knowledge about providence. The individual is able to recognise the activity of God in certain events in his own life and sometimes in those of other people. There are occasions—and they may be failures as much as successes—when he is sure of the hand of God on his life. He has no doubt that a particular event did not occur purely by chance but was somehow intended. Things worked out through the normal natural and human processes, but in some way were worked together by a direction that came from beyond. God's providential action may also be recognised in nature and history. Providence in nature was discussed earlier; providence in history will not be dealt with in this book. It is noteworthy that in the teaching of Jesus providence is largely restricted to God's dealing with the individual.

Jesus' most important teaching on providence comes in the Sermon on the Mount. Here the assertion of God's providential care is set alongside the call to do God's will. Jesus' teaching is not that life is going to be easy or pleasant. It is that we can serve God single-mindedly without having to be anxious about the necessities of life. "But strive first for the kingdom of God and his righteousness, and all these things will be given to you as well" (Matthew 6.33). The things are food and drink and clothing. They are the things people are anxious about. The believer in providence need not be taken up with them; what he is to be taken up with is God's kingdom and his righteousness.

In spite of what has just been said about God's provision of the necessities of life, personal safety is not promised. It was while giving a warning about the likelihood of persecution that Jesus spoke the familiar words, "Are not two sparrows sold for a penny? Yet not one of them will fall to the ground apart from your Father. And even the hairs of your head are all counted. So do not be afraid; you are of more value than many sparrows" (Matthew 10. 29ff). God's will is to be obeyed at all costs and this may involve suffering and death. Yet there is a security in the assurance that finally and whatever happens we are not beyond God's knowledge and care.

Providence is closely connected with vocation and in two ways. One is what has just been referred to: providence enables a person to carry out the task to which he is called by freeing him from the anxieties of life. The other connection, central to both providence and vocation, is God's concern with the individual. In vocation he is called personally to a particular task. Of course he has to make sure that he has grasped God's purpose and that the task to which he thinks he is called really is what God wants of him. The fact that we see a work to be done does not necessarily mean that it is God's work; it is easy to deceive ourselves. Hitler felt that there was a great work to be done for his nation. Only someone specially called and prepared could do it. He was the man raised up by Providence to restore Germany to the position it should rightly occupy in the world. Hitler and his associates made frequent use of the word providence—*vorsehung;* it was in fact his name for God. Because of this Christians in Germany even today, I am told, make very little use of it. Misuse has barred out the proper use of the concept of providence.

In the concept of providence there are three essential features.

(a) The Divine Knowledge

That God is all-knowing or omniscient is a traditional affirmation and not one that is much disputed. But there are great differences of opinion as to just what it involves. Are there events and states of affairs which is logically impossible for God to know? In that case omniscience has limits. Questions arise about God's knowledge both of the present and of the future. We are concerned with both but especially with God's knowledge of the future.

The question arises because providence and providential miracle seem sometimes to require that God has knowledge of the future. An example comes in the next chapter. When Hudson Taylor took over the Ningbo hospital he predicted that sufficient funds would come in to support the expensive in-patient work. Funds did come and had been sent long before the need for them arose. It appears, then, that God foreknew the situation. And that is what the word *providentia,* from which our word is derived, means: foresight or foreknowledge. Certainly God could know the future insofar as it was causally necessitated by events in the present. But it is not completely so if human beings have free will. Again it might be suggested that God knows the future because he makes the future. But since it is being held that the world has a relative independence and every event is not directly willed by God, this suggestion cannot be accepted. So if it is granted that God appears to know events which to us are future, the question is how this could be possible?

In answering this question there are two main issues to consider.

(i) God's relation to time

Augustine was asked what God was doing before he created the world. If he was doing nothing why did he change and not continue like that? Augustine says that he could make a joke of the question and answer that God was preparing hell for those who pry too deeply. But he recognises that it is a serious question and gives a considered reply. It is that to speak of before creation implies that there was time. Yet there was no time before God created the world; time came into being with the world. But God himself is eternal and not in time *(Confessions* 11.12-16).

This view of Augustine was not seriously questioned until quite recently. Now many people have argued that God is not eternal but is in time and time is without beginning or end. God is everlasting; he endures from an infinite past to an infinite future without coming into being or ceasing to be. It should be mentioned that the term eternal is sometimes used to cover this idea also: the alternative view is distinguished by calling it timelessly eternal.

Two main reason, which are connected, have been put forward for rejecting the idea that God is timelessly eternal.

First, it is said that the idea that God is timelessly eternal is not Biblical. This would be important if it could be shown to be true and that the message of the Bible was dependent on a certain view of time and eternity.

The idea that the Bible contains a distinctive view of time and of eternity had its most influential advocate in the Swiss New Testament scholar Cullmann.[1] In his exposition time is regarded as a line on which there are a series of decisive moments chosen by God. And eternity, in contrast to the Greek idea of timelessness, is a continuation of the time line so that eternity is endless time. This understanding of the Biblical view of time and eternity was based primarily on the examination of particular words, Hebrew and Greek. It has been shown by Barr that this method of concentrating on words rather than on sentences or larger units is fundamentally mistaken and that conclusions based on it cannot be accepted.[2] What can be said is that the Bible attaches special importance to certain events and their conse-quences. The event of Christ makes the life of individuals and of communities different. For the writers of the New Testament what is significant is before and after Christ and not any special view of time and eternity.

But does the Bible have any special view of time and eternity? Barr goes on to show that it is far from clear that it does. While there are many references to God's action in time there are no passages in which the nature of time or of God's relation to time is specifically taken up. Yet perhaps one thing may be said. It may well be, as Barr suggests, that the early Christians understood the creation story in Genesis I to imply that the beginning of time was simultaneous with the beginning of creation.[3] If that is the case then at least some New Testament writers can be said to hold the view that God is not in time but is eternal.

The second reason for rejecting the idea that God is timelessly eternal is this: it is said that if this were so he could not be personal. The position is forcibly stated by Gale. "The personal God of the Scriptures qualifies as a person in this sense. He has purposes and interacts with his creatures. The Deity to whom the authors of the Bible prayed was taken to be someone with whom they had communion, someone who comforted, counselled, and warned them, and on occasion answered their prayers ..." Such a two-way interaction makes no sense on the theory of a timelessly eternal God, for all of his states and actions occur within a single timeless present and cannot be the effect of anything that happens in time".[4] It will be sufficient here to take up the two main points that Gale makes, the one about purposes and the one about interaction.

In the first place it is suggested that a timelessly eternal God could not have purposes. The reason for this is that when we have purposes we are usually thinking about something in the future. If it is the purpose of a government to raise the level of literacy in a country that means that it hopes to have more people able to read in the future. But if God is timelessly eternal he does not look ahead to the future as we do. Instead he is aware of all that goes on in time as something like an eternal present. In reply to this objection it may be said, as will be argued shortly, that within this awareness the temporal relations of before and after still hold. This means that while events are not past or future in relation to God, some events, as Ewing points out, may be past or future in relation to other events.[5] It seems reasonable to suggest that Moses was fulfilling God's redemptive purpose when he led Israel out of slavery in Egypt. God's purpose would have a future reference but it would be a future in relation to the state of affairs in Egypt and not an absolute future.

In the second place it is suggested that a timelessly eternal God could not interact with his creatures. Interaction means knowing their circumstances, understanding their concerns, hearing their prayers and responding. How this may be possible is better discussed after some discussion of time itself.

In the early part of this century McTaggart, a distinguished Cambridge philosopher, attempted to prove that time was unreal. With his argument we are not concerned. But in the course of it he made an important observation about the language we use when speaking about time. There are two sets of terms. One has to do with the series past, present and future. McTaggart called this A-series. The other set has to do with the series earlier than, simultaneous with and later than. This he called the B-series. These terms are commonly used to designate two different theories of time.

The A-theory corresponds to the way we ordinarily think and speak about time. It is embedded in our language and expressed, for example, in the tenses of verbs and in adverbs and phrases such as today, next week, a year ago. Time, we understand, passes; it moves from the future into the present and then into the past. We may plan a holiday at a particular date in the future. We look forward to it as it comes nearer. It arrives and we enjoy it. Then it passes further and further into the past. Only in the present is an event real. In the future it will be real and in the past it has been real. But in these two times the event is not real in our ordinary way of thinking.

To be in time involves being carried along in time. That applies to everything, ourselves included; we grow older. As we grow older we change; we age as the expression goes. But the changes, although they take place as we move with time, are not part of this temporal movement; they are something in addition. Some things hardly change during the temporal movement, a granite rock, for example. Perhaps there are things which do not change at all as they move with time. Yet, even if it leaves no mark this temporal passage goes on and objects and events move from being future to being present and then being past. That is a strange idea but it is an integral part of the A-theory of time.

On the B-theory processes go on, cosmic, chemical and physiological, for example, and events take place. But there is no movement of everything in time without there necessarily being any changes in them. Everything is spread out in an unmoving space and an unmoving time. There are spatial and temporal dimensions. As things in space have positions in relation to one another so do events in time. As things move in space, so they move in time. Events take place at different dates and are related to one another as earlier, simultaneous and later.

The B-theory describes how the temporal world would appear from an eternal viewpoint. But it was not introduced in order to enable theologians to solve some of their problems. This kind of theory is commonly held by scientists and philosophers of science concerned with time. The claim is that it represents the way things actually are in the world. Yet it is the A-theory that we normally hold and the A-series that we constantly operate with in ordinary life and find it perfectly satisfactory. Can the two series be related?

Mellor points out the judgements made in A-series terms can be shown to be true only by relating them to dates, which are B-series facts.[6] Suppose I say that the landings in Normandy took place 50 years ago. That is an A-series statement. But it is true only if it took place at a certain date, namely 1944 and the present date is 1994. The example shows how the two series are related. A statement about an event in A-series terms can be put in B-series terms by fixing the moving present to a B-series position which is a date. The event is earlier or later than this; earlier and later are B-series terms.

If it is the B-series that represents the way things really are, why do we think and speak in A-series terms? And why do things look that way? The holiday does seem to come nearer, then to be present and then to recede into the past. Things look like that, as Mellor explains, because we are self-conscious beings. We see events in relation to ourselves.[7] Grünbaum makes much the same point: the passing "now" has meaning only in the context of the egocentric perspectives of sentient organisms.[8] When we are aware of an event occurring now it is the awareness of something taking place simultaneously with our consciousness of the event. This is often of practical importance. If I am not to miss the bus it is important to notice that the driver is getting into it now. From the consciousness of the present we can imagine and think about future events and prepare for them, and we can remember events in the past. Because position in the A-series relates events to our immediate self-consciousness it is essential for knowledge and action and cannot be dispensed with.

If the world as it appears from an eternal standpoint is a B-series world this brings back the problem referred to earlier. It is the A-series that relates events to ourselves. And it is what is happening now as seen by each individual that most concerns him; it is where his interests and needs and those of others chiefly lie. But if God does not have our A-series viewpoint how can he interact with us? He is able to do this because he is present always and everywhere. He knows our situation always and how we are related to events. He looks into our hearts and knows our thoughts and feelings and desires. He hears our prayers and can respond. Padgett, who himself holds neither the timeless eternity of God nor the B-theory of time, makes a valuable point for those who do: if the B-theory is only half-heartedly held there will be conflict with Christian doctrine. This has been developed in languages that are A-theory laden. But if a thorough-going B-theory of both reality and of language is adopted there will be no conflict.[9]

(ii) God's knowledge and foreknowledge

The classical position was set out by the Christian philosopher Boethius, writing in prison before being put to death on a political charge in 524 AD.[10] God in eternity is aware of the whole expanse of time. From his eternal standpoint all times and events are present-like. "But the present instant of men may well be compared to that of God in this: that as you see some things in your temporal instant, so He beholdeth all things in His eternal present" (*Consolation* V. VI. 77ff). Boethius gives an illustration of what he has in mind by suggesting that God is like someone on a high mountain peak. From the ground a person sees things bit by bit; from the mountain everything is grasped at once. God from outside time sees the whole sequence of events taking place in their temporal relations of before and after. But, unlike us, he is aware of it all at once.

Boethius' main interest in his discussion of time and eternity is God's foreknowledge and its relation to human freedom. It appears that if God, because he is not in time, knows events future to us, then the future is not open. We are not free to decide what to do because God already knows what the decision is. Boethius' solution to the problem is that properly it is not foreknowledge that God has but knowledge; he is aware of what we do as we are doing it. He knows our actions not before we have acted but as we act. It is our decision to do something and God knows it timelessly as we do it. So we have unrestricted freedom of choice. Yet because God in his eternal present knows the whole temporal sequence of events, including our free actions, he can be said to know what to us is future.

If God knows events as they happen and situations as they develop, he should be able to act so as to change the course of events. But could he act in one situation in view of what happens in a later situation? In the Hudson Taylor example with which we started, God appears to have influenced William Berger to send money before it was needed. Yet we have seen that God knows events as they happen and not before they happen.

God is outside time altogether and is aware of all events in his eternal present. He is aware of events that to us are past as they occur just as he is aware of events today as they occur. He is aware of them in their temporal relationships. For God, as for us, event (a) come before event (b) as do other events contemporaneous with them. But that is a great difference. We, from our place in time, see events taking place only successively. God is, as it were, above the whole sequence of events in time and sees them all at once in his timeless present. As Boethius, writing of God's knowledge puts it, "grasping the infinite extent of past and future it surveys all things as though happening at present in His simple knowing" *Consolation* V. VI64f). He knows the course of events as they develop and can act in one situation in view of what is happening in another. Looking, so to speak, from above, he grasps both situations at once. Accordingly he can intervene in one because of what is happening in the other even if this is later.

(b) The Divine Care

The believer in providence maintains that God not only knows about our affairs but cares. This is the repeated affirmation of Biblical religion. The 23rd Psalm is about providence, "The Lord is my shepherd, I shall not want". In the Lord's prayer the idea of providence is central. And Jesus' teaching about God as Father is largely an expression of the Divine care.

It is important to be clear, before going further, about what the Divine care does not mean.

It does not mean a general benevolence. That was the way it was widely understood in the eighteenth century. The idea of providence was drawn for the most part, not from the life of individuals but from the impression made by the workings of nature. God was thought of as a powerful and beneficent intelligence who saw to it that provision was made for all his creatures. The whole complex life of the world was under direct and kindly management. This view of things was abruptly called in question by the Lisbon earthquake of 1755. Serious objections were raised against providence understood in this kind of way. But in the era of widespread peace, development and optimism in the century before the First World War this sort of view continued to be held. After that it was no longer possible to think of the Divine care as a general benevolence.

The Divine care does not mean that the believer in providence will necessarily be protected from danger. In times of acute danger people have always turned to the 91st Psalm. In the early Arnhem film, which is an accurate reconstruction of the battle, there is a scene in which Mrs. Katie ter Horst comes down to the cellar where many of the wounded British soldiers are sheltering. Her house had been taken over as a first-aid post and she had used up all she had in the house in caring for the soldiers. Because she has nothing more to give them and there is nothing else she can do for them she reads in English the 91st Psalm. James Agate, a well-known literary and dramatic critic, wrote that this was the most moving thing he had ever seen in the cinema."A thousand may fall at your side, ten thousand at your right hand; but it will not come near you". That is true only

if one understands it to mean apart from the knowledge and care
of God. Soldiers sometimes say that they will not be killed
unless their number is on the bullet. They have the feeling that
there is more to life than chance. It may be based either on fate
or on providence. The believer in providence is as likely to be
killed as anyone else. What he is sure of is that the issues of life
and death are in the hands of God. But he knows also that God
allows the full rigour of events to take place; he will not, except
for a special reason, think that a protection denied to others will
be extended to him.

The Divine care does not mean an escape from difficulties
and suffering. Illness, accident, poverty, disappointment and the
rest of the conditions that seem inseparable from human existence
are as likely to come to the devout believer as to anyone else.
Indeed he may be more liable to such things. That is what the
New Testament suggests; Jesus, Paul and Peter all speak about
suffering, come already or expected. And that has sometimes
been the case. In this century above all vast numbers of men and
women in various parts of the world have suffered and died for
their faith. They believed in providence. But few, if any, expected
an early deliverance from the suffering their loyalty brought
them. They knew the warnings and accepted the fact that for
them discipleship meant suffering.

Again, the Divine care does not mean that the believer
escapes the tragedies of life. The word tragedy gets its meaning
in the first place from drama. But the famous plays we class as
tragedies are so various and have been so variously interpreted
that a single clear meaning for the word does not emerge. All
that can be done is to make a rather general statement that will
apply to most tragic drama: an undeserved calamity which comes
from a combination of circumstances and of action by the victim.
The action is often an outcome of a fault of character, for example
King Lear. But not always; it may come from a·virtue. In *Antigone*
persistence in well-doing does not lead to the heroine's triumph
but to her death. In *Julius Caesar* Brutus' scrupulous righteous–
ness, as well as his folly, brings failure and death. In these and
other plays right action leads not to well-being but to disaster.

In ordinary usage the meaning of tragedy is extended. It generally means a calamity for which the victims have little or no responsibility and which frustrates a fulfilment of life which could reasonably be looked for. An unsafe drug is given in pregnancy and the child is born with serious and permanent deformities. In a country where insurance is not available a farm is destroyed by a flood and the family is reduced to penury. The risk of tragedy in prosperous countries has been reduced in various ways. But even there, the world remains a dangerous place and the structure of human life and human relationships is such that the possibility of tragedy cannot be eliminated.

Yet one is bound to ask, why does not God intervene to prevent suffering and tragedy? The natural and the human world have to be considered separately. First, why are calamitous events in the natural world allowed to happen? The world has a relative autonomy and a life of its own. It has been shaped through the properties and relationships of physical entities and through mutation and natural selection in the case of living things. Good fortune and calamity are distributed according to the workings of the world. They are not distributed according to the needs and deserts of individuals. Suffering does not come as a punishment to the wicked nor as a means of perfecting patience in the righteous. It comes indiscriminately to anyone. This is clearly recognised in the teaching of Jesus, "Or those eighteen who were killed when the tower of Siloam fell on them—do you think that they were worse offenders than all others living in Jerusalem?" (Luke 13.4). That the world has a relative autonomy and works by secondary causes inherent in it was clearly stated by Aquinas. He showed also that, for a number of reasons, a providential order did not mean that there will be no evils to endure.

Yet the question remains, why does God not intervene? The probable answer is that nature must work in a regular way. The world and human life would be entirely different if there were not uniformity and constancy in the workings of nature. Tennant points out that there could be no probability to guide us, no accumulation of ordered experience, no pursuit of premeditated ends, no possibility of character or of culture.[11] It is because the laws of nature operate in a regular way that understanding and prediction are possible. Yet it is this same regularity of working that, in a complex world with different and independent forces, does harm to human beings. For example DNA molecules can replicate millions of times without fault. But there are a number of physical and chemical agents which can damage the molecule. A harmful mutation may occur in a gene and a child may be born with an abnormality. The agents in question operate independently in accordance with their own laws. It is this regularity of working which produces risks for human beings.

There are innumerable risks in the world. Some threaten individuals. Some, such as earthquakes and famine, whole communities. To save people from the painful consequences of the regular workings of nature God would have perpetually to be intervening. That is not to say that he could not intervene sometimes without upsetting the regularity of nature. But, as Tennant again points out, the suspension of pain-producing events so as to eliminate all serious harm to human beings would have to be on a vast scale. It would destroy the natural world order. No longer would it be possible to predict what was going to happen under certain observable conditions and then to act accordingly.[12] The price of an understandable, predictable world, in which both individuals and civilizations can develop, is a regular natural order which sometimes brings suffering to people.

God's non-intervention in suffering caused by human wrong-doing may be understood in the same kind of way. Some of that suffering has been terrible, none being more evident than what has taken place in various parts of the world during this twentieth century. Even so, if human beings are free and responsible the consequences of our actions have to be allowed to work themselves out in spite of the fact that severe suffering will be caused. If God were frequently to intervene to prevent the consequences of wrong-doing taking place there would be no real moral responsibility. In that case we would be something less than human.

If this is so why does God nevertheless sometimes intervene? That he does so is clear, for example, from the cases discussed in the next two chapters. It should be remarked that the interventions asked for and expected were not for saving from personal suffering or tragedy. An instance is Hudson Taylor who sometimes spoke of his five graves in China. He would pray in serious illness for his wife and children but he did not predict special intervention. He did so on certain occasions when praying for work done in God's name. That God does sometimes intervene in answer to prayer is the conviction of thousands of people. Yet why should he do so in some cases when in others, where people are literally crying out for intervention, he does not?

The answer involves taking with the utmost seriousness the personal relationship between God and the believer. This is entered into and maintained by faith and love and unity of will. It is in this relationship that providential action is experienced. Prayer, miracle and providence, it has been said, are fundamental to the Christian's life of personal fellowship with God; to discuss it is to discuss them.[13] A personal relationship has two sides. If God were quite unresponsive to the concerns and expressed desires of men and women we should not have a deep sense of fellowship with God. But if God is responsive we should expect some of our prayers to be answered. A dramatic answer to prayer is a miracle and has always been felt to be such. Providence belongs to the same class of events but is less dramatic. God's response to us is seen in events in the world we recognise as answered prayer and providence. It is the expression of the Divine side of the personal relationship.

This does not mean that God acts in providence to relieve us from trouble or for our immediate happiness. He may answer prayer in a way that we do not expect and do not like. The conditions of life may be exceedingly difficult: hard and monotonous and disappointing. The believer may have to face the most adverse circumstances but still may be sure that God cares. Paul writes, "We know that all things work together for good for those who love God" (Romans 8.28). "Good" certainly does not mean ease or comfort or freedom from the anxieties of life. A year or two before writing these words Paul, under provocation, had given a list of the imprisonments, beatings, stonings, shipwrecks, dangers of many kinds, hunger and

exposure, weakness and anxiety he had experienced (II Corinthians 11.23ff). Somehow, he would say, God worked in all
these things for good.

The good which God works with those who love him is
fulfilment. This is of two kinds. First, there is the task to which
they are called which may be great or small. The task may be
clear from the beginning or guidance may be needed in seeing
what it is. And long preparation may be necessary before it can
be taken up. Mother Teresa worked for almost twenty years as
a teacher in a high school in Calcutta before seeing what her real
vocation was. Yet she would not have been ready for it earlier.
Guidance may be needed also in carrying out the task. There are
many wrong ways that may be taken and the closing of some
ways may be just as important as the opening of others.

The long story of Joseph is an illustration of this aspect of
Divine care. He was sold into slavery in Egypt because of the
jealousy of his brothers. He got on well there but provoked the
anger of his master's wife by refusing her advances and was sent
to prison. In due course he was released owing to his ability to
interpret dreams and became chief executive of the country. His
principal work was to prepare the country to withstand famine.
A widespread famine developed and his brothers were forced to
come to Egypt to buy corn. They did not recognise Joseph. But
when he told them who he was they were terrified that he would
take revenge. Instead he said, "Do not be afraid! Am I in the
place of God? Even though you intended to do harm to me, God
intended it for good, in order to preserve a numerous people, as
he is doing today" (Genesis 50.19f). God had his purpose for
Joseph but he was spared nothing of the hardships and
disappointments of life. The way led through these things to the
fulfilment of his task.

Second, there is fulfilment in personal life. Following the
verse quoted from Romans about God working all things together
for good (8.28) Paul goes on to speak of being conformed to the
image of Christ. This refers not only to sharing his glory hereafter
but also to an approximation to his image in this present life.
Our personalities are not supposed to remain as they were when

religious life began. That often happens both in the case of someone converted as a young adult and in the case of a person brought up in a Christian family and a Christian church. Religious observances are carried out but little or no spiritual growth takes place. It may be that for growth trials are needed. Certainly there are aspects of the personality which could not develop apart from the real trials which form part of human life. Trials are not bound to come but when they do come God can work in them for good. There is no uniformity of personality; each person remains himself. But within this individuality wonderful development can take place and this will be shown in conduct in many different ways. It is part of God's providential care to guide towards this kind of fulfilment.

(c) The Divine Activity

The preceding section may have given the impression that belief in providence is only a matter of the way we look at things. The believer takes them one way and the unbeliever another. But, it may be thought, the believer does not expect anything to happen that the unbeliever does not also expect. That is not the case. Certainly the believer does not expect anything contrary to the way in which things normally go on in the world. There will be no break in the regularities of the natural world, nor will there be any sudden change in the present conditions of personal and social life. But he does expect that sometimes God will bring things to pass that would not otherwise have happened. He believes that God acts in the world

Of course the idea of Divine action in the world has emerged from a primitive way of thinking. In primal religion life is set against a supernatural background and is directed by supernatural agencies. The spirits act directly causing some event to take place, perhaps an illness or an accident, perhaps success in fishing. And the tendency to think like this is alive in us all. It makes us see a providential intention when a combination of events fits our desires. The questions that need answering are: first, is what we interpret as Divine action really a primitive way of thinking carried over into modern life, or is there sometimes really a Divine activity in the events of life? And second, if there is, how are we to understand it? The first question will be answered in the only way it could be satisfactorily answered. Instances are given in Chapter VI and VII of events which were predicted solely on the basis of Divine action, and which were found to occur. It is the second question that has now to be addressed.

It is not being held that God is active in all events. On the contrary the world has a relative independence. The more extreme believer in providence is inclined to think that God acts in all the events of life. This is sometimes referred to as universal providence; every event is directly willed by God. Against such a view it has to be said that while God is present always he is not acting always. He has given the world and human beings lives of their own, not separated from him but nevertheless relatively independent. This is the view of common-sense; we do not think that God is acting every time a dog crosses the road. The independence of the world is taken for granted by the natural scientist and the historian. The scientist can trace out the orderly sequences of nature and the historian can describe the many and complex factors which have gone into the making of the events of the past. And while it is true that God can and does operate through these factors, there is no reason to think that he is always doing so. But there are occasions when God does act and so makes evident the Divine environment of our lives.

God may act both in the human and in the natural world. First, his action on human thinking and willing.

In Chapter VII all the examples mentioned are of this kind. Mother Teresa asked God for money and expected him to influence people. Again in the case of Hudson Taylor, the great majority of the incidents in which Divine intervention is claimed have to do with money and with people's decision to give. The number of cases studied is small and there was a special reason for providential action to occur by the guidance of human minds and wills. But more general accounts of providence seem to confirm that the human mind is the chief locus of Divine action.

This raises the question of the freedom of human decision in a different way from that considered in the first section of this chapter. Does Divine guidance of human decision mean over–

riding freedom? Not necessarily. Decisions are made in particular circumstances and in some cases guidance may be given through circumstances. Attention may again be drawn to the provision of funds for the hospital at Ningbo. In this case we know the circumstances in which the funds were sent. William Berger's father had died leaving him with a great deal more money. There was no desire on the Bergers' part to increase their own expenditure. And so no special influence was needed to make them send money for Hudson Taylor's work; rather they were now in a position to do what they wanted to do.

On other occasions it appears that God influences a person's decision more directly. Farrer calls attention to a prophecy of Isaiah about Assyria (10.5-19). God was to use Assyria for the correction of Israel because of its wickedness. The Assyrians were to be God's agents. But that is not how the Assyrians thought; their intentions were entirely different (v. 7). Farrer suggests that the mechanism of Divine guidance lies in the openness of people's thoughts to pressures of which they are unaware. The Assyrians felt the force of the reasons for military action against Judea. But these reasons might not have occurred to them or a different use of their troops might have seemed more rewarding.[14] It may be that God sometimes guides the decisions of human beings by bringing ideas before the mind.

Is this is curtailment of human freedom? In one way it is not. A person acts in accordance with his own character, the circumstances at the time and for reasons that he is able to state. He does what he wants to do or thinks best to do; he does not act in any way contrary to his own will. And yet in another way he is not free; he could not have acted otherwise. What God intended him to do he did. The fact that God may influence people's minds in this sort of way does not affect the general issue of the freedom of the will. As Langford notes, so long as the interference with people's thoughts and actions is not general but something exceptional, the normal freedom of the will is not affected.[15]

The other area in which God's providential action is claimed is the natural world. In the lives of the two people studied that appears only in the case of Hudson Taylor. And the only clear examples of providential action of this kind in the records has to do with the weather. That the weather should provide examples of prayer and miracle is not surprising; travel by sailing ship was hazardous. What is surprising is that experience of providence in other aspects of the natural world is not mentioned.

People do pray for, and expect, providential action elsewhere in the natural world. I have made no investigation as to whether claims to have experienced such action can be justified but perhaps the claims should be mentioned. Guarding people from dangers on journeys is prayed for with other hazards besides the weather in mind, some human, some natural. Another area of life in which prayer is made is for food and this may be an urgent need. Its lack may be due both to natural and to human failure. We are taught to pray for daily bread although the prayer is not always answered. A third area is sickness. Apparent answers to such prayer are hard to assess. Certainly there are dramatic cases following prayer. But psychosomatic effects are powerful and the fact that prayer is made may itself influence the course of things. When there is Divine intervention it may well be by means of psychosomatic influences and so these cases perhaps properly belong to the first group where the influence is on the human mind. What has to be said here is that the aspects of the natural world where providential action is expected sometimes to occur are not many.

It is suggested by Pollard that the sub-atomic is the level at which it is likely that God acts in providence.[16] For very small objects, such as an atom or electron, it is impossible to specify both the position and the velocity simultaneously. It is not that we do not know enough to do so. It cannot be done because quantum events are not determined by prior causes. In the large scale phenomena of the ordinary world enormous numbers are involved. Because of this quantum mechanics is able to make predictions on a statistical basis about the behaviour of the whole group. But the behaviour of individual particles cannot be predicted. Pollard believes in a universal providence; all events in the world occur under the direction of God. This has already been rejected and a relative independence for the world affirmed.

But with this modification it may be said that Pollard does suggest one possible locus for the action of God in the natural world. Very occasional interventions in chance events would not be detectable amid the large numbers involved.

Beyond setting out a possible locus for the action of God in the human and the natural world we cannot go. We have no understanding of the inner being of God. We cannot therefore understand all aspects of his relationships to people nor to animals and plants and inanimate things in the world and cannot expect to understand just how he acts.

2. Our Attitude to Providence

First, what our attitude should not be. It may be wrong in two ways. In the first place it should not be egocentric. We do all have a tendency to think of the world as centering round ourselves. As children we all start off like that. We want things to happen for our pleasure and for our advantage. And we tend to think that this is the way they do happen. They may happen also for our correction. Allport notes that many children think that a thunderstorm is put on for their special punishment.[17] He goes on a little later to say that to revise one's view of providence and to give up the childhood attitude of self-interest is extremely difficult. Many people never do give it up. God is looked on as an ally for their own schemes and they interpret as providential any fortunate event which appears to further them. Reinhold Niebuhr referred in a sermon to the biography of an actress which was described as religious. She said special providence in all her fights with other people but knew nothing of love and humility. This is an extreme case but an egocentric attitude to providence is not at all uncommon. Perhaps that is how most of us start and many never get beyond it.

It is not difficult to get into a state of mind in which we think that God must intervene to change conditions which are threatening. This may be regarded as an expression of faith. If God does not act and what is threatened takes place, the person may give up his faith. This sometimes happens, for example, when prayers for recovery are not answered and someone greatly loved dies young. For facing the fact that the God-fearing person does not escape calamities and for being able to rejoice in spite of them no better expression can be found than the words with which the book of Habakkuk comes to a close,

> Though the fig tree do not blossom,
>> nor fruit be on the vines,
> the produce of the olive fail
>> and the fields yield no food,
> the flock be cut off from the fold
>> and there be no herd in the stalls,
> yet will I rejoice in the Lord,
>> I will joy in the God of my salvation (3.17f RSV).

That is mature faith. To think that God must ward off a threatened calamity is also faith. But it is immature and its motive power is self-interest.

Another way in which an egocentric attitude to providence comes out is acquiescence in things as they are. It is possible to justify almost any long-standing evil in society by an appeal to providence. If God in his providence directs the affairs of the world it would seem that the present order of things must express his will. Such a view presupposes a Stoic understanding of providence, not a Christian one. The one word obscures the fact that there are two quite different ways of understanding providence. For the Stoic, providence represents the Divine reason at work in the world which orders all things for the good of the whole. The existing state of affairs must be what the Divine reason appoints. The Christian view is quite otherwise. The world has a relative independence. Things as they are in social life do not represent the will of God; a state of affairs that is far from right cannot be his will. Men and women are God's agents in fashioning the world according to his will. If someone claiming to be a Christian thinks of providence in the kind of way mentioned, and uses it as a reason for acquiescence, the basis of his attitude is likely to be self-interest. He likes things as they are and is afraid of radical change. Providence is used as a justification.

In the second place our attitude to providence should not be one of passivity. Although quite different from the attitude just mentioned, the practical outcome in social life is much the same. Passivity is based on the idea that because God is in control of all things we should not interfere. At a presidential election in the United States a woman was asked by a reporter which way she was going to vote. She was not going to vote because God was in heaven and would shortly put all the troubles of the world right. This kind of attitude has been taken by some believers in a number of areas of life: in the nineteenth century over whether to make use of insurance; more recently, over faith healing and whether medicine should be used and over family planning. An earlier debate was over the establishment of foreign missions. Opponents argued that when God wants to spread the Gospel he will do it without our help. Carey replied to this contention in a pamphlet published in 1792, which is generally regarded as beginning the modern missionary movement. His reply was, in effect, that while this is God's work he uses means to get it done. He can take our activity and work through it. There may be occasions in life when the right thing is to wait expectantly. But normally reliance on providence does not require an attitude of passivity; rather we are to make use of the powers that God has given us. The right attitude is that of Nehemiah (4.9), "So we prayed to our God, and set a guard as protection against them day and night".

Second, what our attitude to providence should be. The attitude is twofold. In the first place it is one of confidence in the service of God and neighbour. Belief in providence, as was mentioned earlier, frees us from anxiety about our own affairs. It frees us also from anxiety about whether large endeavours are feasible. If we can be sure that something is the will of God we can be sure that, in the long run anyway, it can be done. That is how it was, for example, with Carey. The attitude is expressed in what has come to be called Carey's motto, "Expect great things from God, Attempt great things for God". In fact the words are the two heads of a sermon preached before leaving England. But they sum up his whole life in India of astonishing activity. To bring about any important change generally requires long years of steady and often disheartening work. Belief in providence can be a source of vigour by liberating us from anxiety. Like Moses, the man or woman of providence endures as seeing him who is invisible (Hebrews 11.27 RSV).

In the second place the attitudes should be a readiness to accept whatever life brings. Here providence has a different significance. It is because important events in life cannot occur without God allowing them that we must accept them willingly. The conviction that nothing of real importance in our lives can occur apart from God's knowledge and permission has always been held. Bonhoeffer, for example, wrote from prison about eight months before his execution, "It is certain... that no earthly power can touch us without his will".[18] Because we can be sure that God knows and cares we should be able to accept without resentment whatever happens. Events such as illness, bereavement, disappointment and failure should not lead to bitterness. Our attitude to providence should be, as Garrigou-Lagrange puts it, obedience to God's known will and abandonment to whatever God may will and the future may bring forth.[19]

This has been the attitude of spiritual leaders. Caussade wrote that what was important in the spiritual life was to submit with faith and love to the designs of providence. To grow up spiritually we simply had to make use of what God gives us to do or to suffer at each moment.[20] He thought of God's direction as extending to the small events of life. But even if life is largely autonomous obedience to God's known will and acceptance of what the future brings and God allows remains basic to the spiritual life. In this spirit Caussade submitted without complaint to the increasing blindness of his later years. Carey and his colleagues in 1812 suffered a disastrous fire at their printing works. Buildings, presses, type, paper, books were all destroyed. More important was the loss of manuscripts. They included materials for a great polyglot dictionary of the Sanskrit group of Indian languages and much of the translation of one of the epics. The calamity was accepted without despair. The type-founders and translators began work again and within a few months the press was once more in full working order. Bonhoeffer, two days after the letter referred to above, wrote "Please don't ever get anxious or worried about me, but don't forget to pray for me—I'm sure you don't! I am so sure of God's guiding hand that I hope I shall always be kept in that certainty. You must never doubt that I'm travelling with gratitude and cheerfulness along the road where I'm being led".[21] That is the attitude to providence of a spiritual leader.

References

1. O. Cullmann, *Christ and Time*, 1946, 3rd ed. London, 1962, chs. 1-3.

2. J. Barr, *Biblical Words for Time*, 2nd ed. London, 1969, ch. 3.

3. *Ibid.*, pp. 78f, 152.

4. R. Gale, *On the Nature and Existence of God*, Cambridge, 1991, p. 54.

5. A.C. Ewing, *Value and Reality*, London, 1973, p. 281.

6. D.H. Mellor, McTaggart, Fixity and Coming True, in *Reduction, Time and Reality*, ed. R. Healey, Cambridge, 1981, p. 86.

7. *Ibid.*, p. 88.

8. A Grünbaum, Time, Irreversible Processes and the Physical Status of Becoming, in *Problems of Space and Time*, ed. J.J.C. Smart, New York, 1964, p. 419.

9. A.G. Padgett, *God, Eternity and the Nature of Time*, London, 1992, p. 80.

10. *Boethius: The Theological Tractates* and *The Consolation of Philosophy*, eds. H.F. Stewart and E.K. Rand, London, 1918.

11. F.R. Tennant, *Philosophical Theology*, Vol. II, Cambridge, 1930, pp. 199f.

12. *Ibid.*, p. 202.

13. H.H. Farmer, *The World and God*, 2nd ed. London, 1936, p. 10.

14. Austin Farrer, *Faith and Speculation*, London, 1967, paperback ed. 1988, p. 61.

15. M.J. Langford, *Providence*, London, 1981, p. 100.

16. W.G. Pollard, *Chance and Providence*, London, 1959, pp. 53ff.

17. G.W. Allport, *The Individual and His Religion*, New York, 1950, paperback ed. p. 32.

18. D. Bonhoeffer, *Letters and Papers from Prison*, 3rd ed. London, 1971, p. 391.

19. R. Garrigou-Lagrange, *La Providence et la Confidence en Dieu,* Paris, 1932, p. 236.

20. J-P. de Caussade, *Self-Abandonment to Divine Providence,* paperback ed. Glasgow, 1971, pp. 35f.

21. D. Bonhoeffer, *op. cit.,* p. 393.

Chapter VI
Case Studies :
Claims for Providence—A

An understanding of the concept of providence may suggest that it could occur. But that providence actually does occur requires the examination of particular cases. This is undertaken in the following two chapters. The people whose experience is studied are not ordinary. They took faith in God to an extreme. In any age, as van Buren remarks, there are the many who make up the largest part of all establishments, religious and otherwise, and the few strange ones who stand in awe in the presence of God.[1] It is from these strange ones that we are most likely to learn about any action of God in providence and miracle.

The two people we are concerned with, although very different from one another, have one thing in common. For the support of their work they made no effort to raise money; they asked God for it. They did not simply do what they thought needed doing even though they had insufficient funds; they decided as a matter of policy not to ask people for money. It is not being maintained that this is the right way to proceed. Certainly it was not Paul's way. For his own support he raised money by working. And he undertook a large-scale fund raising project. He wanted the new mission churches to send money to the mother church in Jerusalem. He asked them for it. He made arrangements for its collection. He saw that the money was accounted for and was taken to Jerusalem by representatives of the giving churches (1 Corinthians 16.1-4; 2 Corinthians 8 and 9). All I am saying about the people we are interested in is that, right or wrong, they did in fact depend wholly on God for their own material needs and those of their work.

In doing this an implicit prediction was made. The prediction was that God would act in response to complete trust. In these two chapters we are concerned with one question and one question only: was there or was there not a Divine response in providence or miracle? No distinction need be made here between providence and providential miracle; the question is simply whether there was any Divine action. The chapters are all about money because the issue was raised in these terms. And money has a special value in this connection; it is something objective and quantifiable as well as being essential to life and work.

1. Narrative

The first person whose life will be examined for evidence of providence is Hudson Taylor, founder of the China Inland Mission. Detailed information is required for understanding the person and assessing the evidence. This is available and has to be set out in order that an informed judgement of the claims may be made.

The primary sources are the large amount of material preserved in the archives of the Overseas Missionary Fellowship. In addition I have drawn freely on the recent seven volume biography by A.J. Broomhall.[2] I have also made use of the older two volume biography by Hudson Taylor's son and daughter-in-law, Howard and Geraldine Taylor.[3] They knew him intimately and took great care in collecting and verifying information. The book is something of a classic and is still available in a one volume abridgement. It is the product of late nineteenth century pietism and is intended to contribute as much to religious devotion as to biography.

Hudson Taylor was born as Barnsley in 1832. His father was a pharmacist who later founded the Barnsley Building Society. He was a Methodist lay preacher and took a keen interest in Protestant mission work in China, then only beginning. Conversation at table must often have been on that topic. The parents, James and Amelia, had dedicated their baby son to be a missionary in China. But as he grew up they did not think him robust enough for such work and gave up the idea. They did not tell him what they had done until over thirty years later.

His mother reports that when Hudson was seventeen he made a deliberate act of consecration. There was a sense of awe in the Divine presence and, as distinctly as if a voice had uttered it, he felt that the words were spoken to him, "Then go to China". That was a turning-point in his life.

To prepare himself for service in China he started to study medicine. He had some experience from assisting his father whose work went a good deal beyond what we now expect of a pharmacist. In 1851 he was invited by a relative, who was a surgeon in Hull, to be his assistant. He worked with him for sixteen months. The surgeon thought highly of his work and asked him to stay longer. But Hudson decided to go to the London Hospital and prepare for the examination for membership of the Royal College of Surgeons. He was already in touch with the newly formed Chinese Evangelization Society (CES). Before going to Hull it had offered a grant for the fees if he would come for study at a hospital in London. He had refused because he did not have the means of supporting himself in London. In 1852 he visited London at the invitation of George Pearse, one of the honorary secretaries of the CES and made up his mind to take the course at the London Hospital.

On Sundays he went to friends he had met in connection with the CES. They lived in Hackney and Tottenham, then both villages outside London. At Hackney were George Pearse, who was a stockbroker and William Berger, a starch manufacturer; they were to be of the greatest importance in Hudson Taylor's life and work. At Tottenham were the Howard brothers, John Eliot and Robert, who were manufacturing chemists; they were youngish and had young families. Also at Tottenham was Miss Stacey and a group of Quaker ladies. All these people were to be lifelong friends. Miss Stacey noticed that Hudson often looked pale and tired and made a second home for him. He appreciated enormously the warm friendship at these places.

The medical work went on very well but Hudson began to wonder whether he should complete the course. That would take another two years. Certainly it would be an advantage to have the diploma, but he thought that it would not be essential in China. He had the knowledge and some experience; one of his teachers at the Hospital thought that he was ready then to take the examination.

But this was not his main reason for thinking of giving up the course. It is given in a letter to his mother from London written on May 1st 1853. The CES was paying the fees and would in due course send him to China as one of its missionaries. The Society had, and Hudson saw that it was bound to have, bye-laws defining its relationship with its agents. For instance, bye-law 6 stated that the missionary was to be ready to go to such a place and at such a time as the Board should decide. Hudson felt that this would set a limit to his direct dependence on the guidance of God. He would be a servant of the Society and not of God. And to be educated at their expense with no money of his own to repay, it would not be possible to release himself honourably from his obligation.

The CES was very understanding in its attitude. The General Secretary, Charles Bird, asked him to consider whether passing the College of Surgeons examination would not repay the extra time. But the Society was willing to send him out without the qualification if that is what he thought best. Nor would there be any objection to his going into the interior if the opportunity should arise. That is what the Society was founded to do.

Missionary work had been going on in China since the early centuries. The Nestorians, coming along the trade routes from the Middle East, were at the capital by 635 AD. An important Nestorian monument erected in 781, was found at Xian in Shaanxi in 1625. It sets out their doctrines and their early history in China. In 841 severe persecution began and before long nothing was left of the Nestorian Church in China. They returned when the Mongol emperors became rulers of China in the thirteenth century. There were churches and monasteries in many parts of the country. In 1368 the Mongols were replaced by the Chinese Ming dynasty. Again there was persecution and the Nestorians disappeared from China.

The first Roman Catholic missionary was a Franciscan, John of Monte Corvino, who arrived in 1294. The Christian faith was established in several cities. But, like the Nestorians, the Catholic communities suffered when the Mongols were driven out and this work came to an end. In 1552, less than two centuries later, Catholic missionaries returned. Sometimes work could be done openly and there were periods when it was very successful. Sometimes there was persecution and the priests lived in secrecy, hidden by Chinese Christians at the risk of their lives. But the Church continued with martyrs among both Chinese members and foreign missionaries.

The honour of beginning Protestant work for the Chinese, Latourette suggests, must be divided between the Serampore missionaries and Robert Morrison of the London Missionary Society (LMS).[4] In 1805 an approach to China from the West was being planned at Serampore but was given up as too dangerous. The following year Joshua Marshman began the study of Chinese with a view to translating the Bible and saw the first Chinese translation in modern times through the press.[5] He published an introduction to the Chinese language and an edition of Confucius with an English translation.

Robert Morrison sailed for China in 1807. All British ships going beyond the Cape were in the hands of the East India Company and it was strongly opposed to missionary work. Carey had travelled to India in a Danish ship and Marshman and Ward in an American one. Morrison had to go to America to get a ship. He landed in Canton, then the only port open to foreigners apart from the Portuguese city of Macao. He translated the Bible, prepared a dictionary and a grammar and wrote some pamphlets. The East India Company, which operated in China as well as in India, recognised his ability and offered him a position as translator. This he accepted in order to secure his foothold in China. For five years he was the only Protestant missionary.

In 1832, twenty five years after Morrison arrived, the LMS had only five missionaries to the Chinese and they were not all in China. Others had been sent but there had been sickness and death including that of the second missionary William Milne. Morrison married a British girl in Macao, Mary Morton. They lost their first child on the day of its birth. Mary Morrison died of cholera in 1821 and with her a premature infant. Robert Morrison died in 1834 at the age of fifty two.

Only two other British Societies had representatives in China in those early days, the British and Foreign Bible Society and the Church Missionary Society (CMS). There were two Continental missionaries to the Chinese of whom the best known is Karl Gutzlaff. His activities, writing and speaking led to the formation of the CES and several Continental societies. American missions began in 1822. At first, like the British, numbers were small.

In 1839 the first opium war broke out and lasted until 1842. There were several causes. Increasing industrial production in Britain meant that new markets were needed and China put severe restrictions on trading. Western nations were regarded as outer barbarians and in their relationship with China they were treated as tributaries. Diplomatic representation in Peking was not permitted and when the Emperor was approached by a representative of the Queen a ninefold *ketou* was required. Yet while there were these restrictions and irritations the basic cause of the war was opium. The East India Company, which ruled India, had a monopoly of opium production and the revenue it produced formed a very important part of government finances.[6] The Company did not want to be directly involved in the trade and auctioned the opium in Calcutta. It was taken to China by powerful trading companies in armed ships. The British government, of course, knew and supported what was going on.

A long campaign against the opium traffic made the public aware of the situation. In 1843 Lord Shaftesbury, then Lord Ashley, introduced a resolution in Parliament to have the trade stopped. He tried again in the House of Lords in 1857 before the second opium war. But it was not until 1913 that the opium traffic was finally brought to an end. The first opium war Lord Shaftesbury, speaking for many, described as cruel and debasing and the peace which followed as wicked as the war itself.

Meantime something of great importance was happening. In 1834 Liang A-fa, a convert of Morrison and Milne, gave some pamphlets to a young schoolteacher, Hong Xiu-quan, who was a candidate at the state examinations in Canton. He read the pamphlets and put them aside. Two or three years later he had visions during a long illness. Then in 1843 his attention was again drawn to the pamphlets and he found that they explained his visions. He started preaching and for some months he had teaching from an American Baptist missionary. As a result of his activity a religious movement sprang up in the area. It had many Christian features. In a doxology regularly used one God, Father, Son and Spirit is worshipped. There was to be no idol worship and idols were destroyed wherever the movement spread. Nor was ancestor worship permitted. The Sabbath was observed and a meeting was held with Bible reading, the Lord's prayer and an address. Adults joining the movement were baptised. The poor were respected and cared for and there was a strict code of conduct: opium smoking was forbidden and there was to be no drunkenness or theft. Yet how far the movement was really Christian is not easy to say. Hong claimed to be the younger brother of Jesus and sent down to earth. He was Lord not only of China but of the whole world. His cousin, Hong Ren, another leading figure, had been an evangelist and was well known to LMS missionaries. He certainly regarded the movement as a Christian one.

Other elements, besides the religious, soon came into the movement. It included a people's uprising in the face of poverty and corruption; this is likely to have been one factor in the extraordinary attraction of the movement. Then there was a strong nationalist element. Quite early a man with military training, Zhu Jiu-dao, brought in members of the Triad Society which aimed at restoring the Chinese Ming dynasty and removing the Manchus who had ruled since the seventeenth century. It became a military campaign, the Taiping Rebellion, while still carrying evidence of its Christian origins.

At first the Rebellion, which lasted from 1850 to 1864, was astonishingly successful. It captured the Ming capital Nanjing which became its headquarters, and it came near to overthrowing the government. Unfortunately as the years dragged on the religious and moral elements faded. Mass slaughter and destruction became widespread as it struggled to survive. Missionaries had tried to make contact with the leaders but only succeeded when it was too late to have any influence. The foreign powers were at first neutral but later supported the Manchu government. What if they had adopted a different policy and supported the Taipings? Very different views have been taken. One is that the Taipings could never have governed the country. Someone in a better position to judge than many was W.A.P. Martin. He was an American missionary who lived in China for fifty seven years. He became the first President of the Government Tangwen College in Beijing and was an expert on international relations as well as a trusted friend of China. He thinks that had the Taipings been supported early it would have been an immense benefit to China. As it was, an opportunity was lost that does not occur once in a thousand years.[7]

These events were of enormous interest in the West. Many people in the early years of the Rebellion thought that a new era was about to open in China. Among them was the Committee of the CES. They were therefore anxious to send as many missionaries as possible to China and as early as possible.

(a) Perils at Sea

The Chinese Evangelization Society took a passage to Shanghai for Hudson Taylor in the sailing ship *Dumfries*. She was a three masted vessel of about four hundred and seventy tons. They set sail from Liverpool on Monday 19th September 1853.

A high wind blew up as soon as the ship got out to sea. After three days it dropped and on Saturday they had a favourable breeze. But all that day the barometer kept falling and in the evening the wind began to freshen again. By noon it was blowing a gale and all possible sail was taken in, leaving only as much as would keep the ship steady. Hudson Taylor gives an account of the storm in his Journal of the voyage. The entry under Monday 26th reads: "... The barometer kept falling till it reached 28.97 and the wind increased till it was a perfect hurricane;—the Capt'n and the Mate said they never saw the sea look so wild. Between 2 and 3 p.m. I went on deck, and the scene was beyond description. The sea was lashing itself with fury, and was white with foam. There was a large ship astern of us, and a brig to our weather-side. The ship gained on us but drifted more. The waves were hills on each side of us and threatened to swallow us up, but through Divine grace, the ship bore up bravely. On account of the heavy sea, we were making little or no headway, but we were drifting quickly, irresistably, about two or three miles towards a lee shore—and the wind being westerly. The Captain said, 'unless God help us, all is up' ... The water was now becoming white—the land was just ahead—and the captain said, 'Now we must try to turn her and tack, or—it is all up. The sea in turning might sweep the decks and wash everything overboard—men too—but we must try'".

The next event is described a little more fully in a letter to his friend Benjamin Broomhall (Shanghai, March 12th 1854) than in the Journal entry. "... We were in Caernarvon Bay, a place universally dreaded by mariners; a strong current sets in— it is full of rocks,+very few vessels that once enter ever come out again. The captain, a pious man, tried in vain to tack the ship, he therefore wore ship (turned her the other way) when we were among the breakers, and we cleared the shore by not more than two ships length. At this moment, most providentially, the wind favoured us two points: had it veered half an hour sooner, when we were on the other tack, it might have destroyed us before we could have got round; but just occurring when it did we had the fullest possible benefit on both tacks. By the mercy of God we were thus enabled to beat out of the Bay".

The journey to China took over five months. A good deal of it was monotonous. They did not sight land until Tristan da Cunha, and then not again until Sandalwood Island (Sumba, Indonesia). The route took them to within 120 miles of Australia and then up through the islands of Indonesia to the Pacific Ocean and the China Sea. This part of the voyage was dangerous. For one thing pirates might be met. But there were greater dangers. One was that the islands were not all correctly charted at the time. Another was that currents were variable and sometimes strong. And when there is no wind there is nothing that can be done to stop a sailing ship drifting. Hudson Taylor refers to this stage of the journey in a letter to his parents (Shanghai, August 17th 1854). He is replying to a question of theirs: "I cannot say positively whereabouts we were at the end of January. We sighted the first isle of the Archipelego on Jan. 12 + arrived here on Mar. 1st, between times we were mostly among isles, + had two or three very narrow escapes from shipwreck. Once, on the third night, we ran to within three miles of an island incorrectly laid down on the chart. Had it continued thick and dark, a very short time would have seen us wrecked, + probably all lost—the shores being nearly perpendicular, we should have struck and gone down in deep water. A sketch of it as it appeared next morning, was lost in the 'Dumfries'. The second and third escapes were when lying becalmed, + drifting by strong currents ..."

The second incident mentioned in the letter to his parents is described in the Journal entry for Monday, January 16th: "About 4 o'clock Capt. Morris came to my room almost distracted there being no wind and we were drifting on to Canbay at the rate of four knots an hour. So I prayed earnestly for a breeze, and felt assured my prayer was heard and went on deck and told the Mate we should have one soon. It came directly and has been a steady 7 knotter. Praised be the Lord".

The third incident is referred to in the Journal for Sunday, January 29th: "Had a light breeze for a few hours during the night and made to noon 38 miles. Then we were only 8 miles s'th latitude; but a strong S.E. current has drifted us fast towards New Guinea. Raining this morning, and when it cleared up, became calm. About 2 p.m. had to lower the boat and tow the ship's head round, so as to retard her drifting as much as possible;—as much more, and we should be ashore on that inhospitable and barbarous coast. He, however, who has protected us so long, will not leave us now, I feel confident... The carpenter and I prayed for a breeze, and our prayers were heard. One immediately sprang up and by 6 p.m. we were making 8½ knots; it did not long continue so strong".

They reached Shanghai on March 1st 1854 and Hudson Taylor landed from a pilot boat.

The *Dumfries* never got back to Britain. An announcement in the *Times,* June 13th 1854, reads: "The British ship *Dumfries* of 468 tons which left Shanghai on 3rd inst (this is from the 'China Mail' dated Hong Kong, April 22nd) with full cargo of tea, about 560,000 lbs, was totally wrecked in the Pescadores on the evening of the 11th. Crew saved". Hudson Taylor records something of what happened in a letter to his sister Amelia (Shanghai, July 1854). "The late carpenter of the 'Dumfries' called on me today... From him I got the only particulars I have heard of the loss of the 'Dumfries'. It was 9½ p.m.,—dark + blowing heavily;—she struck, they launched the long boat, got the captain's compass, quadrant, chronometer, + a keg of water into her, + the ship went down. They pushed out of the way, and just saved themselves, for, directly, the mainmast fell, so that had they continued at her side two minutes longer, it would have fallen on them and sunk the boat. The only thing the carpenter saved was his Bible, + the steward (a black) saved the captain's gold watch which had been forgotten. The carpenter says that he was up to the waist in water before he left the ship; and when they got off, the captain asked him to thank God for delivering them. After some days + dangerous adventures, they were picked up by a ship and taken to Hong Kong + so no lives were lost. The poor man having lost his tools has been obliged to go in a ship as a common sailor ..."

(b) Funds in the Early Period in China

Shanghai was one of the five ports opened under the 1842 treaty. In the twelve years since then there had been enormous development. An international settlement was built facing the river north of the old walled city. Roads were laid out, drains were made and a great deal of building took place. Dr Lockhart, an LMS missionary, built a hospital across the small river which formed the southern boundary of the International settlement, between it and the Chinese city.

In 1853 the Chinese city was taken by the Triads. The main body of the Triads was not connected with the Taipings but took the opportunity provided by their engagement of the Imperial forces. Nonetheless the Imperial government was able to send

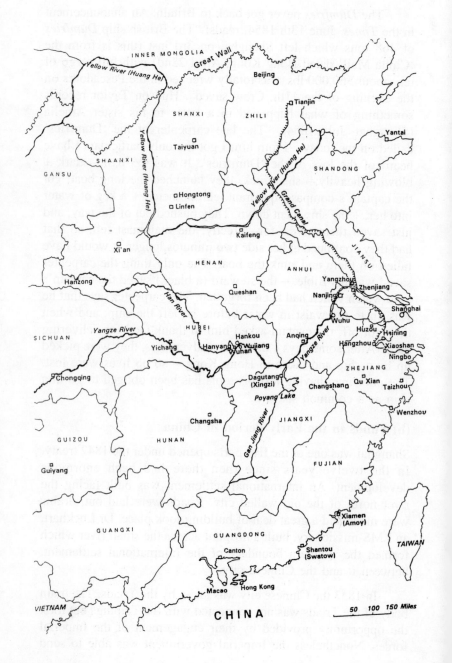

large numbers of troops. They encamped on two sides of the ancient city and had the Triads hemmed in between the main river and the International settlement. When there was fighting the casualties on both sides were taken to Dr Lockhart's hospital. Neither side wished to attach the International settlement. But merchants started selling arms to the Triads and mercenaries joined them. In consequence, an attack was made by the Imperial forces but it had been fought off by British and American marines and sailors.

That was the situation when Hudson Taylor arrived. He had letters of introduction to three people in Shanghai. But one had died, one returned to the United States and the other was away from home. However, he met a young LMS missionary, Joseph Edkins, who welcomed him warmly, as did others, and Dr Lockhart invited him to stay with him for the present. Next day he went to the consulate and found one letter from home awaiting him. There was none from the CES and no letter of credit enabling him to draw money. He had not been given one to take with him nor did he get one for the next two months.

In a letter from home later on Hudson Taylor was told that a Dr and Mrs Parker and their family were coming to join him. He had no notification from the Society and did not know when they were expected to arrive. Nor did he have authorisation to draw money to prepare for them. Then suddenly in November he got a message that they had arrived. He hoped that the Parkers would carry an authorisation to draw money or that it would be awaiting them; that is what the Parkers had been assured. But no authorisation awaited them. The LMS missionaries again helped by looking after the family for a few days until reasonably satisfactory arrangements could be made.

In the middle of December 1854 Hudson Taylor went with Joseph Edkins on a boat journey of about a hundred miles from Shanghai. They wanted to test the feasibility of working beyond the Treaty limits. This meant seeing what the mandarins would do and seeing how they were received by the people and by any troops that were about. They went openly in European clothes. They preached and distributed New Testaments and pamphlets in the towns they passed or could be reached easily on foot. And Hudson Taylor looked after patients who came for treatment. People were generally friendly but sometimes noisy crowds collected and on one occasion they had to escape by jumping on to a boat. The journey lasted for eight days. It was the first of many, sometimes much longer, beyond the Treaty ports that Hudson Taylor was to make. Sometimes he went with Edkins or another missionary, sometimes without. This was to be his principal work for the next two years.

William Parker sometimes accompanied Hudson Taylor when he went out of Shanghai. But he wanted to start his real work as soon as possible. His idea was to have a hospital, schools, chapel and mission houses as others had; there was scope in Shanghai for everyone. Hudson Taylor agreed with the plan because it would provide a base from which to go into the interior. Shanghai was on the Yangzi River coming from the west and near Grand Canal going north. But when the plan was put to the Society it was learned that they neither had the funds nor did they want to establish work in Shanghai.

In June 1855 a CMS missionary, Hudson Taylor and William Parker set out on an evangelistic tour in the direction in Ningbo. This was another Treaty port, to the south of Shanghai across the wide Hangzhou Bay. There was a group of British and American missionaries there working harmoniously together. Following the visit a group of missionaries and merchants wrote to Dr Parker asking him to come as community surgeon. He replied that he would not be justified in leaving Shanghai unless a hospital could be developed and maintained. It would cost about $ 260 a year to support. To get the present day equivalent the figure has to be multiplied by 40 or 50. In August a letter came saying that they would guarantee the money required. Ningbo was the only Treaty port without a hospital and the CES were not against the plan. Dr Parker was not happy about leaving Hudson Taylor but decided that Ningbo was the best place for him to work, at least for the present.

Hudson Taylor accompanied Dr Parker part of the way to Ningbo. For the first time he had got his head shaved and was wearing Chinese clothes. Missionaries sometimes wore Chinese clothes to make them less conspicuous on long journeys. But this was a temporary matter. Hudson Taylor was thinking of something more. He wanted to be one with the Chinese and would wear the clothes and live as they did all the time. He knew that he would be derided by the merchants; he was going native. They thought of themselves as belonging to a superior race and this was expressed by western dress and a western way of living. He knew, too, that he would be criticised by many missionaries. Over the years a style of living had been developed that was regarded as normal and proper. To live like the Chinese implied a criticism of the conventions and was bound to be resented. It needed courage to make the break.

After working in Shanghai and subsequently in Shantou Hudson Taylor had to go to Ningbo to see if he could buy some medical supplies from Dr Parker; his own had been largely destroyed in a fire. At Ningbo he met new missionaries of the CES, John and Mary Jones and their three children. Another child had been lost from dysentery at Hong Kong on their way. A close friendship with them at once developed.

When he had the medical supplies Hudson Taylor planned to go to Shanghai and sail to Shantou. But he learned that the colleague with whom he had been working had been arrested, put in prison and then handed over to the consul at Canton. It seemed likely that Hudson Taylor would get the same treatment if he returned. He thought it best to stay in Ningbo where other members of the mission were stationed.

The CES, to which Hudson Taylor, the Parkers and the Jones belonged, was in a very unsatisfactory state. The Committee understood little about China. The Foreign Secretary, George Pearse, corresponded patiently and courteously but he was a busy man. Only the General Secretary, Charles Bird, was full time. Unfortunately he was verging on a nervous breakdown. The Society was in debt and did not provide its missionaries with the salary and expenses promised, yet it sent out fresh ones. Hudson Taylor wrote pointing out the difficulties caused when the Society did not send what was promised. Dr Parker also wrote briefly and vigorously. To his sister, Hudson Taylor confided in September 1856 that he did not think that the Society could last a year and that for some time he had been thinking of resigning.

Before coming to China Hudson Taylor was confident that God would provide for him in emergency. But he thought that ordinarily his support would come from a missionary society and the normal arrangements that were made. He joined the CES with the clear understanding that they would provide a regular salary and be responsible for the expenses of the work. He wrote to George Pearse in September 1856 that he thought that every missionary ought to be provided regularly with a stated sum by the Society or Church he was sent out by. He then could depend on it and act accordingly. He did not think that to be connected with a society to which he could look at stated intervals for a stated sum implied any want of faith in God. That was no more so than at home accepting a salary to provide for necessary needs.

John and Mary Jones, he found, had an entirely different view of things. They did not depend on the Society and the Society had no financial obligations to them. In their letters there were no requests for funds and no complaints when nothing came—only gratitude when it did. They were the Society's representatives doing the work its members wanted done and they would be glad to receive any money it was able to send. But their dependence was directly on God and not on the Society. They had been influenced by George Müller who ran a very large orphanage in Bristol without appealing for funds; his reliance was on God alone. John and Mary Jones were prepared to do as he did. They too took seriously the statements of Christ about God's provision for those who seek first his kingdom. And so away in China, far from relatives and friends, and without any arrangement for a definite sum of money coming regularly to them, they were confident that God would supply all they needed. No further arrangements for their living expenses were necessary. In acting in this way they were making a firm prediction that God would somehow provide for the needs of their family and of the work they were undertaking.

That made Hudson Taylor think again. If he resigned he could not depend on support by individuals. William Berger had sent a good deal of money and George Müller had started sending to him. But that was not intended as his main support and there was no promise in either case of its continuing regularly. He had been thinking that he might join another mission. Now the question was, could he, like John and Mary Jones, rely on God to provide, in one or another, for the needs of himself and his work? This is what he finally decided: he would depend, not on human organisations or individuals, but directly on God.

He resigned at the end of May 1857 and the Jones shortly afterwards. Hudson Taylor wrote that he was not resigning from any disapproval of the Society or its principles. He would be glad to receive anything that the Society sent either in the way of counsel or of financial aid. But it was unable to provide him with a regular salary. That being so he did not think there was any value in a formal connection with the Society and this was to some extent a tie. If on an excursion into the country he were arrested and sent to the Consul, there would be a heavy fine for which the Society would be responsible. By resigning he would not have to take into account the interests of the Society and would be free to do as he thought best.

The Society was sorry to lose Hudson Taylor and the Jones. But they accepted the resignations graciously and said that they would continue to send what they could. Wilhelm Lobscheid, who worked in South China and was the senior CES missionary, had resigned in March. The Society still had the Parkers and the Halls who were new missionaries. But after another year the Society was disbanded.

Hudson Taylor and the Jones were now on their own. They would be an independent mission to Ningbo but co-operate closely with others. Hudson Taylor rented a house in Bridge Street where Dr Parker had a dispensary. There was also a room for meetings and he lived in the attic above. The Jones, when the house they were in for the present was required, rented a house in the poorest part of the city. The plan was to work together to build up a Church that would undertake the task of spreading the gospel in the interior. This meant, in the first place, a great deal of evangelistic work in the city and the surrounding area. But much more was involved. Converts came from a religion with different ideas, different values and a different way of life. A change of religious allegiance, however sincere and profound, does not at once alter the whole life. They hoped that by working and worshipping with the converts and by teaching and pastoral care they would build them up in the faith.

Besides all this there was humanitarian work to be done. Hudson Taylor treated patients in the dispensary and visited them in their homes. Opium addicts were helped to break the habit. He also assisted Dr Parker in the hospital. Another piece of work they undertook for a time was giving a meal to destitute people. Every morning, except Sunday when they were occupied with other things, between forty and eighty people came for a bowl of hot rice gruel.

It was in connection with the feeding programme that Hudson Taylor had his first test of whether he could depend on God alone for funds. It occurred on Saturday, November 4th 1857, and is described in a letter to his home on November 18th. The meal was given that Saturday and things needed for the Sunday were bought. After that Hudson Taylor and the Jones did not have a dollar between them and they had provision only for the Sunday. The post, which might bring a credit note, was not due for another week. Nevertheless they did not ask the poor not to come on Monday for they were sure that somehow funds would be provided. And so it was. The mail arrived on the Saturday, a week earlier than expected. It contained a credit note from Mr Berger for $214 for the Jones and they were able to draw enough cash in time. "On Monday the poor had their breakfast as usual, for we had not told them not to come, being assured that it was the Lord's work, and 'Jehovah Jireh' (the Lord will provide)".

A description of how Hudson Taylor appeared to another missionary is given by W.A.P. Martin. He was in Ningbo at the time and knew Hudson Taylor for fifty years. "When I first met him he was a mystic absorbed in religious dreams, waiting to have his work revealed—not idle but aimless. When he had money he spent it on charity to needy Chinese, and then was reduced to sore straits himself. When the vocation found him it made him a new man, with iron will and untiring energy".[8] To call him a mystic is right, for a mystic is someone for whom religion is centered on union with the Divine. That this was so with Hudson Taylor can be seen in his little book on the Song of Songs, *Union and Communion.* His love for the Divine Lord was expressed not only in a life of service but in his regular and unhurried devotions. He said once, "The sun never rose on China without finding me at prayer". To say that he was aimless is not wholly true. But his aim then was limited in comparison with the very large and clearly defined aim that was to come.

While in Ningbo in August and September 1856 waiting for funds to buy drugs and instruments from Dr Parker, Hudson Taylor used to go with the Parkers every week to have dinner with a Miss Aldersey. She was an elderly lady who became a missionary after the death of her father. She worked for six years among the Chinese in Java and came to Ningbo when the port was opened to foreigners in 1843. The following year she opened a school at her own expense and invited two young English girls to help her. They were the daughters of Samuel and Maria Dyer, early LMS missionaries who had worked in Pelang and Malacca. First the father died and three years later the mother and the girls were sent back to their uncle and aunt who were their guardians. The girls wanted to continue their parents' work and when Miss Aldersey invited them they were given into her responsibility. Their passages were paid and an allowance for their maintenance was regularly sent. When Hudson Taylor met them Burella was twenty three and Maria nineteen.

Maria was attracted to Hudson Taylor from the first. He still had his heart fixed on a girl in England. They were writing but her letters were getting less encouraging. In July 1856 he received a firm rejection but still he hoped that she might change her mind. Then in October he heard from his sister that she was not changing her mind. This time he accepted the painful fact that the rejection was final. Now his position was different. He was free to take an interest in the vivacious Maria Dyer and he soon fell in love. In Ningbo the missionaries of the different societies frequently met and they met the staffs of the consulates too. But according to the conventions of the time Hudson Taylor and Maria could hardly ever be alone together and so neither was quite sure of the other's feelings.

In January 1857 Hudson Taylor and the Jones had to go to Shanghai. There they heard that new missionaries were coming to join them but there was no knowing when they would arrive. They would have to be met and escorted to Ningbo. While in Shanghai Mary Jones had a severe attack of smallpox. John nursed his wife and Hudson looked after the children. Not being able to move Hudson decided to write to Maria. He told her of his love for her and asked her to consent to an engagement. And he pleaded that she should not send a hasty refusal.

Maria was overjoyed when she got the letter. She was fond of Miss Aldersey and told her about it straightaway. Miss Aldersey strongly disapproved of Hudson Taylor and felt that she had to save Maria from making a terrible mistake. She had suspected something was up when Maria turned down the eminently suitable Robert Hart, a young consular official who was to become, perhaps, the most influential foreigner in China. Hudson Taylor had no professional qualifications, no denomination and was not connected with one of the established missionary societies. He wore Chinese dress all the time, had strange ideas and talked of living in the Interior. Miss Aldersey would write and inform Maria's uncle and ask him to find out more about Hudson Taylor. Maria could write if she wished. But she must write to Hudson Taylor refusing his proposal and asking him not to raise the matter again.

Maria was in a difficulty. She was twenty, Miss Aldersey sixty. She was a formidable woman and used to getting her own way. And she had some responsibility for Maria. Maria felt that she had to do as Miss Aldersey said and her friend Mary Gough thought so too. She would try to write a letter that satisfied Miss Aldersey and yet somehow convey that this was not her own wish. The letter passed Miss Aldersey's scrutiny and was sent to Shanghai. Now Miss Aldersey went further and asked Maria not to write to her guardians. So she kept the letter she had begun and did not write for three months.

Maria's letter reached Hudson Taylor about the end of April 1857. The first reading was devastating. But as he went over it again and again he began to feel that there was more to it than at first appeared and wondered whether Miss Aldersey was not behind it. But for the present there was nothing he could do.

When Hudson Taylor and the Jones got back to Ningbo he was able to find what Maria's real feelings were and that Miss Aldersey had been behind the letter. He went to see her but her opposition to the marriage was in no way reduced. She did all that she could to stop it. But they were not deterred and got engaged even before they heard from Maria's guardians. When their letter came it said that they had made enquiries about Hudson Taylor and that they heard nothing but good. All that was asked was that they should wait until January, when Maria came of age, before marrying.

So they did that. The wedding was a very happy occasion with everyone present except Miss Aldersey and relatives of hers who were working there. And they were reconciled before long.

Two weeks before the date fixed for the wedding an incident occurred which to us, looking from the outside, does not appear much out of the ordinary. But to Hudson Taylor it was very important. He told his son, a year before be died, that no such severe trial ever occurred in later life. Its significance lay in the fact that having come, apparently so close to destitution he felt that he had to offer to release Maria from the engagement. But, with her eyes open, she unhesitatingly accepted all that was involved.

The incident is described in a letter to his sister the following year, dated May 10th 1859. "... For some time before money had not been plentiful; and a few weeks before all our money was spent. On Wednesday morning we had breakfast + a very light one it was, but nothing for dinner. Mr Jones + I went out to try and sell a stove for old iron, to buy some food with, but singularly enough the bridge—a floating bridge of boats—was unmoored, + undergoing repairs. The two of us had only one cash between us, and as the fare across on the ferry boat was 2 cash (half a farthing) not one even of us could go. So the Lord saved our stove. We came back, and the walk and the hunger together made me faint and very ill. We made some cocoa and took some and engaged in prayer,—'Give us *this day* our daily bread'. While we were praying a knock at the door interrupted us. It was the postman with a letter from Engd. containing $40-0-0! Then did we weep—but our tears were tears of joy and thankfulness. One thing that had tried me with reference to that day, was that it was arranged that my dear Maria should come and take tea with us that night + I had no money to cross the river and alter the arrangement ..."

Not many months later Maria too was involved in a similar incident. It is described in a letter from Ningbo, dated 8th May 1858, to Mr Berger. "An alteration in the arrangements for the homeward mail, gives me the opportunity of answering without delay your kind letter of March the sixth, which with the enclosed bill for dollars to the value of £71-11-0 reached us on Wednesday evening last. Your letter brought us great pleasure, as it did the proof of your continued love and our Father's watchful care.

The day it arrived we had used our last cash; and while my dear wife and I were on our knees at night, praying for the blessings we need, and amongst them for pecuniary supplies, we were interrupted by a loud knock at the front door of the house. On going to see what was the matter, I was told that it was a letter from the Consulate. We had not before been visited at so late an hour, and at first I thought it must be a notice of political change of some importance, in connection with the war. But on opening the packet it proved to be two letters—yours, and one from Mr Pearse. You may imagine the joy! The messenger must have been enjoying himself with some of his friends, I think, for the letter should have reached us sooner. But it was so ordered that while we were asking, the answer came ..."

Hudson Taylor and Maria lived in the attic in Bridge Street improved by reflooring and dividing into smaller rooms. Hudson

Taylor and the Jones continued their work and Maria added her own contribution. She ran a school for children. For women in the neighbourhood she started a sewing co-operative to provide income; she collected orders and supervised the work. And she ordered a small printing press from England and paid a woman to print leaflets in the Romanized type. They were in the local dialect used by uneducated people.

Dr Parker's medical work was greatly appreciated in Ningbo and beyond. His main activities were among poorer people. He examined and treated them entirely free and did an enormous amount of work. This was supported by the work done among the well off. He was consulted by merchants, consular officials and wealthy Chinese and he visited foreign ships in port. With the money raised he was able to build an up to date hospital just outside the city wall and facing the river. A house was built in the compound where he and his family lived.

On 26th August 1859 Mrs Parker was wakened in the early morning by an attack of cholera; she died the same evening. Dr Parker was desolated. He thought that he should take his five children, one of whom was seriously ill, back to their grandparents in Scotland. He asked Hudson Taylor if he would continue the outpatient work. It would be impossible to keep the inpatient side going because it was very expensive. There was the staff to pay and food as well as drugs and other things to supply. The cost was met entirely by Dr Parker's private practice and this was not open to Hudson Taylor. He thought and prayed over the matter for some days and then told Dr Parker that he would keep both sides of the work going. He had no regular source of income but was confident that in some way God would supply the funds.

Hudson Taylor did carry on both sides of the work. Before the supplies and money left by Dr Parker ran out he received more. In a letter to his mother dated October 31st 1859, he says that $100 had been given for the hospital and $170 had come from Mr Berger. He had received similar sums from him before but this time there was something further. Hudson Taylor wrote later that Mr Berger had said that his father had recently died leaving him with a considerable increase in income. He did not wish to increase his own expenditure so he asked if his friends in China would inform him if there were ways in which they could properly use more money.

As it happened Hudson Taylor was not able to stay long at the hospital. He was not in good health and it was very exhausting. Maria had written to his mother on September 30th, "He comes upstairs, perhaps between 10 and 11 p.m. tired out and poorly, and after sitting or lying down a little while goes down again to see some of his hospital patients and make up some medicine for them ..." After nine months he was seriously ill and was told by a doctor he consulted that he must return to Britain.

In July 1860 Hudson and Maria and their baby Grace, sailed from Shanghai. With them was Wang Lae-djün, a young convert. He was to help both with the translation work they planned to do and with teaching the dialect to any recruits who might return with them. They were looking for five.

(c) Funds in the Early Period of the Mission

After coming back from Ningbo Hudson Taylor's doctors told him that return to China was out of the question for at least some years. So the family took a house in the east end of London near the London Hospital. Here Hudson Taylor completed his medical training, getting the diploma in October 1862. At the same time he began revising the colloquial Ningbo version of the New Testament. He had a working knowledge of Greek as well as a good grasp of the dialect. With him were Wang Lae-djün and Maria who was fluent in the Ningbo dialect. They were joined by Frederick Gough of the CMS who had taught at Cambridge. He came back from China with his wife who was seriously ill; she died four days after arrival. He had already lost a baby but had a little daughter who was being looked after by relatives.

During these years Hudson Taylor was increasingly concerned that so little was being done to carry the gospel to the interior provinces of China. Protestant mission work after half a century had gone little beyond the coastal provinces, although journeys had been made into the interior. The Roman Catholics had been far bolder. Hudson Taylor, accompanied later by

Frederick Gough, called on the secretaries of all the leading missionary societies. They urged that a special effort should be made to occupy this as yet unreached field. But the same objections always met them: financially it was impossible and candidates were not coming forward. Further, the country was not open. All that could be hoped for was to keep up the existing agencies on the coast and even this often seemed beyond their power. By the end of 1864 the number of Protestant missionaries in China had dropped from 115 to a little over 90.

With this defeatist attitude on the part of the existing societies and feeling, as he did, the great need of the people of China for the gospel, an idea began to take shape in Hudson Taylor's mind. Ought he himself to try and form some kind of agency, perhaps of a different sort? Was this his work? Some years later he wrote about the Divine call in a letter to Henry Soltau (between Nanjing and Zhenjiang, April 29th 1873), "Now when God calls to work it is not always by the *command*, clear + unmistakable, 'Go!' It is often by the *question*, 'Who *will* go?'" And he would not have *us*, who are taught by his Spirit, led by fancies or impulses, perhaps more often of the flesh than of the Spirit; but as Romans XII teaches, he calls to a reasonable, rational service". That is how it was in his case.

He made no quick decision. He well knew the difficulties. He had seen the Chinese Evangelization Society fail and be disbanded. He knew what conditions of life in China were: the isolation, the disturbed state of the country, the deaths. He did not need to be reminded that without a strong organisation at home those overseas were liable to be forgotten. And when sickness came or riots or lack of funds it would be he who would have to bear the responsibility. Already he was committed to the work he and the Jones had been doing in Ningbo. For this six men and women went out while he was in England and others were being prepared. But this was a limited work. The question was whether to attempt in addition something on a far larger scale. That was what the inner struggle was about. Was this God's call? Did the promises in the Gospels still hold? Was God like that? Still he hesitated.

A letter to his mother dated June 1st 1865 shows what was in his mind. "... It is much pressed on me to try and get twenty more European missionaries besides these four, so as to send at least two into each province of China proper, in which there is *no* missionary, and two into Chinese Tartary; and to try and send with them an equal number of Chinese helpers, making in all forty eight persons (besides those on the way) requiring support. The expense of these would exceed £5,000 a year. Will you earnestly pray God to guide aright—whether to attempt this or not".

Up to this stage he had not finally committed himself. His struggling over the question was causing sleeplessness; indeed so much so that his health was beginning to suffer. His friend George Pearse noticed this and invited him down to Brighton, where he now lived, for a weekend. At Brighton also that weekend was another friend, J.M. Denniston, a Presbyterian minister. Hudson Taylor attended the church at which Denniston had been invited to preach. But the contrast between the congregation of over a thousand, as it were at ease in Sion, and his vision of the state of the people in China was more than he could endure and he left the service. Yet some word there must have reached him. For he said to Denniston's widow long afterwards that he had been the means of deciding him to form the China Inland Mission.

He went out on to the sands at low tide and there the decision was made. The record of it are some words written in pencil on a page of his Bible. "Prayed for 24 willing skilful labourers at Brighton, June 25th 1865". He returned to London next morning. The following day he went with George Pearse and opened a bank account in the name of the China Inland Mission.

In forming a new mission Hudson Taylor was anxious that funds should not be diverted from existing societies; that would have defeated his object. Accordingly he decided that no appeals would be made for funds and no collections taken at meetings. But there was a further reason for this decision. Having begun in the faith that God was calling him to undertake his work and that God would be responsible for it, he would proceed differently from other missions and rely directly on God for funds. This stance meant that the workers to be recruited would have no guaranteed salary; they too would have to be prepared to trust in God to supply their needs. This was one principle of the new mission.

A second principle was indentification with the Chinese people. It was to be expressed by the wearing of Chinese dress and more generally by living in China as Chinese and not as British. Roman Catholics wore Chinese dress; Protestants did so occasionally and in part when going away from the Treaty ports. Hudson Taylor was the first Protestant missionary to do so fully and all the time; it included shaving his head and wearing a pigtail. When he returned to China with the new mission not everyone in his party was able to bear the ridicule of people including members of the older societies. To Hudson Taylor and Maria it was apparent that the question at bottom was who an individual wanted to be identified with.

A third principle of the new mission was that the direction would be on the field and not in Britain. This was something quite new and of far reaching significance. The Director could be in intimate touch with all that was going on and decisions could be made on the spot. He would know the detailed circumstances and problems of the workers and be able to act quickly. No doubt the introduction of the principle was the result of his own difficult early years in China.

Such an arrangement was possible only because there was a very able man willing to manage the home side of the mission. This was William Berger. He handled the correspondence, received and transmitted the funds, selected the candidates and sent them out, published the *Occasional Papers* and undertook the whole of the work that supporting a mission entails. Without a man of his ability and dedication the mission could never have gone on. There was a relation of complete mutual trust between him and Hudson Taylor; each was quite confident that the other sphere was being adequately directed. And there was a corresponding relation of intimate friendship between the two wives, although Mrs Berger was much older. She took an interest in all members of the mission and would prepare and send out parcels for everyone.

The launching of the new mission and the publication later in the year of Hudson Taylor's small book *China : Its Spiritual Needs and Claims* aroused great interest. At the same time it gave rise to an enormous amount of work. He was planning to leave for China, with Maria and the four children they now had, the following year. They would take with them a group of young missionaries. In order to arrive at the best time of year for newcomers they would leave in May. To the end of 1865 he was still working on the Ningbo New Testament. Now he had frequently to speak at meetings, in many cases away from London; carry on a vast correspondence; look after accounts; talk with callers; and have candidates stay for varying periods for selection and preparation.

During this period Maria was ill. In September 1865 she was found to have serious chest trouble and needed rest for several months. She stayed with the Bergers in their country house at East Grinstead. There was no question of delaying departure; medical opinion was that a sea voyage lasting several months would do her good.

Sixteen new missionaries were finally chosen to travel at this time. There was one married couple, Lewis and Eliza Nicol, five single men and nine single women, a very unusual proportion in those days. They were setting out with no church backing and with an organisation that was quite new. No fund raising was permitted and regular support had not been sought. Salaries were not guaranteed, only a promise to share what came in. To many people it was madness. But they went fully aware of what they were doing, trusting in God to provide the funds that were needed.

All the accommodation had been taken in the *Lammermuir*, a beautiful three masted sailing ship. It left London on 26th May 1866. Until they reached the South China Sea the voyage was relatively uneventful except for the conversion of Mr Brunton, the feared and hated first officer and a considerable number of the crew. Then they were struck by first one and a week later by a second typhoon. Emily Blatchley describes this in a letter to Mr Berger dated 18th October 1886.

"That Friday night we shall not soon forget. We had been carrying a good deal of sail, quite unprepared for a storm. Now, the wind was reefing our sails for us, after its own fashion; and in the darkness we could do nothing. Our starboard bulwarks were washed away, leaving a wide and free entré for the waves, which thenceforth kept up a continual surging sea on our main deck. Early on Saturday morning (the 22nd) the jib-boom was carried away; the fore-topmast did not stand long after that was gone; then the main-topmast was broken off, and hung over us threatening every minute to fall and stave in the deck or side of the vessel. But we still had no suspicion of it being another typhoon, until, in the afternoon, the wind began slightly to veer round: and then the sailors gave up all hope. Our decks were in a terrible state; and the heavy seas rolling over them, made it perilous to attempt to secure the great spars, casks, + c, which had been washed loose, and were threatening much harm to the vessel from the force with which the waters dashed about them. Mr Taylor went and talked to the men, cheered them, and inspired them with fresh courage ... But for Mr Brunton and Mr T there would be nothing done. Into every most dangerous position they are the first to go".

They got to Shanghai on 30th September. Captain Bell had invited the party to stay on board as long as they wished. But that was not necessary. William Gamble, manager of the American Presbyterian Press, met them and looked after the whole group and all their baggage. Hudson Taylor had to go to Ningbo and now there was a regular steamship service. He was taking two young women, one to join her fiancé and the other to join her mother. He got back to Shanghai two days later. While at Ningbo he met the missionaries he had sent out and the members of the church.

Ningbo was the mission's base in the sense that the church built up there was to be the first source of pastors and evangelists. But the headquarters would move. The plan was to begin at Hangzhou, a hundred miles from Ningbo and Shanghai and capital of the province of Zhejiang. It was a big city and three mission families were already there, Anglican, American Presbyterian and American Baptist.

Three weeks after landing the party set out in four canal boats, each with good accommodation. It was intended to proceed slowly, taking about four weeks for the journey, so that there would be a gradual introduction to life in China. With them was Mr Tsiu, a Christian teacher from Ningbo, from whom they could learn something of the life as well as the language, and four other Chinese helpers. Unknown to them Carl Kreyer, the American Baptist stationed at Hangzhou, had heard of their coming. He had to be away but put his house at their disposal. Before his return they were able to rent a large and suitable house of their own.

Once settled Hudson Taylor started a dispensary. Soon he was treating up to two hundred patients a day. He carried out small operations and removed cataracts as well as doing other eye work. The printing press they had brought was set up and William Rudland put in charge. He was slower in learning the language than the others. Hudson Taylor thought that working in the Romanized script and working with a Chinese printer would help him and so it proved. Maria opened an industrial school for women, mostly sewing. In the last working hour the women were taught to read by Jennie Faulding. She made friends with all kinds of women and was frequently asked to their homes even those of officials. Her principal work was running a boy's school.

Evangelistic work was going on and baptisms were taking place. The intention was always that the church should be thoroughly Chinese with a Chinese pastor, self-governing and with Chinese style of buildings. Wang Lae-djün, who was with the Taylors in London from 1860 to 1864 and lately worked in Ningbo, came as pastor and stayed for the rest of his life. When he came the membership was eighteen with fifteen applications for baptism. By the end of 1867 the membership was almost forty.

The provincial capital was deliberately chosen to start the work. Then they would go to the chief prefectures and after that to towns and villages. The response there was likely to be quicker. But if they could establish themselves in the chief cities the rest of the work would be much easier; the officials in the smaller places looked for guidance to their superiors in the big cities. So, as soon as they were ready, it was to these cities that Hudson Taylor put down a young missionary with one or more Chinese companions.

By the end of 1867 great progress had been made. Including the work of the missionaries who came earlier, buildings had been obtained and work begun in six prefectural cities and in two county and three market towns. They were spread over an area the size of England.

This outcome was not obtained without cost. Hudson Taylor had dysentery from time to time, sometimes severe, especially when under strain. Maria, who in February had a baby, also Maria, was happy and very active but seldom really well. Often she had cough and fever and in August was seriously ill with it. The weather was very hot and all but two of the Hangzhou group went for a little holiday in the hills nearby. There Grace, now aged eight, developed meningitis. She did not recover and was taken back to Hangzhou for burial. Emily Blatchley, Hudson Taylor's secretary, was ill for a long time. Two other women were ill and John Sell, just before he was to be married, caught smallpox and died.

There were difficulties with a group of the new missionaries. They thought Hudson Taylor too autocratic and very different from the man they had travelled with. He and Maria, of course, were the only ones who knew anything about China and he was so overwhelmed with medical work that there was not much time for discussion. But it was especially the wearing of Chinese clothes, when other missionaries were not doing so, that upset them. The most difficult man was Lewis Nicol who was resentful, made complaints, some to William Berger, and said things which were quite untrue. Mr Berger thought that the Nicols should not be retained in the mission. Hudson Taylor bore with them for two years, hoping for a change of attitude, but finally dismissed them and gave them their fare home. Three of the women, who had always sided with the Nicols, resigned.

There was a serious disturbance at the city where the Nicols were located and a riot at another. The following year, 1868, there was a major riot at Yangzhou, about 150 miles north of Hangzhou. The headquarters of the mission was being moved on and Hudson Taylor would have liked to have had stations both at Zhenjiang, at the junction of the Yangzi and the Grand Canal, and at Yangzhou a little further up the Canal. Negotiations for a house at Zhenjiang fell through at the last moment but one was obtained at Yangzhou. The house was a large one with courtyards and a number of buildings. They moved in cautiously in two stages.

All went well at first. Then handbills and posters appeared stating, among other things, that foreigners scooped out the eyes of the dying, opened foundling hospitals to eat the children and cut open pregnant women in order to make medicine out of the infants. Hudson Taylor wrote to the City Prefect asking him to put a stop to the posters else great injury was likely to be done. The following day he was warned by well-wishers that a riot was expected the next day. Hudson Taylor proposed sending the women and children away to safety but all the women insisted on staying.

The riot was stirred up by the gentry. On the evening of August 22nd a crowd of eight to ten thousand people collected, some armed. They broke into the house, looted it and set it on fire. Some of the women had to jump from the first floor windows. Because it was dark, the household, some of whom were injured, were able to get to neighbours' home and hide there. Meantime Hudson Taylor and a companion had been able to make their way to the Prefect's residence. He came with soldiers and dispersed the crowd. Next day people collected again. Once more the Prefect was appealed to. This time the party was sent to Zhenjiang with the belonging that had escaped damage.

In 1870 there was sickness among almost all the missionaries, including Hudson Taylor and his family. They decided to send the four older children home, leaving with them only Charlie, who was a little over a year old. Emily Blatchley volunteered to return to England in order to look after the children and help with the home side of the work. Before the little party reached Shanghai Samuel, a boy of five, died. Because he was for long delicate he was often taken with him by his father and became something of a special companion, as Gracie had been. Another baby, Noel, was born a few months later; he died after a week. Three days afterwards Maria died.

Looking back a year later Hudson Taylor wrote to his mother (Zhenjiang, 21st June 1871), "As I think of last year, and of my loved ones gone before, my heart aches, oh! so wearily; and T' in-pao [Charlie] is in Ningbo, and the others in England. It makes me feel lonely, notwithstanding the full assurance that all is well, and that He will never, does never, leave me. I have seemed to realise those thin, loving arms almost around me again, as they were when she gave me her parting blessing. These long weary days of anguish of heart seem to have swallowed up the many happy years we had together. They appear like a dream".

In August 1871 Hudson Taylor returned to England on furlough. He was far from well and he wanted to see his children. With him were his son Charlie, now nearly three, and Li Lanfeng who was to live with him and get personal tuition. On the same ship were the Meadows family from Ningbo and Jennie Faulding. This had not been intended. They were to have travelled in a ship leaving in the middle of July. But Jennie, who had recurrent malaria, got a serious attack. She was stationed at Hangzhou where her school was greatly appreciated. And so was she; wherever she went women were drawn to her. Hudson Taylor had always thought highly of her. And she had always admired him, even in the early difficult days when by no means all the party did. Now on the voyage, as often happens, their feeling for one another developed into love, although Jennie knew that it would not be the same as with Maria. They became engaged and were married in London in 1872.

There was a special reason for Hudson Taylor to return just then. William Berger, after six years, was no longer able to bear the responsibility of the home side of the work. He was fifty one when he took it up and during these six years it had grown a great deal. It now had thirty foreign and fifty Chinese workers with thirteen main stations. The Bergers' contribution to the well being and growth of the mission had been immense. Now for health reasons they were going to settle in Switzerland.

For the time being Hudson Taylor undertook the manage-ment of the Home Department. After some months a Council was formed with the idea that its members would divide among themselves the work previously done by William Berger. In addition there was Emily Blatchley. She was in London primarily to look after the Taylor children. But she lived at the mission offices and her intimate knowledge of people and conditions in China enabled her to handle a large part of the day to day work and to advise the Council members. In point of fact for the first year or two the real responsibility for the Home Department fell on her.

Hudson and Jennie Taylor left England at the beginning of October 1872. They got back to China at the end of November after an absence of fifteen months. Things at first were far from encouraging. Not only had there been a good deal of sickness among the missionaries; they had not maintained their distinctive position. He wrote shortly after his return (Hangzhou, 16 December 1872), "Almost all our people have put on English dress; it is hard to stand laughing at. McCarthy and Williamson are, I think, the only *men* who have not changed. It is disappointing, but God reigns and carries on his own work". James Williamson had come out with the *Lammermuir* party and John McCarthy later in 1866 with his wife and four children.

Nor had the Chinese Christians acquitted themselves much better. Hudson Taylor wrote to his mother, on a boat on the way to Hangzhou, on 25th January 1873, "Poor Yangzhou, it is not what it once was! I hear very poor accounts of some of the members, but they are more to be pitied than blamed; for they have not been fed or watched over as young Christians need. May the Lord help me to seek out and bring back, some of the wandering ones.

It is very slow work in new places: but sometimes the slowest at first, afterwards take the lead of more promising fields".

Almost all this period in China was spent on the move; the Taylors had no settled home. Hudson Taylor was called from place to place to give medical attention. And he visited every station and outstation with the purpose of restoring and encouraging the Christians. The kind of thing he was doing and aiming at may be gathered from a letter to his mother (Zhenjiang, July 15th 1873), "The Lord is prospering us in the work; it is steadily growing and spreading—especially in that most important department, *native* help. The helpers themselves need much help, much care and instruction; but they are getting *more* efficient, as well as more numerous; + the future hope of China doubtless lies in *them.* I look on all of us foreign missionaries as platform work around a rising building: the sooner it can be dispensed with the better; or rather, the sooner it can be transferred to other places, to serve the same temporary purpose there, the better for the work sufficiently forward to dispense with it, and the better for the places yet to be evangelised. As to difficulties and sorrows their name is legion. Some spring from the nature of the work, some from the nature of the workers. Here Paul and Barnabas cannot see eye to eye; there Peter so acts as to need a public rebuke; while elsewhere private exhortation is required to restore a wanderer, or to quicken one growing cold. The extension of the work involves no little labour, too. The renting, leasing or purchase of buildings or land + the subsequent building on it, involves much thought + correspondence + supervision. And how many, or how serious difficulties may arise before the work is fairly established in any place, it is impossible to foresee ..."

For a long period, and especially after the Bergers' retirement, when the London office was not so well run, funds were low, there the many references in Hudson Taylor's letters at this time to his having nothing or next to nothing in hand. For example in a letter to William Berger (Nanjing, March 14th 1873) he writes, "I think I have never, since I have been in China seen the opportunities for furthering the work look so promising. And though I have not a cent of mission money in hand, I cannot but go forward, trusting the Lord will meet and supply all the need of the work".

In 1873 Jennie Taylor received a legacy yielding about four hundred pounds a year; she decided to devote it to Christian work in China and elsewhere. A member of the Council who had been asked to act as a trustee questioned the wisdom of this course. But the Taylors could hardly have urged their fellow workers to go to China without a guaranteed salary, relying on God alone, while they themselves were financially secure. The only personal use they made of money from the legacy was sometimes to pay for passages between China and Britain. This was also done for others. Their losses from theft could also be made good from this source.

Because of continuing shortage of funds some members of the Council were thinking of making appeals. Hudson Taylor never wavered from his position. He wrote to several members asking them not to appeal. For example in a letter to John Chalice, the Treasurer (Zhenjiang, April 24th 1874) he says, "I am truly sorry that you should be distressed at not having funds to send me. May I not say, 'Be careful for nothing + c'. I would say we should use *all* care to economise what God does send us; but when that is done bear no care about real or apparent lack. After living on *God's faithfulness* for many years, I can testify that times of want have ever been times of special blessing, or have led to them. I do beg that never any appeal for funds be put forward, save to God in prayer. When our work becomes a begging work it dies ..."

An account of the way funds came in during the first half of 1874, with special reference to the second quarter, is given in a long letter to his mother of which the following is part (Shanghai, July 11th 1874). "You may not know that our work is now so extensive that it cannot be carried on, without much difficulty and trial, at a less cost than £100 a week. This may seem a large sum; but our work is a large work. We have more than fifty buildings—houses, chapels, and schools—to keep in repair, and four fifths of them, to pay rent for. More than a hundred labourers are supported. I need scarcely say that the travelling expenses involved in the work in China, now extended to five provinces, are not small, not to speak of those incurred by the return of invalided missionaries to England. To meet these demands with £100 a week requires the utmost care and frugality ...

On making out my Mission accounts on April 1st, I found that I had 25 dollars and 29 cents (about £5.10s) in hand. I knew that most if not all of the members of the mission must be urgently needing funds for their own daily wants, as well as for the expenses of the work. I constantly cast these cares on God, and hoped that when I reached Shanghai I should find his answer in the shape of remittances; for, as I was travelling, my letters had to await me there. On 7th we arrived, and received the letters of several mails. You may imagine the interest with which, after seeking the Lord's blessing on them, they were read. I found a remittance from the secretaries of £15.11s.8d, consisting wholly of special donations; £7 for two of the missionaries, and the remainder made up of small sums for the support of particular native helpers. I further learned that there were no funds at home for the general purposes of the Mission. Now, I knew that £500 would have been instantly absorbed; that 170 mouths had daily to be fed; that the life of Mrs Stevenson appeared to hang on an immediate return home; that there were no more mails due for nearly a fortnight (for while the French and English mails leave England at intervals of a week, at this time of year they often arrive at Shanghai nearly together). Knowing, then, that there were no funds in hand at home, and that the total mission funds received from home for the past quarter had only been £422.1s, need I say that I required the precious resource of again casting *all* the care on him who cares for each of us? or that in so doing the assurance that his grace was sufficient for me, and for *each* of the needy ones, fills my heart with love and joy?

Next morning I awoke about five, and found the burden coming back again; but, in accordance with Phil.IV.6, I made my requests known to God, and found the promise of verse 7 fulfilled. Some of the passages, too, which occurred in the course of my morning's reading, seemed to have been written on purpose for me. When my dear wife awoke, I told her of the assurance I felt that help was at hand, though I had not the least idea of how the Lord would send it. And so it proved. Before noon a letter reached me, which, having been addressed to Ningbo instead of Shanghai, arrived some days later than the letters of the same mail, which had come direct. It contained cheques for me to forward inland to many members of the mission, to the value £260, besides several other sums. These kind gifts greatly cheered me, and relieved me of anxiety concerning the personal wants of those to whom they were sent, though they still left an urgent need, about which we continued to wait on God. I asked the prayers of some members of the mission, with special reference to Mrs Stevenson, who required an immediate change; and in the full conviction that the Lord would provide, their outfits for the voyage were proceeded with".

The passage money and travelling expenses of the Stevensons was made up by gifts, mostly from members of the mission.

The letter continues, "But to return. We were kept waiting on God till May 5th when £104.2s were received from the secretaries, of which £100 was for the general purposes of the Mission. None but those who know what it is to bear the burdens of others, can tell the joy with which we distributed this small sum—small as compared with the wants of more than forty stations. A kind friend augmented it by a gift of 6 dollars the same day; and 26 dollars were also forwarded to me, which had been given to support a girl in the girls' boarding school. On the 15th, 22 dollars 22 cents reverted to the funds, which had been temporarily appropriated in February to an object for which it was no longer required; and Mr Judd, on leaving Nanjing for Wujiang, was able to hand in 240 dollars 71 cents, a surplus of funds given him in December, and which had not been required. In these ways, by the sale of stationery, and by profits on exchange, the most urgent necessities of May were met, leaving us *all the promises of God* to meet the expenses of June, and nothing more.

I asked urgent prayer of some of the brethren for £ 500 to meet the manifest and unavoidable outlay of that month. Perhaps never, in the history of the Mission, had we *all* been so low together. As it proved, the outlay of the month *required* above £100 more than the sum I had named; and, therefore, the Lord, who meets all our wants, supplied it too. And in China I received,

Saturday evening prayer meeting had dwindled to nothing. Before long, news was received of a riot at Huzhou. James Meadows and Aurthur Douthwaite, who had recently come, had to fly for their lives while their property was destroyed or carried off. This was not the end of the discouragement. On the voyage Hudson Taylor had pain in his back and it was necessary for him on arrival to use crutches. Gradually paralysis set in and before the end of the year he was totally paralysed in his lower limbs; he could only change position in bed by means of a rope hanging from above. No doubt he had fractured his lumbar spine in his fall on the boat and dislocation, as sometimes happens, took place gradually. To his friends it did not appear probable that he would ever walk again. And Jennie Taylor wrote to William Rudland, who was seriously ill, "It seems very unlikely that either we or you will ever see China again".

Hudson Taylor continued to work from his bed. He had a large map of China hung opposite him. He was unable to sit for several months but he could dictate letters and people came in to help. Council meetings were held at his bedside. He interviewed people there. He conducted a class in Chinese round his bed. And from there he planned the next stage of the Mission's programme. So the time when its Director was lying in bed paralysed became one of the formative periods in the history of the Mission.

Before leaving China a decision had been made to advance. The first step in implementing it was an appeal which appeared in *The Christian* and several other papers in January 1875. It stated that there were nine provinces in China, each as large as a European country, with no Protestant missionary. There were Chinese Christians, from these provinces, converted in existing stations, who were anxious to take part in the evangelisation of those regions. The appeal was to pray for eighteen suitable men to lead the way. There was no appeal for funds; indeed it was stated that during the past year £4,000 had been contributed for that purpose.

Hudson Taylor's idea was that the actual work of evangelisation would be done largely by Chinese Christians. But they were mostly young in the faith. For leadership and oversight, both pastoral and administrative, missionaries were required. And for this purpose he proposed in the first instance to send them two by two, following the pattern Christ had set in the Gospels, for mutual support and encouragement. The work would be begun by experienced missionaries, but only four were suitable or could be spared and they would need replacement. So eighteen new missionaries were required, fourteen for new work. Not surprisingly this led to criticism by members of long established missions. But if they would not move, Hudson Taylor argued, what else was to be done? So the candidates were carefully selected and specially prepared. During 1875 Hudson Taylor had correspondence with more than sixty candidates. Between twenty and thirty young men and nine or ten women spent periods varying between a few days to several months with the Taylors. By December 1875 the eighteen had all been selected.

The offices in London were now the scene of vigorous activity. Candidates came there for selection. Those chosen had to be prepared and got ready for the journey. There was much correspondence, both with China and at home. A monthly magazine, *China's Millions,* was launched with Hudson Taylor as editor. It was illustrated and well produced and was something quite new at the time containing news, articles, Chinese stories and other features. It came to replace the *Occasional Papers.* To look after the Home Department Benjamin Broomhall, Hudson Taylor's brother-in-law was brought in. The two houses adjoining the office were taken. A little later a secretary, William Soltau, was installed. And now Hudson Taylor, after nearly five months in bed, was able to get up.

The immediate financial requirements of the new work was well provided for. The £4,000 mentioned in the Appeal for Prayer had been given by Jennie Taylor. Part of the capital of the legacy referred to earlier had now come under her control. She decided to devote it to the new work and sent it to the China Inland Mission account in Shanghai. And £800 had been given earlier by a Mrs Emma Grace specifically for work in fresh provinces. But the established work had to be supported and for the last two years the Taylors were in China, funds were very low; sometimes for weeks together there was not a dollar of mission money in hand.

The mission was now being greatly enlarged. On January 1st 1875 there were 21 missionaries in China, 3 on their way and 12 on leave after five to ten years in China, 36 in all. By December 1875 eighteen more were being prepared or were on their way to China. On April 5th 1876 the last of the eighteen sailed.

In the course of a year the number of missionaries increased by half as many again. And, of course, more Chinese staff were needed. This meant that support had to be maintained at a much higher level. That is the crux of the matter. Hudson Taylor did not first get the increased income and then work out how many people could be supported. He worked out how many men and women were needed for the job at that time and recruited them. The whole basis of his action was trust in God. This amounts to a prediction that God would provide what was necessary. Nor was the prediction falsified. From 26th May 1873 to 25th May 1874 the income received in Britain was £4,426. The following year it was £7,311. It never fell below about this level and continued to increase.

By June 1876 Hudson Taylor was thinking of returning to China. He had to watch over the young missionaries and guide the pioneering work as well as to deal with problems at the older stations. He left London on September 8th expecting to return before next summer as he was still not in good health. Jennie Taylor remained in London to look after the family. In addition to the older children she had herself a child, Ernest, born on January the year before and was expecting another.

(e) Funds for Expansion : the Thirty

Hudson Taylor got back to China in October 1876. By then a number of the pioneers had begun their journeys. He did not underestimate the difficulties and risks involved in what was being done. He wrote to his wife from a boat near Anqing on January 6th 1877, "... no less than 6 or 7 of the unoccupied provinces are being simultaneously attempted and there can be no such extensive evangelism unattended with danger". In point of fact several of the pioneers were seriously ill on their journeys and Edward Fishe died at Guiyang in Guizhou province. But no one was killed or seriously injured. It was not the case that Hudson Taylor did not care for his men. He cared deeply and had the greatest pride and confidence in them. In April 1877 he called a conference at Wujiang for them and invited members of other missions nearby to take part. It was arranged that the majority of the Eighteen would be returning from their first journeys. Hudson Taylor followed their experiences into the minutest detail. At the end of the Conference all were ready for fresh departures.

In February the same year John McCarthy had set out with Yang Cunling, an ex-soldier, to walk right across China from east to west. In planning the route he was ready to go to any of the young pioneers who were in difficulty and intended to visit others also. They were at Yichang with Nicoll and Cameron during a riot; it followed a visit to the city of a British consul and a small group of officials in western clothes. At the end of May, they found Brounton quiet in Guiyang, eight hundred miles from the nearest foreigner. By August they had reached the province of Yunnan in the far west. McCarthy made a point of spending two days in the village where Augustus Margary, a consular official, had been killed and Yang Cunling bought some eggs from the mother of the man who was supposed to be responsible. As they went they preached. Yet McCarthy was never asked for his passport and never had to appeal to an official for help or protection.

The first part of the journey was to end at Bhamo on the Burma side of the frontier. In April 1875 John Stevenson and Henry Saltau, who had been Secretary in London, set out for Bhamo. It was hoped to make it a starting point for reaching western China. But they were forbidden by the British political agent there to go into China. After waiting some time Stevenson, whose family was in Britain and unwell, left to join them. McCarthy had intended to go back through the southern part of Yunnan but he also was forbidden to cross back into China. So, after six months in Bhamo, he too returned to join his family in Britain.

It was reckoned that in about eighteen months the pioneers had travelled 30,000 miles everywhere preaching and distributing tracts. The purpose of these itinerations was twofold. In part it was to spread ideas widely, to give them time to be grasped and to repeat them by coming again and again. In part the purpose was reconnaissance; to gather information so that suitable places could be chosen to begin settled work. The extensive work of itineration was to give way in due course to the intensive work of the settled station.

The work was now large scale and funds were low. In the course of a letter to his wife (Taizhou, August 1st 1877), Hudson Taylor wrote, "I now acknowledge the £150 of May 25th + £100 of May 31st. The Lord very speedily send more as I have only 2 cents in hand + all funds are dry".

Once again the home side of the mission was not being managed efficiently and Hudson Taylor was clearly needed there. But he had not been able, partly through sickness, to visit the older stations where there were difficulties. So he set out to make a tour of them before his return. He took the opportunity of escorting to her station Elizabeth Wilson, a lady who had come to China some months earlier. Thirty years previously she had made a vow to go to China as a missionary. But she would not leave her parents who were sick and never told them of her intention. Now coming out in middle age she was received by the Chinese women wherever she went with the greatest cordiality and respect. Hudson Taylor saw here a pointer to another new departure. If men could live in the interior of China women could do so too with no less safety and no less effectiveness. For many years this was seen as a shocking flouting of settled opinion.

Hudson Taylor sailed on November 9th 1877. He had arranged to accompany the grieving Annie Fishe and her two children. With them also were Anne and George Crombie, both sick, and their children who also were sick. They reached London on December 20th.

Shortly before leaving China Hudson Taylor wrote an open letter to Friends of the China Inland Mission.[9] "... several wants have much impressed themselves on my mind during this visit to China. I need scarcely say that the first and foremost is for more labourers. To effectively inaugurate the work at least one missionary to each prefecture is needed, and though this number may not be at once attainable, we must continue in prayer until they are given us. During the present year, 1878, if the Lord tarry, it is extremely desirable to strengthen weak points of our work by the addition of twenty four new missionaries. Again, many of the converts are women and for their instruction and help we need additional female workers. Those already in China have their strength fully taxed and their hands more than full, and cannot attempt any more than they now have in hand. At least six, if possible twelve, lady helpers should join our sisters this year".

The number of new missionaries sought in 1878 was not so precise as on other occasions and the term The Thirty is not in the records. It is used here for convenience and by analogy with the others.

As the year went on candidates were selected, equipped and sent out. Enough money came in just to make ends meet. On October 4th 1878 Hudson Taylor wrote to Jennie who was in China, as will be explained shortly, "... Not much has been coming in for some time past for the general fund, but God has answered prayer + helped us through so far".

Just a week later another party sailed. The same day Hudson Taylor wrote to two young men accepting them for work in a particular province. He told them that he had nothing in hand for outfits and passages but invited them to come to London and be prepared for early departure. By the evening post a letter came containing money to send out two new workers as well as other donations.

In 1877-78 the total income of the mission, Britain and China, was £8,754. In 1878-79 the figure was £10,701. This was not the large increase hoped for. It was enough to send out more than thirty new missionaries. And the mission was sustained at its greatly increased strength, although strict economy had to be exercised.

By the end of 1878 fourteen new men and fourteen new women had sailed. Four more sailed in March 1879. In February Hudson Taylor left England. He had meetings in Holland and the south of France. At Marseilles he was joined by the party of candidates. They sailed on March 9th.

Hudson Taylor had been ill in France. At Singapore he was dangerously ill with dysentery; the doctor there was doubtful whether he would reach Hong Kong alive. But he decided to go on and by the time they arrived he was better. A letter from Jennie awaited him saying that she was in Shanghai. Then the dysentery returned making him very weak. He was advised by a LMS doctor to go to Yantai to escape the summer heat. It is by the sea on a peninsula in north China and has an excellent climate most of the year. It could be reached by ships on their way to Tianjin.

When Hudson Taylor was coming back to Britain in 1877 one of the things he was thinking about was the very severe famine in north China. It began in 1876 and was to last until 1879. The area affected covered large parts of several provinces, the worst affected being Shanxi. When the news of the famine reached Shanghai it shocked all members of the foreign community. A committee for famine relief was formed to collect and distribute aid. Consular officials, merchants and missionaries served on it. Subsequently another committee was formed at Tianjin. Some missionaries had already started relief work in the winter of 1876-77. A member of the LMS went home to raise funds in Britain.

The authorities did a great deal but probably the more effective work was that done by the two relief committees which received funds in China and from abroad. The distributors were missionaries. About thirty Protestants took part in the work of whom twelve belonged to the CIM. Few, if any, other foreigners had travelled in these regions. In addition to what was raised by the committees, funds were sent direct from the missionary societies to their agents. The work was not without danger because of the risk of typhus. Five Protestants died of it and at least an equal number of Roman Catholics. But it was reckoned that many thousands of people were kept alive who must otherwise have died.

But what of the destitute children? They needed more than food. Timothy Richard, an English Baptist missionary and one of the earliest and most active relief workers, was already giving special attention to children and old people. It seemed to Hudson Taylor that what was needed was an orphanage where no destitute or starving child would be refused. But in China if girls were to be admitted, this was the work that could only be done by women. And especially in view of what was already happening to children, to begin such work required someone with experience and with unusual qualities of understanding, sympathy and discretion. There was only one woman in the mission who had all the qualifications: his wife. So after much thought he suggested her going.

Jennie Taylor found it very difficult to decide whether it was right for her to go. She had two young children of her own and was looking after Hudson Taylor's older children and Millie Duncan, both of whose parents had died. Hudson was not in good health and carried immense responsibilities. Many friends advised her against going, William Berger among them. But weighing it all up she decided that she ought to go. And then, when she had made up her mind, she had an unexpected visit which brought all her misgivings back again. She did not know what to do. The question was so difficult and so much hung on it that she asked for quite specific guidance.

How she got it is described in a letter to her mother in law (London, 22nd April 1878). "Your kind letter this morning was just God's direct answer to prayer + was cheering to dear Hudson too... I asked God to confirm me in going. I felt like Gideon,— that my strength in China would be 'Have *I* not commanded thee' + I wanted some fleeces to strengthen my own faith + as answer to those who would have me remain. I asked God to give me, for one thing, money for getting a few things for Amy + myself as we had none to spare [she was proposing to take the baby with her but Amy developed whooping cough and had to be left], + to give me liberally—£50 so that there might be money in hand for use when I went away. On Thursday morning at prayers I asked them all to join with me in asking God to answer a prayer of mine + I would tell them when the answer came. That afternoon £10 was brought me (the sum we allow for outfit) with the words, this money is for you to get any thing you need for your journey + c. I thanked God + watched eagerly for the £50 that I was expecting. Friday it did not come, Saturday it did not come... This morning I glanced over the envelopes for one that might contain the £50 for ourselves, + thought I was still to wait. I then began to open + among the first chose yours not thinking there would be money in it... I had said to God '£50 just now would be worth more to me than a fortune at another time, it would be a guarantee of all other needs being met'".

So, having got the £50 Jennie Taylor went. The day before leaving she received a thousand pounds towards the orphanage she hoped to found. It was given by a friend who was not wealthy but who understood her sacrifice. With her went a group of new workers. They sailed on May 2nd 1878 and reached Shanghai on June 13th. After going to several places for consultation Jennie Taylor set out for the famine area. With her were Anna Crickmay and Celia Horne who had arrived in 1876 and Frederick Baller who had come three years earlier. This was the first time foreign women had gone so far inland. She had received a letter from Timothy Richard welcoming the enterprise as the answer to many prayers. But things were not easy. The Chinese distrusted foreigners and were suspicious about what the children were wanted for. The Prefect put out a proclamation attributing their efforts to evil notions. But he was reprimanded by the governor of the province who himself issued a proclamation in their favour.

It had been Hudson Taylor's intention to join his wife in Shanxi when he reached China and to work there for a period. She did not know which boat he was travelling by or when he was due to arrive. But in February 1879 she had a premonition that he was seriously ill. By this time the work among the orphans was properly established and rain had come the previous year. So she left her companions in charge and made her way to Shanghai to be on hand when he arrived.

(f) Funds for Expansion : the Seventy

Hudson Taylor gradually recovered at Yantai. The place where the mission buildings developed is generally called Chefoo from the name of a fishing village nearby. That became his head–quarters during this period in China.

Difficulties sometimes arose at stations which demanded personal visits. But pressure of administrative work practically confined him to Chefoo and the two business centres that were maintained with missionaries in charge. And he visited stations between them. One of the business centres was at Shanghai. The other was at Wuhan also on the Yangzi but six hundred miles inland. From there people were continually coming and going to the more distant parts. He often mentions in his letters his hope that when this or that matter is settled he will be able to go to those far off places where the missionaries were now settling in. But other problems always cropped up to prevent it. However his residence at Chefoo was to have an important consequence for the future. A school was started for missionaries' children. It became widely known and children of consular officials and of merchants were made welcome as well as those from other missions. And buildings were provided to make Chefoo a health resort for the mission.

During this time the operational plan was steadily being carried out. It was a plan for the evangelisation of the whole of China and it took fully into account the work of other societies. An outline of it had been published in *China's Millions* in 1875, at the time the Eighteen went out. The work had started in Ningbo. The first extension was to Hangzhou the capital of the province; this was occupied for a number of years until handed over to another mission. Then they extended to the capitals of the four circuits into which the province was divided. Subsequently they attempted to occupy as many as they could of the prefectural and county cities. What was being carried out in Zhejiang, the first province, it was intended to put into effect in all the provinces.

During the whole of this period in China funds were low. The sending out of the Thirty had enormously increased the size of the mission. The income had increased but to nothing like the same extent. So there was constant stringency. Furloughs were postponed, all but essential expenditure was cut to a minimum and the amount of money available to missionaries for personal use was reduced. Nonetheless no one appears to have suffered from it and the work went on developing. But the shortage of funds was a constant anxiety. It is referred to in letters throughout this period.

Not long after his return to China Hudson Taylor wrote to Benjamin Broomhall (Chefoo, Italy 19th 1879) "Many thanks for your note of May 30th which, with the remittances, I was *very* glad to receive. We have been holding special prayer meetings once or twice a day to pray for funds, and are thankful for a little, though it is very difficult to divide small sums, the number is now so large".

The following year in the course of a letter to Louisa Tomalin, (Wujiang, March 20th 1880) he wrote, "Mrs Copp has put on foreign dress, and does not mean to put if off again... There is a rumour that Messrs Clarke and Riley have been recalled from Chongqing by the Consul at Yichang. I hope it is not true. When shall we get through our difficulties?... Funds seem getting lower: we need much prayer. But God cannot fail us, let us trust and not be afraid".

The next year George Nicoll and his wife were staying at Chefoo after having been for some time in the interior. He recalled in reminiscences that one day in the autumn of 1881 Hudson Taylor said to his wife, "Mrs Nicoll, what would you do if you had a very large family and nothing to give them to eat? That is very much the situation with us just now". He went on to say that Hudson Taylor used to spend hours in prayer at that time. Then when they most needed it Tls 50 came in from a Consul who had never given before and Tls 400 from a missionary in North China, neither of whom knew of the special need. And Tls 100 came from a missionary in Chefoo. The total value was about £140.

But also throughout this period opportunities for advance were everywhere opening out. Things were literally going according to plan. Hudson Taylor wrote to Benjamin Broomhall (Wujiang, March 6th 1880) saying that they were feeling the need for more workers, both men and women. The very next sentence went on to say that he was hoping that he would shortly receive a further remittance as the needs of the month were far from being met.

Others in the mission felt strongly that there should be no thought of increased numbers until the funds improved and money was not so tight. They were opposed even to the normal reinforcements being sent. These continued and there were now ninety six missionaries making the mission the largest in China. There was a suggestion of some loss of confidence in the judgment of the Director in not calling a halt to any further increase in numbers. Yet the idea was not irresponsible; it was taking seriously the presence of the living God which was the basis and the end of all their endeavours.

Jennie Taylor, having done the work she came out to do and seen Hudson Taylor through his illness, returned to Britain in October 1881 to look after the family.

Hudson Taylor towards the end of November went to a little conference he had called at Wujiang. The conference, which was to last a week, was for workers in north and central China.

On Friday afternoon November 25th Hudson Taylor was out with his secretary A.G. Parrott for a walk on the hills. They were talking over the needs of the various stations and reckoned that to carry on the work adequately fifty or sixty more men and women were needed. On the Sunday, along with two others, they went over the whole country, province by province and station by station, noting the reinforcements needed to maintain the older work and to develop what was opening out before them. They estimated that forty two men and twenty eight women were required, making seventy in all. And recalling that Jesus had once appointed other seventy also (Luke 10.1) the conference took that number as a firm target

Of the ninety six missionaries twenty six were wives with families which limited their work outside the home. So there were seventy full time. Clearly the mission was not in a position to absorb another seventy all at once. They reckoned that a period of three years would be necessary to receive, train and place so many newcomers. It was now the close of 1881. So the years 1882 to 1884 were fixed as those in which the seventy were to be asked for. Then they bound themselves to pray daily for them until they should arrive. This also meant praying for the funds to sustain the mission at double its present size. They were also to pray for large reinforcements for other missions. All those present at the Conference joined willingly in the vow.

Before the Conference closed on the Wednesday they did a rather curious thing. Having prayed together for the seventy new workers they felt that they should give thanks together when the last of the new recruits arrived. But it was most unlikely that this would be possible. In all probability they would be scattered over many hundreds of miles in the distant parts to the north west, the south west and north east. Some might be in Europe. So they held the thanksgiving meeting before breaking up. In one way this was a meaningless procedure. But in another way it was very significant. For it implies a perfect definite prediction. It was most unlikely on any human reckoning to be fulfilled. For it was exceedingly improbable that funds would come in to support the mission at almost double the size.

Hudson Taylor was not going, or willing to go, by human probabilities. He was pretty sure that when funds were low not all members of the Council in London would agree to a rapid further expansion. The day after the conference ended he wrote to Jennie (steamer, Fuh-wo, December 1st 1881) "We have our definite lines of work: we must not leave them not get weary in them. If any leaves us on account of them, they, not we, are the losers. If any members of our home Council cannot go along with us they too will sooner or later need to go too. God remains faithful. Do not be cast down, Darling, if you meet with difficulties at home. All things are working together for good, as in due course we shall see".

It had been decided at the conference to issue an appeal for workers in the names of as many as possible of the mission. On account of the immense distances over which the members of the mission were scattered it is not surprising that it took a long time to circulate the proposed appeal. In fact it was not published until February 1883, more than a year after drafting. But in the end the great majority signed, including some of those who had been most strongly against enlargement of the mission. Of those who did not sign, most were sympathetic but did not wish to be tied down to a particular figure. Just how this change of opinion was achieved is not evident from the records. No doubt there were many letters and visits to stations. It was said that Hudson Taylor always got his way in the end. Some of the women members of the mission attributed this to personal charm. But clear reasoning about what was being proposed is likely to have been the main factor.

Although the appeal for the Seventy had not yet been published, the idea of doubling the active strength of the mission was becoming known in Britain. It caused concern to some well-wishers. They felt that the seventy men and women might be forthcoming but that the funds to support them might not. News of the fears reached Hudson Taylor in Chefoo at the end of January 1883. He recalls that they were mentioned at a prayer meeting at which some half a dozen people were present. They prayed that God would set his seal on the matter for the encouragement of the timid ones. It was asked that some wealthy person might give liberally to this special object. The date of the meeting was not noted at the time but it took place either at the end of January or the beginning of February.[10]

Hudson Taylor had hoped to be back in Britain by the beginning of 1882 but did not feel able to leave China for another year. He sailed from Chefoo on February 6th 1883 and caught the French Mail at Hong Kong. On reaching Aden he got news in a letter that an anonymous donor had given £3,000 towards the Seventy. He learned that it was sent on February 2nd when he got to Marseilles. Jennie came to Paris to meet him and they stayed for a few days together.

Once in London he was plunged into a round of meetings and conferences of various kinds and in various parts of the country. Of a meeting in Salisbury in September a friend remarked that the people felt they had received so much that they would give anything. At the end of the year Hudson Taylor wrote to Jennie from Glasgow (December 9th 1883) "Another happy day has passed and my four services are over ... I have a busy day before me, and two meetings, but neither of them exhausting. I must write to the papers on the opium question and make some calls and answer some letters if possible tomorrow ... Monday afternoon. I am just worn out with yesterday's meetings, a sleepless night and writing a long newspaper article on the opium traffic. P.S. I have to leave in a minutes to dine and hold two meetings".

With the increase in the size of the mission Hudson Taylor was occupied also with its future organisation. In August 1882 he had written a circular letter to all members of the mission making certain proposals and asking their opinion. This was followed by a second letter. After his return to Britain he discussed the matter with the London Council. With their approval a third letter making definite proposals was sent in August 1883. The most important idea was for a superintendent and a council of experienced missionaries in each province and a China Council made up of all superintendents and the Director.

By the time Hudson Taylor arrived in Britain the first of the three years for the Seventy to be sent had gone by and the task of selecting and preparing the candidates had begun. Of course it built up over the three years. There are differences in the way the numbers are reckoned. But, taking the lowest count, in the first year nine new missionaries sailed. In the second year the figure was eighteen and in the third year, 1884, it was forty six making seventy in all.

But the main question was never whether enough suitable people would come forward; it was whether there would be funds to maintain the mission at almost double the previous size. In 1881-82 the total income of the mission was £10,696. It had been pretty well constant at that level for four years. In 1883 the mission's financial year was changed. The first twelve month period for which figures are available is January to December

1885. The figure is £20,403. It never dropped below that and continued to rise.[11]

There was a kind of bonus to the Seventy. During the period they were being recruited the mission was joined by the majority of those later referred to in the press as the Cambridge Seven. The first to apply was D.E. Hoste. He was an officer in the Royal Artillery, educated at the Royal Military Academy, Woolwich, and was not a Cambridge man. But he had a brother at Trinity who was a friend of those there: Stanley Smith, Montague Beauchamp and C.T. Studd. From St John's College came Willian Cassels. They were joined later by Cecil Polhill-Turner of Trinity Hall and his brother Arthur who had been at Jesus College and was an officer in the Dragoon Guards. In groups of two or three they spoke at universities and other places all over Britain. These meetings created an extraordinary stir. Probably this was on account of the social and sporting prowess, at the time both highly thought of. Studd was captain of the University cricket team and played for England. Smith was stroke of the Cambridge boat. Beauchamp was known as an oarsman and Cassels as a rugby player. It had been decided that the first group of them would sail in December 1884. But Hudson Taylor was asked to allow them to continue their touring and they all left together in February 1885. He had gone on January 20th. He visited the Bergers at Cannes before joining the ship with its party of new missionaries.

(g) Funds for Expansion : The Hundred

One of Hudson Taylor's main tasks during this period in China was to put into effect the new organisation that had been planned. This required much consultation and involved long journeys and took a lot of time. The first appointment was the deputy China director; he would be in full charge when Hudson Taylor was out of the country. John Stevenson, in Britain at the time, who had come out in 1865 was chosen; the appointment was widely welcomed. James Brounton, who had pioneered the work in Guizhou province was made Treasurer and located at Wujiang at the centre of the vast mission area. Eight men were appointed as provincial superintendents; in some cases adjacent provinces being combined. Not everyone liked the changes. Older missionaries who had been used to dealing directly with Hudson Taylor did not like having to go to a superintendent, especially if he was a younger man. But the new arrangements proved to work well.

Changes were also needed in some of the mission's establishments to allow the handling of greatly increased numbers. A much larger headquarters was needed in Shanghai and in 1886 a two acre site was bought in an undeveloped area. There was already a language school with accommodation for women in Yangzhou and a corresponding one for men at Anqing; plans were made to have them both enlarged. The increased accommodation was soon required. Wherever Hudson Taylor went he was told of the need for reinforcements. In May 1885 he cabled London for thirty more be sent as soon as possible. During the year forty new missionaries arrived in China.

John Stevenson got back to China in December 1885. Before taking up his duties as Deputy Director it was thought that he should make two journeys. One was to visit the older stations in eastern Zhejiang where there were difficulties with a few missionaries. The other journey was to the far off stations to see the work and meet as many missionaries as possible; this took over seven months. It was arranged that he and Hudson Taylor should meet in Shanxi.

Hudson Taylor had been planning to visit Shanxi for some years. He was always held up by administrative work. But with the new arrangements he was able to make long journeys. He was with Stevenson at conferences in Hongtong and Linfen. Then, in August, he was off on a journey westward to Hanzhong in Shaanxi. With him were his son Herbert, W.J. Lewis his secretary, Montague Beauchamp and C.T. Studd. As it was very hot Hudson Taylor was only able to travel by night. The others could not sleep by day and got behind. Only Montague Beauchamp who had known him since boyhood remained with him all the time. The mission archives contain his reminiscences of the journey.

"The great difficulty was in getting food and we constantly lost our way and there was nobody to ask the road. No muleteer

would come at night. We had very little baggage and the pack
mule was behind with the others. No inns being open at night we
often used to lie down on the roadside. A remarkable thing about
Mr Taylor was his power of endurance and his ability to sleep
in the daytime. At any time he could rest in an inn, put up an
umbrella and mosquito net and have a good sleep. No matter
what the surroundings Mr Taylor was always the same man with
the same spirit—with food—without food, with rest or without
it—always the same. I often used to carry him through the rivers
which were all in flood, the wet season being on. Still he would
not be hindered—he would push on.

We arrived at Hanzhong while the conference was going
on. All the missionaries were living there very comfortably and
congratulating themselves. Mr Taylor dropped into their midst
like a bombshell and scattered them. Mr and Mrs Pearce, Dr and
Mrs Wilson, Mr Easton and the ladies in their house. I remember
Mr Taylor saying we were not out in China just to settle down
to girl's schools. The ladies must be up and out among the
women".

From Hanzhong Hudson Taylor returned by boat a 1,000
miles down the Han river to Wuhan. He took with him Pearce's
little daughter Annie who was far from well and did everything
for her. He reached Wuhan on October 14th and found 201
letters awaiting him.

The first meeting of the China Council took place in the
middle of November. One 'of the things done was to start
preparing a Book of Arrangements. The mission, although little
more than twenty years old, was becoming a large organisation.
By far the greater number of its members had been out for less
than five years and needed to know what to do in a variety of
circumstances. And time is saved in administration if there are
regular procedures which are accessible to people. But some
members of the London Council did not see it that way. They
had thought of the mission as being like a large family with
Hudson Taylor dealing personally with each member. Now it
seemed that love was to be replaced by law. The feeling was so
strong in some cases that on his return to Britain Hudson Taylor

felt that he had to visit members of the Council individually to explain why the book was needed and that it would not change the character of the mission.

The China Council did something else. It set its seal on the proposal to pray for a hundred new missionaries to come out in the following year. How the idea originated is not certain. The first mention of it comes in a letter from John Stevenson in September 1886. It is likely that the idea was his and was the outcome of what he saw on his extensive travels that year. Certainly the idea did not come from Hudson Taylor. He was hesitant at first, doubtless because the funds were barely sufficient to meet the needs of the existing greatly extended work. Other people regarded it as impossible. A very experienced American Baptist missionary said to Hudson Taylor, "You will not get them, of course, but you will get more than if you did not ask for so large a number".

By this time Hudson Taylor was convinced that the Hundred should be prayed for and that they would all come. After the meeting of the China Council Hudson Taylor, Lewis and Stevenson went to Dagutang to work on the Book of Arrangements. Stevenson recalled later that one day Hudson Taylor was dictating a letter and used the phrase "a hundred new missionaries in 1887". Lewis, looked up in astonishment. Then Hudson Taylor said, "If you showed me a photograph of the whole hundred taken in China, I could not be more certain than I am now".

That was a clear prediction and it involved funds as much as personnel. During this whole period in China money was tight. Funds had increased over the preceding year but not sufficiently to keep pace with the rapid increase in numbers. Shortage of funds is mentioned often in Hudson Taylor's letters. There was enough when used carefully but some reinforcements had to be kept back until more money came since the mission would not go into debt. A hundred new missionaries would require an additional £10,000 income.

The China Council had suggested that Hudson Taylor return to Britain to help forward the sending out of the Hundred. He left China on January 6th 1887 by the French Mail and met Jennie in Paris. On February 10th they reached London.

A very busy year lay ahead. Benjamin Broomhall, the General Secretary, had arranged meetings all over the British Isles which would go on throughout the year. A lot of time was spent in the selection of candidates. Nothing was more important than choosing the right men and women except perhaps not choosing the wrong ones; earlier mistakes had been made. There was a large amount of correspondence; an average of thirteen or fourteen letters sent every weekday. There were many meetings of the London Council, some of them difficult because of the dislike of several prominent members of the Book of Arrangements.

And, of course, it was an exceedingly busy year for the mission staff. They had plenty of experience in sending out new missionaries but never on this scale. For the hundred to be sent there were six hundred applications. The candidates had to be brought to London, accommodated and interviewed. Those selected had to be prepared for the journey, passages booked and speakers at farewell meetings arranged. The work was got through and party after party left. By the end of 1887 a hundred and two new missionaries had been sent. The strength of the mission was now 265.

In 1886 the total income of the mission was £22,423; in 1887 it was £33,717. It did not fall below that figure. In 1891 and 1892 the British figure fell but it was made up by increased giving in China and to a less extent in North America where a branch of the mission had been started. The mission was maintained at its greatly increased strength.

In the 1888 annual volume of *China's Millions* there is a frontispiece. It is a photograph showing the hundred new missionaries in China. There had been no such pictures on previous occasions when a definite number of new missionaries had been prayed for and had arrived. A likely reason for the innovation is not hard to supply. Hudson Taylor had made a prediction in those terms and what was predicted had come about.

(h) Sequel

There is no need to go further; there was no more striking providential events of this kind. John Stevenson looking back on the time of the Hundred, said to Howard and Geraldine Taylor, "We all saw visions at that time. Those were the days of heaven upon earth; nothing seemed difficult". But the mission did not come to a standstill and neither did the Church in China. Something needs to be said briefly about this as well as about Hudson Taylor's later years.

Four of Hudson Taylor's children were with the mission in China. Maria, married to a former secretary of Hudson Taylor, lost a baby at Wenzhou in 1897 from dysentery and died of it herself shortly afterwards.

Hudson Taylor continued his work which included visits to Britain, North America and elsewhere. In April 1900 he gave the keynote address at the Ecumenical Conference of Foreign Missions in New York. This was followed by addresses at other places. At Boston he suddenly lost his train of thought and had to stop. He had been seriously ill three years earlier and Jennie had taken him to Davos in Switzerland where he quickly recovered. So she took him there again and this time recovery was slow. As will be described shortly, it was a period of terrible suffering for missionaries and even more so for Chinese Christians. Reports reached him in Switzerland but responsibility for action had to be left to John Stevenson in Shanghai. Yet even when weak Hudson Taylor had a grasp of affairs and could take decisive action. In August 1900 he cabled appointing Hoste to act as General Director during his incapacity. He knew that he would have the backing of prominent members of the London Council who had been urging him to appoint a successor. He knew also that the appointment would be acutely embarrassing both to Hoste and to Stevenson. Hoste refused the position at first but later accepted it. The Councils supported the appointment.

In July 1904 Jennie died and was buried in Switzerland. Hudson was naturally heartbroken. But his health continued to improve and early the following year he was able to go to China with his son Howard and his wife. He visited a number of centres

in inland China and was enthusiastically welcomed by Chinese
Christians. It was singularly appropriate that he died peacefully
at Changsha, for this was the capital of Hunan, the last and most
difficult province in which to establish work. His body was
taken to Zhenjiang to be buried beside Maria and his children as
he had always hoped.

When Hudson Taylor died the mission had over 800
members. It had become international with Councils
corresponding to the London one in Toronto for the United States
and Canada, and in Melbourne for Australia and New Zealand.
There were individual members from a number of other countries.
In addition there were associated missions in Britain, Germany,
Denmark, Norway, Sweden, Finland and the United States. They
had their own organisation but followed the CIM policies and its
direction in China. The CIM, under Hoste's direction continued
to grow. By 1934, a year before he retired, it had 1,368 members
and was at that time the largest mission in the world.

The mission had for long actively supported the movement
against the opium traffic. Speeches were made at meetings,
articles were written for newspapers and from the beginning
China's Millions had published letters from missionaries and
special articles on the effects of opium on the Chinese people.
Benjamin Broomhall was on the executive council of the Society
for the Suppression of the Opium Trade. In 1888 he and James
Maxwell of the English Presbyterian Mission formed a comple–
mentary organisation, The Christian Union for the Severance of
the Connection of the British Empire from the Opium Traffic.
Its aim was to arouse the Churches, the public and members of
parliament to the need for action. They started a periodical
National Righteousness which Broomhall edited in addition to
his other work. In 1895, at 66, he retired from the CIM to devote
the rest of his life to the struggle against the opium traffic. A
resolution urging the government of India to stop granting licences
for the cultivation of the poppy and to stop selling opium was
carried in parliament in 1891. But vigorous campaigning had to
go on for another twenty years before parliament acted decisively
to end the traffic. Benjamin Broomhall died the same year.

The opium traffic made Britain hated and led to war and humiliating peace treaties. Other humiliations came from France and Russia. More recently China had been defeated by Japan which, unlike China, had thoroughly modernised. And Germany had seized territory causing great resentment. At the end of the century there was widespread anti-foreign feeling. It was intensified by drought in some places which was blamed on foreigners. A secret society came into prominence, "The Righteous United Fists", called by foreigners Boxers. Before long they had the support of the Empress.

Foreigners everywhere were in danger. The legations in Beijing were under siege for two months and just managed to defend themselves before relief came. Inland there were engineers building railways and some others in secular work. But the largest group of foreigners living inland were missionaries and of Protestants far the greatest number belonged to the CIM and its associated missions who were spread throughout the country. It lost by violence, in many cases decapitation, a total of seventy nine men, women and children. Many others suffered terribly as they made their escape from their attackers. A detailed account of one family's experience is on record.[12]

But it was not only foreigners who were attacked; there were those who had accepted the foreign religion. The brunt of the Boxer attack was borne by Chinese Christians. Many were farmers who lost everything: livestock, implements and grain and were made destitute. Houses were burned down and people were robbed of all they possessed; in some cases even the clothes they were wearing were taken away. Some were shut up in the appalling conditions of Chinese prisons at the time; some were beaten with bamboo rods; hundreds were killed because they refused to recant—relatively few did so. The Catholics lost most Christians, the CIM most missionaries.

In August 1900 Beijing was taken by a combined western and Japanese force and the Boxer uprising was quickly brought to an end. Large indemnities were imposed. Only the United States acted generously. The first payment was returned to be used for education and further instalments were not taken. Among missions there were differences in the attitude to compensation. Some asked for large amounts. The CIM decided not to claim anything in compensation and not to accept anything if offered. That did not apply to Chinese Christians; they belonged to the country and were not in the service of foreigners.

Numbers have continued to grow during the turbulent years of this century. They cannot be estimated accurately because there are large underground churches, both Protestant and Catholic. But it is reckoned that there are now more than fifty million Christians in China.

2. Assessment of Evidential Value

To be of evidential value an event should have the following features.

First, there is a prediction that something prayed for will happen. Ordinarily petitionary prayers do not have any element of prediction. Certainly we hope that they will be answered. We may believe that they will be. But we know from experience that many prayers are not answered. Sometimes the reason becomes apparent later; often it does not. Hudson Taylor's prayers for people seriously ill were of this kind; he made no prediction about recovery. The prayers we are concerned with here are quite different. They were unusual even in Hudson Taylor's life.

Second, something does happen which completely fulfils the prediction.

Third, it is most improbable that what happened would have come about from natural or human factors alone.

Most of the incidents regarded as providential have to do with funding. To be able to asses their evidential value certain aspects of funding need looking at in more detail.

When the mission was started there were to be no requests, no appeals and no collections. God alone was to be asked for money and would move people to give. But people who do give want to know how things are going on; they give just because they are interested in the work. And so information had to be given. Meetings were held, *Occasional Papers* were published and later a well produced magazine was brought out regularly. This, of course, stimulated giving. And so while there were no direct appeals to people there were indirect appeals.

Hudson Taylor believed that there was both a human and a Divine side to funding. He well understood that information promotes giving and that without it interest wanes and giving dries up. But he put his emphasis .on the Divine side. In times of shortage there were no special appeals; there was special prayer. And when an extension of the work was undertaken he did not predict that sufficient funds would come because people would see the need for it and respond generously. He predicted that sufficient funds would come because God would respond. He could extend the work when funds were low for this reason. This may be seen on each occasion when there was expansion.

In the case of the Eighteen, at the time the decision was made to call for 18 new missionaries funds were low and had been for two years. The initial expenses involved in sending out and supporting the Eighteen were met by the gifts of Mrs Grace and Jennie Taylor. But the mission would have to go on being maintained at a higher strength, half as many again. There was no human reason for thinking that the necessary funds would be forthcoming. Hudson Taylor acted because he believed that God would see that the funds were provided.

But could the fact that the income did rise substantially be accounted for by purely human factors? There was a general revival of interest in foreign mission work at the time. The bold expansion might well arouse interest. A new type of missionary magazine was produced, better than anything before. It could be said that while the prediction of sufficient support was made on the basis of God's presence and power, the fulfilment of the prediction did not require any Divine factor to explain it.

Much the same considerations apply to the Thirty. Although the mission was being maintained at the new level of staffing money was very tight. It was not a situation in which any other mission, or any other organisation, would think of expansion. Hudson Taylor planned to send out about 30 new workers because the opportunities for extension were there. He predicted that sufficient funds would be provided to send out the additional missionaries and to maintain the mission at almost double its existing strength.

Again the question must be asked, can the increase in funding be explained without any Divine factor? Hudson Taylor's presence in Britain and his speaking at meetings is likely to have stimulated interest. Then because new missionaries were to be sent out some people would give more, although it is likely that others would think the idea foolish and would not support it. The famine in China would focus interest on the country. But that would not necessarily bring more money to the mission. Hudson Taylor had no objections to appealing for money for the famine and did so vigorously. It is likely that money which otherwise would go to the general fund would be earmarked for famine relief. All in all it is at least possible that the increased funding could be explained without Divine influence.

When Hudson Taylor and his colleagues at the conference in Wujiang prayed for 70 new missionaries there was no human likelihood of the mission being maintained at almost double its existing strength. Many members of the mission were against any increase in numbers for this reason. But the prediction was made that they would come and would be supported.

Once more the question has to be put: granted that the prediction was made on the basis of God's presence and power to act, could its fulfilment be explained by purely human considerations? A great deal of interest was created by Hudson Taylor's many meetings up and down the country. It was continued by the enthusiasm aroused by the Cambridge Seven. Whether this could account for the continued support of the mission at the new level is difficult to judge; enthusiasm tends to wane. But it is at least possible.

In the case of the hundred there was a quite definite prediction that 100 new missionaries would be sent in the year and that there would be funds to send them out and to support them. The prediction was completely fulfilled. But it might be said that the boldness of the plan and Hudson Taylor's extensive speaking engagements would be enough to account for the interest shown and the funds provided.

There was one striking feature about the funding in this case. It was estimated that £10,000 was required over and above the 1886 figure. The office staff were under enormous pressure in getting the Hundred selected, prepared and sent out. It would be much increased if they had to thank people for small donations making up the extra £10,000. So it was decided to pray that the additional funds should come in large gifts. In fact the whole amount came in eleven gifts. The smallest was £500 and the largest £2,500.[13] Still, it could be argued that the one occasion when this happened could be put down to chance.

In each of the four cases just looked at there were factors which would increase the likelihood of additional funds being given. But in no case is it clear whether or not these factors would be enough to provide the money required if there was no Divine factor at work. By themselves they might or might not be sufficient to account for the predictions being fulfilled.

Four other cases have to be taken into account. In the early period in China, John and Mary Jones and Hudson Taylor were prepared to live with no Society and no individual guaranteeing support. They predicted that sufficient funds would come for themselves and their work. In the four instances described money came just when needed. Of course there was a certain probability of this happening. The mail would arrive when the Jones and Hudson Taylor were at different stages through their resources; sometimes it might come just as they were at the end. But there was also a possibility that it would come a few days or weeks after the exhaustion of all they had. This did not happen.

Two further occasions may be mentioned. In the early period of the mission funds were often short. But always sufficient came. Details have been given for the first half of 1874.

Earlier still, when the *Dumfries* was drifting among the Indonesian islands, Hudson Taylor prayed earnestly for a breeze. He felt sure that the prayer would be answered and told the Mate that a breeze would come soon. It did come.

Ten cases have been referred to in which a prediction was made. In each case it might or might not have been fulfilled. In certain cases it appears more likely that it would be fulfilled than in others. If there was no Divine factor at work it would be expected that in some cases the prediction would be fulfilled, in others not. But they were all fulfilled. It is a little like expecting a family of ten to be made up of girls and boys and finding that they were all girls. This would suggest that there was some special factor at work. Nor are there any occasions referred to in the extensive archive material when a prediction was made and was not fulfilled.

In addition two incidents have been described in which no predictions were made but in which there were striking answers to prayer. One is the *Dumfries* in Caernarvon Bay. The wind veered two points just at the critical time. Almost anyone experiencing the event would regard it as a miracle.

The other is Jennie Taylor's prayer for guidance. She asked for two sums of money. This first was for things needed for the journey; she was given £10 which was the amount normally provided for outfit. The other amount she asked for was £50 for the family. Just this amount was given her. There was some chance that she would be given money since people knew that she was going. But the sums were precise and the second came from a wholly unexpected quarter.

In these twelve incidents belief in the reality of God's providence was rigorously put to the test and was not falsified. They do not prove the reality of providence but they do provide evidence.

References

1. P.M. van Buren, *Theological Explorations,* London, 1968, p. 166.

2. A.J. Broomhall, *Hudson Taylor and China's Open Century,* London, 1981 to 1989.

3. Dr and Mrs Howard Taylor, *Hudson Taylor in Early Years,* London, 1911. *Hudson Taylor and the China Inland Mission,* London, 1918.

4. K.S. Latourette, *A History of Christian Missions in China,* London, 1929, p. 210.

5. J.C. Marshman, *The Life and Times of Carey, Marshman and Ward,* Vol. I, London, 1859, pp. 244f.

6. W.H. Moreland and A.T. Chatterjee, *A Short History of India,* 4th ed., London, 1957, p. 408.

7. W.A.P. Martin, *A Cycle of Cathay,* Edinburgh, 1896, pp. 141f.

8. *Ibid.,* p. 214.

9. *China's Millions,* London, 1878, p. 2.

10. *China's Millions,* London, 1885, pp. 8f.

11. M. Broomhall, *Our Seal,* London, 1933, pp. 167, 171.

12. A.E. Glover, *A Thousand Miles of Miracle in China,* London, 5th ed., 1909.

13. *China's Millions,* London, 1888, p. 95.

Chapter VII

Case Studies :
Claims For Providence—B

1. Narrative

The second person whose claims for providence will be examined is Mother Teresa. She is so well known that a fairly brief account of her life and work is all that is needed. My most important information comes from observation of her work and discussion with her. I have also spoken with Father Van Exem, her spiritual adviser from the very start, with senior sisters and with volunteers who come to help. Of books and articles read I have drawn mainly on Eileen Egan's *Such a Vision of the Street*. The author has known Mother Teresa for many years and accompanied her on many journeys. The references are to page numbers in the British edition of this book.

(a) Development of the work

Mother Teresa was born in Albania in 1910 and came to India as a very young missionary in 1928. Her training was to be at the Loreto Convent in Darjeeling. This is the hill station in the Himalayas to which the Government of Bengal used to move from Calcutta in the summer months. There in 1931 she made her first vows of poverty, chastity and obedience as a Loreto sister and came to Calcutta. Her lifetime vows were made in 1937.

In Calcutta the Loreto Convent stands in spacious, well-kept grounds behind a high wall. In the compound are two schools, one with the teaching in English and the other in Bengali. Mother Teresa taught in the latter for almost twenty years and for some years was principal. It was a happy and satisfying life. She loved teaching and she loved the girls. She enjoyed the fellowship of like minded people engaged in a common endeavour. And while people in religious orders do not have possessions, and the living conditions are simple, they can be quite comfortable. With this goes the security of belonging to an Order which knows and cares for its members.

Just over the Convent wall on one side is what can only be called a slum area, known as Moti Jhil. It was a vast labyrinth of narrow lanes with single roomed houses. The main road through was not metalled. The houses had no water, no sanitation and no electricity. There was no relief from the stifling heat in the hot months. The place was filled with people, poor, undernourished, in threadbare clothes, often without shoes. There was no school for the children and no doctor or nurse ever came. All this could be seen from the Convent. Some of the girls in Mother Teresa's school belonged to a religious society. Under the guidance of a priest they visited the area and did what they could to help the people living there. But Mother Teresa, because of the Convent's rule of enclosure, was not able to go with them.

In September 1946 Mother Teresa was going up to Darjeeling for her annual retreat. In the little train which moves slowly up the mountain she had what she describes as a call within a call. She was convinced that God was calling her to devote herself wholly to serving the poorest of the poor. She might have done so while living in a convent of a different kind. But she felt that something more was required of her. She was to serve them not from the security of a convent but sharing something of the poverty and hardship of their lives and trusting in God to guide and to provide.

When she returned to Calcutta Mother Teresa gave some papers to Father Van Exem. He was an expert in Islam and had been appointed to a parish only the day before. Although he did not feel it was his real work he had agreed to say Mass daily at the Loreto Convent. He took the papers and promised to give his opinion on them the next day. They had been written during the retreat at Darjeeling. They contained not only an account of her call but in considerable detail all the ideas which she was later to put into practice. The work was envisaged as applying only to Calcutta. Later what was done in Calcutta was taken as a model, with appropriate modifications, for work all over the world.

Father Van Exem fully supported Mother Teresa both then and during all the subsequent years. But neither would do anything without the full consent of all the ecclesiastical authorities concerned. This took time, partly because it was intended to. It was not for two years that she was able to set out on her new work. Before doing so Father Van Exem suggested that she should go to a mission hospital in Bihar for some months to get experience in caring for people with different kinds of illnesses. This she did. When she was confident that she had sufficient experience, and with the agreement of the hospital, she returned to Calcutta where somewhere to live had been found. The same year she became an Indian citizen.

Mother Teresa began her new work by going to Moti Jhil. There, with the agreement of the parents, she gathered some children and began to teach them. The children were quite big and had never been to school, although without education children are condemned to remain in the lowest stratum of society. Various things were taught despite having nothing to teach with; a stick was used to trace Bengali letters in the mud. Next day she went again. One of the mothers said to her, "I do not know what is happening. My child woke up at three in the morning and asked, 'When is Sister coming?'" That day someone gave a table and a chair and later a cupboard. Someone from outside gave money and a room was rented. So the school continued and grew large.

From the beginning Mother Teresa looked after people dying in the streets. Hospitals would not take them because there was nothing they could do. But Mother Teresa and the young women who joined her could make them feel wanted and cared for. For nearly four years they tended them in the streets, bringing food and medicines and making them as comfortable as they could.

One day Mother Teresa saw a shrunken, emaciated man die in the rain, alone, in a pool of blood and vomit. She felt more than ever that she must have a place to which she could bring people who were dying in the streets. So she went to the Corporation and asked them if they could provide a place where people could die in dignity and love. It happened that the Corporation had a large disused building which had been a place for pilgrims to rest in, next to the great Kali temple and this was offered to her. She accepted it and within twenty four hours had patients and helpers in. In the first five years more than eight thousand people were taken care of.

The work at Kalighat is exceedingly demanding. Sometimes when a patient is brought in, the smell from suppurating sores is overpowering. People have to be bathed and dried and clothed. Then there is shaving, hair cutting and nail trimming to be done. Sores have to be dressed and sometimes maggots picked out. Some patients are incontinent and require periodic washing and changing of clothes and sheet. Often feeding is necessary and can be painfully slow as can the giving of medicines. As time went on more patients lived than died. But those who died did so in an atmosphere of respect and love.

Caring for unwanted babies is another important activity. The babies come from parents, from hospitals, from prisons, from the police, from doorsteps where they have been left and even from rubbish dumps. They generally get two or three a day. Some of the babies are tiny—two pounds or less and require skilled attention. Often they are premature and drugged from something the mother has taken to get rid of the child. Some inevitably die—but no longer unwanted and uncared for. The main impression of the children's home is one of being well cared for, happy children. The bigger children run about cheerfully and people come in to play with them. Most of the children are adopted either by Indians or by people abroad and are made happy in their new homes. Some, such as those with disabilities from poliomyelitis or hydrocephalus, continue to be cared for in the children's home.

Children who are badly undernourished are taken in temporarily. They come both from city slums and from villages.

When the children are ready for it their parents take them back. Some are severely undernourished and have to be kept for a longer period.

Leprosy work was not started for some years. One day five lepers presented themselves. They had been put out of their homes and work and had no shelter and no means of livelihood except by begging. This happens to people in all levels of society when they are found to have leprosy; they are asked to leave home and go away to be unknown and uncared for. Mother Teresa felt she had to do something for lepers. It was arranged that patients should collect at specified locations. These stations were visited by a mobile clinic with a specialist in leprosy who gave his services. The work grew rapidly. Just outside Calcutta a leprosy station became, in due course, a largely self-supporting leper community. A Missionary of Charity Brother, who was a doctor, lived with them. The centre also looked after 20,000 out patients. At another station a school was opened for the children of lepers. A further development was a leper colony. The Government gave thirty four acres of land in Begal two hundred miles from Calcutta and buildings were provided by donations. Here hundreds of leper families could live in separate houses and receive treatment under medical supervision.

Other programmes have been developed. There is a feeding centre where more than a thousand families are fed every day. It is done on a ration card system. A sister visits each family and food is given in accordance with the information collected. There are dispensaries and there is a mobile clinic to reach people where they are. There are schools in addition to those mentioned. And in a very poor dock area, where work is irregular, women are helped to earn and provide for their families. All this had been built up in the Calcutta area to meet specific needs.

Very shortly after Mother Teresa began her work in Calcutta she was joined by a number of young Indian women. They came one by one and almost all were her former pupils. Within a few months there were ten. The group so far had no official recognition. But after a year's observation and consultation with a number of people, the Archbishop was ready to have the group recognised as a congregtion of the archdiocese. Formal recognition would have to come from Rome. The new society was named by Mother Teresa Missionaries of Charity and a written constitution was drawn up. The Archbishop himself took it to Rome and recognition was granted in October 1950. The Missionaries of Charity were limited to the archdiocese of Calcutta which meant that they could not work outside India. In point of fact for nearly ten years work was limited to Calcutta.

Then it spread very rapidly. It was extended to areas of special need in different regions of India. The kind of things done in Calcutta were undertaken but adapted to meet particular situations. Young women had begun coming from other parts of India and other parts of the world. Then in 1963 men were taken. Mother Teresa thought that there were things which were better done by men and a new branch was added, the Missionaries of Charity Brothers. An Australian Jesuit priest, then in Bihar, was invited to head the Society and took the title General Servant.

Work could not be taken up outside India without special papal recognition of the Missionaries of Charity. An approach was first made in 1960 and recognition was granted in 1965. An invitation had already been received from a bishop in Venezuela. He was looking for Sisters to work among the poor and neglected people in his diocese. The Sisters had to be willing to live among them and under the simplest conditions. Mother Teresa went to Venezuela to see whether there was work that her Sisters could do, a place to live and a church. The group of Sisters arrived within a year and very quickly became an accepted and valued part of the community.

This has been the general pattern for starting work in a new area. An invitation is received from the Roman Catholic bishop. Mother Teresa, or a deputy, visits the area to see whether there is a real need and one which they are able to help meet. She asks only for two things. First, a place for the Sisters to live and work. Something close to the people and quite simple is what is wanted. Second, there has to be a priest to celebrate the Eucharist. This is central to the life of the Missionaries of Charity. It gives them the strength to endure the hardships and difficulties involved in much of the work. In emergency situations Mother Teresa will go at once and then suggest to the bishop that an invitation should be given. But normally the first move comes from the bishop. It is by no means only in under-developed countries that extreme poverty and suffering is found. In developed countries there are people who suffer as a result of such conditions, as long unemployment, chronic illness, disabilities, confinement to a room, alcoholism and drug taking and whose needs the social services have been unable fully to meet.

At the time of writing work is done in every state in India and in ninety other countries. It is organised in regions with regional supervisors. There are 441 houses and 3,068 Sisters. And so far from growth being at the end there are 150 applications from different parts of the world awaiting assessment.

(b) Basic Principles

Mother Teresa told me quite definitely that the whole work rested on two principles. These principles were not simply her own but were accepted by all the Sisters and Brothers.

First, care for the poor. This is what Mother Teresa was sure she was called to do. And this is what she had been doing consistently and unremittingly ever since she left the Loreto Convent. When she formed her own Order the principle of care for the poor was incorporated in a special vow. To the older and searching vows of chastity, poverty and obedience a fourth vow was added. It is "to give whole hearted and free service to the poorest of the poor". The life of a person in a religious order is controlled by the vows deliberately taken. And it is this fourth vow in especial which was intended to, and does in fact, control the lives of the Missionaries of Charity.

Mother Teresa felt from the beginning that only if she and her Sisters were really poor could they fully understand the lives of the poor. Their own standard of living should not be too far removed from that of the people they tried to serve. Food is simple although a proper diet is insisted on; that was something learned from the mission hospital in Bihar. Furniture is quite basic. On more than one occasion good furniture has been provided by a well-meaning diocese only to be given back and something much simpler taken in its place. Nor are washing machines used. In Bengal there are no fans in the rooms although in the hottest months it can be almost unbearable without them. But the poor have no fans so neither should the Sisters. As to possessions all the Sisters have is three simple cotton saris and underwear and a pair of sandals. They have a plate and a spoon. And they have a small crucifix and a rosary. These meagre conditions of life do nothing to dampen spirits. One of the deepest impressions made by the Mother house in Calcutta, where the Sisters live, is its cheerfulness.

The fourth vow is called the vow of Charity. Charity, from the Latin *caritas* is the old word for Christian love; it is used, for example, in the authorised version of 1 Corinthians 13, Paul's chapter on love. It is love which is the motive power for service of the poor. "Why do you do this?" asks a dying man. "Because I love you" is Mother Teresa's reply. No one who has spoken seriously with her can have any doubt that this is true. She has a deep love for people and a constant concern for their well-being. It is not so much a love for people in general as for individual people and especially those forced to live in poverty and hardship. At the mobile clinics, for example, she knew the patients and could see who was missing and needed searching for; she cared for each of them.

This love of people is felt and acted on not only by Mother Teresa but also by the Sisters and Brothers. It is a love awakened and maintained in response to God's love. "We love because he first loved us" writes John and he is referring to the love of others (1 John 4.19f). People are loved for themselves. But they are seen also as fellow creatures of God and as brothers and sisters of Christ. The words "As you did it to one of the least of these my brethren, you did it to me" (Matthew 25.40 RSV) are taken very seriously. Because their love is a response to the love of God and of Christ it is important that that love is not forgotten amid the business of life. As in all religious orders a pattern of life is followed which ensures that this is the case. The Missionaries of Charity have a regular sequence of prayer and work and recreation and this is done as a community. It may

well be that living as a religious community is the best way for
such love as is shown by the Missionaries of Charity to develop
and be sustained. It is a love which endures poverty and which
continues joyfully and wholeheartedly amid tasks which are often
both trying and monotonous.

The second basic principle is reliance on Divine providence.

When Mother Teresa left the Loreto Convent it was not
only an act of love and obedience; it was at the same time an act
of faith that God would provide. In the early days some of those
working with her were anxious about what would happen when
the food ran out. But Mother Teresa always told them to keep
nothing back when people needed it. God would provide. Nor
were they ever without food for themselves and those they cared
for. Throughout her work Mother Teresa has depended directly
on God for the maintenance of the work. And Sister Frederick,
Assistant Mother General, in conversation made exactly the same
point. She emphasised that they were completely dependent on
providence; without that the work could not go on at all.

Mother Teresa's reliance on providence is brought out by
a number of things that she does not do.

She does not accept maintenance grants which are
sometimes offered by Churches or Church related bodies. Eileen
Egan was present when papal recognition was first asked for in
1960. She mentions that the Cardinal investigating the matter
wondered how the Sisters could live and work without dependence
on a regular outside source of funds. Mother Teresa, she reports,
kept insisting that dependence on God's providence had seen
them through thus far (p. 135). Again Egan reports that when the
Sisters came to work in New York in 1971 the Cardinal there
informed Mother Teresa that the archdiocese was ready to supply
five hundred dollars a month for the support of each Sister. The
grant was refused because it was on providence that she depended
(p. 241). I was told by Sister Frederick that some years ago the
Church decided to allocate a considerable sum of money for
every new vocation. This applied to all orders. Since the
Missionaries of Charity had five hundred vocations the sum
would be a large one. It was to be a maintenance grant. Mother

Teresa asked permission to use the money for a new building. This was not possible. Therefore the money was refused. Shortly before writing this, Mother Teresa was visited by representatives of the Knights of Columbus, a Catholic society in the United States. They said that the Society had recently decided to send twenty thousand dollars annually for her work. She thanked them warmly but declined the offer. Her principle was to depend on providence alone.

Recurring government grants are not accepted for the same reason. In the early years she did accept a grant for children in her homes but this was given up. There was an additional reason for doing so: acceptance of the grant would involve spending more on some children than on others.

Nor are endowments accepted. She was once offered a very large sum of money by a wealthy Indian businessman. The capital was not to be touched but a large income would be provided. She replied that she was grateful for his thoughtfulness but that she could not accept the money. All the years God had taken care of them and if she accepted it the security would no longer be in God but in the money. In this case too there was an additional reason for refusal: she could not keep money in the bank when people needed it. The man was taken aback. But before he died he sent the money allocating it to be spent on particular pieces of work.

Again, Mother Teresa does not allow her co-workers to do fund raising for the work. The co-workers are groups of people who have not taken vows but are expected to care for, and share their possessions with poor, sick, lonely and neglected people in their own vicinity. There are many thousands of co-workers round the world. At the beginning some groups did fund raising but Mother Teresa asked them to stop. This came as a great surprise; many co-workers thought that fund raising was their principal task. The only fund raising that is permitted is for local needs such as an outing for house-bound people. But although they are not to raise money the co-workers help by acknowledging and transmitting the donations which come in without being asked for.

Mother Teresa does not take money into account when invited to start a new piece of work. If she is satisfied that the work is really needed and that it is one that her Sisters can do she agrees to take it up without waiting for funds to be available. Some money is brought for immediate needs and in a poor area money may continue to be sent from the centre where it comes in. An opening donation is generally offered and is accepted but regular support is refused. I asked Mother Teresa quite specifically whether she went forward without waiting for funds. "Yes", she replied, "we simply start".

Mother Teresa does not maintain a large balance of funds on which she could draw in a difficult period; she uses the money as it comes in. All the funds are transferred to the actual work.

While Mother Teresa does not accept maintenance grants and endowments and while she does not allow money to be asked for, she does, of course, accept donations. That is what keeps the work going; she wants people, she says, to give till it hurts. Sometimes people and organisations give very large sums and this is gratefully received. And if a person asks what particular piece of work he or she can give for they are told what is needed at the time. Mother Teresa does not mind asking for certain things for special purposes, for example land or buildings. But she will not ask people for money to support the work; she asks God. From the beginning her reliance has been on God alone.

2. Assessment of Evidential Value

Her life and work has enormous humanitarian value. Does it in addition have any evidential value?

The first point to note is that a prediction was made. It is that God will provide. The work accordingly is carried on without any financial planning. There is no estimate of probable expenses, and as has been made clear, no effort is made to raise the money needed. Money simply comes into the bank and goes out again. That does not mean that there is no accounting. In India, for example, each house sends its accounts to the Motherhouse in Calcutta every month for auditing. And, under the Foreign

Contibutions Act, all money received from abroad has to be reported in detail to the Government. There are people trained to do this work. But accounting for money received is quite different from limiting expenditure in accordance with estimated income. There is no such estimate. For the basis on which the work is carried out is that in one way or another God will provide what is needed.

Second, the prediction has been fulfilled. Over a period of forty years it has not been falsified. There have been no closures of work for lack of funds. There have been some closures for other reasons. In Sri Lanka, for example, the work was discontinued because the Government wanted all the Sisters to be nationals and this was not in accordance with the spirit of the work. But there have been no closures for financial reasons. Nor has there been any limit to expansion for lack of funds. On the contrary, as just described, expansion goes on without considering funds. And always the funds needed have come in.

The straightforward conclusion is that the prediction has withstood the test of time and that Mother Teresa's experience does provide evidence for the reality of God. But, before this can be accepted a question has to be asked. May there not be natural explanations that will by themselves account for the maintenance and development of the work?

In the first place it may be pointed out that there are other charitable organisations which have grown very large without dependence on providence. And again it has to be said that where there are needs which are known and organisations which tackle them effectively, people will respond generously. But it has to be remembered that in the first ten years of her work Mother Teresa was not widely known. Yet she was able to do extensive work in Calcutta; the money did come. Nor do other large charitable organisations put the restrictions on funding which Mother Teresa does. In particular they do not refuse money and they rely heavily on appeals and other fund raising activities. It is doubtful whether sufficient funds would be forthcoming without them. That puts in doubt the soundness of an argument based on comparison with other organisations.

In the second place it may be argued that the essential requirement for the kind of work done is confidence. It does not have to be confidence that God will provide. Confidence that people will respond to efforts made to help those in real distress would be all that is required. It would enable such work to be started and to expand without having to wait until funds came in. Certainly confidence would enable the work to be started. But for work to be carried on for forty years with rapid expansion, the funds needed would actually have to come in and come in on time. It is not confidence in the long run that counts but the money expected actually arriving. There is an abandon in Mother Teresa's confidence which enables her to take on new commitments without any financial planning. It is fortified by the fact that funds have always come in as required. And that is a matter not of confidence but of experience.

Mother Teresa did not set out to find experimental evidence for the reality of God. She set out to serve the poorest of the poor. For her the reality of God was not in doubt and reliance on the providence of God for the work she was sure he was calling her to do was natural. Certainly such reliance is exceptional; Father Van Exem thinks that Mother Teresa's outstanding characteristic is her absolute faith in God. But forty years of remarkable activity has given her no reason to amend her faith. "I have put God to the test," she told me.

Chapter VIII
Creation and Evil

The most serious objection to belief in the reality of God is the fact of evil. There is a great deal of suffering in the world. When people are directly involved it may come as a very sharp challenge to belief. But it raises a real problem for others also. Evil as suffering does not count against all forms of religious belief. It is especially to Christianity that it is a challenge. This is because God is understood as being both good and omnipotent. It would certainly appear that if God were good he would want a world without evil and if he were all-powerful he would have it so.

The problem of evil arises in connection with providence: why does God not intervene to prevent suffering? This was discussed in Chapter V. Here we have to take up the further question: why did God create a world with so much evil in it? Before discussion this question something should be said about creation itself.

1. Creation

To create means to bring into being. The arguments discussed in Chapter III are arguments from the world to a Creator. The cosmological argument moves from a succession of dependent beings to ultimate self-existing being. The teleological argument moves from the ordered complexity of the world to Divine direction. God brings into being the world and all the things in the world both living and non-living. Here we have to discuss, so far as is possible from the standpoint of the world, what creation involves.

The Christian doctrine, from about the beginning of the third century, has been that the world was created out of nothing— *ex nihilo* in the celebrated phrase. Frances Young makes clear that the doctrine is not, as is sometimes supposed, a Biblical or a Jewish one; it is an early Christian doctrine. It appears first in the writing of Theophilus of Antioch in the latter part of the second century and in Tertullian shortly afterwards. Tertullian was faced with alternatives that had already been set out but answered differently. Either the world was created out of the Divine being or it was created out of pre-existing matter. His answer was to reject both; the world was created out of nothing.[1]

The doctrine does not specify how the world was made. What it does is to exclude two contemporary ideas on the origin of the world. One is that the world is an emanation from the being of God. As the sun gives out light without apparently suffering any diminution so it is with God. This is not an idea which is compatible with the Biblical understanding of God. It is at variance in two ways. In the first place, so far from the world being an emanation coming from God by necessity, it is understood to have come into being by the will and power of God; there is a conscious intention to create. In the second place, emanation gives the world too close an affinity with God; rather the world is understood to be quite distinct from God and of a different nature.

The other idea excluded by the doctrine of creation out of nothing is that the world was made from pre-existing matter. This came from Platonism, widely held at the time. Plato had given in the *Timaeus* what he called a likely account of creation. This became understood literally. The world was made by a divine craftsman, the Demiurge. It was made out of pre-existing matter on the pattern of the eternal Forms. Wiles points out that the idea of pre-existing matter had a special attraction: evil could be attributed to the recalcitrance of primal matter so that God is not responsible for it. Tertullian and Origen, both of whom explicitly stated that creation was out of nothing, were fully aware of this. They rejected the easy way out and held that the world depends on God alone.[2] Ultimate being is God and not also pre-existing matter.

It has been made clear by Torrance that the doctrine of creation out of nothing leads to the idea that the world is both contingent and rational. The word contingent means not by necessity. Something or some event just happens to be as it is; it might have been quite different. There may have been, in Leibniz's phrase, other possible worlds. But it is this particular world which God chose to bring into being. As created by God it might be expected that the world would have a rational structure and so it has. But in a contingent world there is no way in which the rational structure could be grasped *a priori*. It is found only by patient scientific investigation. What this brings to light is a marvelously complex rational structure and one that our minds are able to apprehend.[3] In biology especially both contingency and rational order are readily apparent.

The Early Church and the Mediaeval Church knew very little about the world in comparison with what we have learned from scientific study. This scientific knowledge should enable us to go further in understanding how creation was carried out. It is generally held that the world originated with the Big Bang in which space and time as well as matter came into being. Not all theories require an abrupt beginning. This is a matter for natural science to decide, not for theology. What it does hold is that the world owes its origin to God who is ultimate being. He saw to it, as it were, that the world had certain specific features, such as the laws of physics, which made possible subsequent development.

On the subsequent course of creation science has thrown a great deal of light. The matter which was formed following the Big Bang was briefly described in Chapter III. It was mentioned that hydrogen, the simplest atom, has a nucleus made of one proton with one electron in orbit. The next simplest atom is deuterium which has an extra particle in the nucleus, the neutron. Protons and neutrons are themselves complex with the elementary particles, the quarks and gluons, as their constituents. It is possible that quarks themselves may prove to be composite. Whether or not this is so, the basic matter of the universe so constituted and its development in other atoms, proves to have been of extra–ordinary potentiality. From it came the whole rich complex world.

In the development of the world there are, from a theological point of view, two main principles.

First, there is a large measure of independence. Things happen as a result of their own secondary causes. God does not control everything in the world as believers in universal providence affirm. But here is something more. The world is to a considerable extent free in the development of its forms and structures. It is not only the behaviour of existing creatures that is to a large extent free; creatures have a relative independence in how they develop.

It is especially in living things that the idea of development is most familiar. And it is in these that the course of development has been studied in great detail. Some account of it was given in Chapter III and not much needs adding here. The primary source of development is mutation. Unless changes took place in the genetic material each generation would be a copy of the last. There could be individual variation due to other changes in the chromosomes but this does not make a new species; that requires mutation. Natural selection gives direction to evolution by determining which of the new forms are to survive. But it is mutation that is responsible for the newness.

Evolution by chance mutation and natural selection allows a great deal of openness in the forms arrived at. Not every new form that comes into being is well adapted to the environment and not all survive. Others are adapted in surprising ways. It is well known, for example, that both human beings and mosquitoes are involved in the life cycle of the malaria parasite and there are some life cycles stranger still. Other new forms have enhanced powers of various kinds and can maintain a place in the world.

There are far more species with no members still alive than those represented today. Of course it is only we who regret the extinction of a species. The individuals who make up a species have no concern beyond themselves and their immediate offspring when young. But that is not to say that the living world is just as if the extinct species had never been. R.A. Fisher, chief architect of what is called the evolutionary synthesis—between Mendelian genetics and Darwinian natural selection—brings out this point. The extinct species "must have left indelible memorials in their effects on species still surviving. Who knows if the mammals would ever have evolved but for the creative activity of the dinosaurs!"[4]

The second main principle in the creation of the world is direction. Not much need be said here as the evidence for direction was discussed in Chapter III in connection with ordered complexity. It was argued there that the immensely delicate and complex order in the world could not have come into being without some intelligent direction. In particular it was suggested that the very precise values of the forces at the beginning of the universe, the origin of life and the development of the human central nervous system required some sort of direction to account for them. The argument is reinforced by the great number of beautiful plants and animals that there are in the world.

There is also a religious consideration. Anyone who has been aware of God's guidance in his own life and especially of striking answers to prayer, cannot think that we have been brought into being solely by natural influences. It is not possible to think that finally it was good luck that produced self-conscious creatures, capable of fellowship with God. While granting the importance of chance in the evolutionary process there must also have been a directing purpose.

If it is granted that a directing purpose must have been at work the question arises as to how it was exercised. This also was briefly discussed in Chapter III. One possibility is that the direction was embodied in a single Divine action at the beginning of the creative process. Things were so ordered that self-conscious life would emerge without the need for any further Divine action. Everything was pre-programmed at the start. No doubt something like that did happen; some kind of direction must have been given in the originating creative act which continued into the subsequent development of the world. But if it was complete the world would have had no independence in its development which we have been asserting that it did have. And if in the creative process there was an important element of spontaneity further direction would have been needed at some points. In such a world a single Divine action would not have been sufficient; there would have to be providential action if the purpose of God in creation was to be realised.

2. Natural Evil

The evils which come, or come largely, from natural causes are of many kinds: earthquakes and hurricanes, famines, diseases, mental and physical disabilities present from birth, animals preying on one another, and many more that we are all familiar with. How can we hold that such a world is the creation of God who is both good and omnipotent?

As was said when discussing Providence in Human Life, the evils which befall people are not, at least for the most part, sent by God. They do not come in order to correct us nor to provide an opportunity to develop patience and sympathy, although they may have these effects. They come from the workings of the world. When discussing creation it was stated that the world had a large measure of independence; God does not control everything that happens in the world. Both in the development of its forms and structures and in the behaviour that comes from the way they are constituted, the world is to a considerable degree autonomous. The evils arising in the natural world which come to people are the outcome of this autonomy.

Could God have created a better world than this, a world with as many good things in it and fewer evils? Leibniz maintains that our world is one out of an infinite number that it would have been possible for God to create. A possible world is one that is logically possible; if there are self-contradictions in it, the world is not possible. God, Leibniz suggests, chose to create the best world out of an infinite number of possible ones.[5] The best world is the one with the greatest balance of good over evil. A possible world might be one with no evil. But it would be less good than our actual world. That is because some great goods are connected with evils. Freedom of the will is a great good but it is also an important source of evil so that we cannot have the one without the other. Leibniz thought that everything that was evil in the world was connected with what was good. This is because God would create the best possible world and he believed that he had demonstrated the reality of God. But it has been pointed out that this is not our position; the reality of God is the main question at issue. So we cannot say that all the evils in the world are necessary ones in the sense of being connected with great goods. Nor can we say, without further argument, that this is the best of all possible worlds.[6]

But now it looks as if there are not many possible worlds that could be created. McLean has drawn attention to the relevance of the anthropic reasoning referred to in Chapter III.[7] As mentioned there, a number of conditions in the development of the universe had to be precisely as they were for life and consciousness to be possible. The delicacy of adjustment in some cases is very remarkable indeed. It seems unlikely that there could be many other worlds substantially different from this one that could produce living and conscious creatures. Some eminent cosmologists, Stephen Hawking, for example, think it likely that it could only be done by the laws of physics and initial conditions that made this world. McLean presented his case modestly as an addition to Tennant's position on the problem of evil which will be discussed very shortly. But McLean's ideas stand on their own as an important contribution. This world, with its good and evil features, is one of very few possible material worlds. It is unlikely that a better world—one with life and consciousness but with fewer evils—could have been created.

Natural evils come about in the world in two main ways.

(a) The Natural Regularities of the World

Tennant has drawn attention to the natural regularities of the world as being the prime cause of natural evils. The evils are the by-product of the regular functioning of nature. It is logically impossible to keep the regularity and remove the evils that go with it and God cannot do what is logically impossible. The regular functioning of nature is vital. The laws of nature, which express its regularities, are essential to the structures and processes of the world. Without them the natural world would not be an orderly and dependable system but a chaos in which, in so far as a world at all like the present could develop, anything might follow anything. It is not only the natural world that would be affected; the development of human life and civilisation is dependent on the regular working of nature.

But if this regularity makes possible the development and functioning of the good things in the world, it makes possible also the evil things; we cannot have the one without the other.[9] McLean, in the article already referred to, gives an excellent example of the kind of thing that Tennant had in mind. DNA, because of its ability to replicate itself, enables cell reproduction of all kinds to take place in living organisms. If a cell is damaged by a factor in the environment so that it becomes malignant, its reproduction of itself is also made possible by DNA which is an integral part of all living cells. What's sauce for the goose is sauce for the gander.

The regular functioning of nature may lead to suffering in many ways.

Earthquakes may bring disaster on a vast scale and in a very short time. Tens of thousands, and sometimes hundreds of thousands of lives may be lost in a single earthquake. In a city there is extensive damage to houses, offices and factories. It is, in fact, the collapse of buildings and the fires that follow which account for most of the loss of life. Earthquakes are caused by huge plates of the earth's crust moving and rubbing together along particular fault lines. They are the outcome of the regular behaviour of natural forces.

So it is with volcanos. Molten silicate material under pressure makes vents, or escapes from existing ones, in the earth's crust. This may cause destruction in which lives are lost and homes destroyed. But many volcanos erupt under the oceans.

Hurricanes are violent windstorms. Especially destructive are cyclones or typhoons as they are called in the China seas where they are relatively frequent. In cyclones, the winds blow in a circular manner around the centre and the whole system moves causing disaster as it goes. Houses collapse, trees are blown down and crops are destroyed. Torrential rainfall coupled with high seas may cause flooding in low lying coastal areas such as the Bay of Bengal, with a great deal of damage and loss of life. Hurricanes are caused by intense depressions which result in the disastrous winds.

Floods may come from the sea especially in a hurricane as just mentioned. More commonly they come from rivers where the water level is very high as a result of excessive rainfall. They cause loss of life to people and animals and extensive damage to crops and to buildings. The Yangze and the Yellow rivers in China have flooded on many occasions and brought extensive devastation.

Famine results from the loss of the staple food supply in a region. It is often a long drawn out calamity as the food supply becomes less and less. The main cause of famine is widespread crop failure. This may be the result of flood and especially of drought and from the destruction of crops by disease and by insects. Like the other evils mentioned, famine comes directly or indirectly from the regular functioning of nature in an autonomous world. Famine may also come from war which is a moral evil.

(b) The Evolution of the World

Beginning from nothing how is a complex world of plants and animals and human beings to be made? We do not know whether a special creation of each species would have been possible. But that is not in fact the way it was done; it was done by gradual development. In Chapter III the early history of the universe was sketched as was the development of living things. The evolution of the physical universe presents no challenge to affirming the goodness and power of God nor does the evolution of plants. But the evolution of sentient animals does. We do not know whether mutation and natural selection was the only way by which the complex structures and lives of animals and human beings could have been built up. But, again, that is how it was done and suffering is involved in the process.

Mutation, as mentioned earlier, is the source of newness in plants and animals. Only some of the changes brought about by mutation are sufficient to produce a new species. Of those that are produced not all survive and reproduce. Smaller changes also are by no means always beneficial to the creatures that have them. There are, for example, a number of deformities and diseases in human beings that are the result of mutations. Mutation plays a necessary part in the creation of this full and varied world. But it does not do so without a cost in suffering.

Evolution takes place not only because new forms are produced by mutation but also because they are sorted out by natural selection. Most are rejected; the creatures that have them are at a disadvantage. But other changes are advantageous. Mutations, for example, that lead to more sensitive hearing are incorporated into a species because those animals that have them are more successful in the struggle for existence.

Did there have to be a struggle for existence if the living world was to evolve progressively? The answer is yes, for evolution is not necessarily progressive and indeed may not occur at all. If there were no factors in the environment making it difficult for creatures to survive and reproduce new forms and new species would not develop. Existing species of lizards, for example, have shown little change over millions of years. They are so well adapted to their niche in the environment that they cannot be bettered. There are many ways in which the environment is hard and new and better structures are developed in adjusting to it. The weather is an important part of an animal's environment. If it becomes colder animals may develop coats of hair as a protection. But changes in the weather are not steadily progressive over the long periods of evolutionary time and so do not elicit a steadily progressive response.

Dawkins points out that there is one part of the environment which does change progressively. This is made up of animals themselves.[10] Among them are both predators who need to eat and their prey which need to avoid being eaten. The two sides develop in parallel as the generations go on. An improvement in structure or function on the one side made by cumulative selection is met by a corresponding improvement on the other side. The characteristics that develop progressively in this way among predators include speed, visual acuity, teeth and claws; those of the prey, speed, alertness, burrowing and nocturnal habits. Tigers have developed in size, in camouflage and in cunning so as to keep up with improved capacities in their prey, animals such as antelopes. And they in turn have developed in the swiftness of their reactions and in their ability to run. Of course this kind of change takes place over the very long periods of evolutionary time and is often intermittent.

One of the structures which has developed in the ongoing struggle between predators and prey is the brain. The brain has become bigger and more complex. A monkey with its big brain is much less dependent on in-built reactions than animals with smaller brains. It can think what to do in a particular situation rather than respond in a more standardised way. Whether the brain could have developed in any other environmental situation is impossible to say. But it was in the struggle between predators and prey that it did in fact develop.

We have a paradoxical attitude towards predators. On the one hand we may be appalled when we think of the killing that goes on day after day or when we see it pictured in a documentary film. On the other hand we think that the world would be a poorer place if it did not contain predatory animals like lions and tigers. Tigers in India are protected even though they kill quite a lot of human beings. In 1978, towards the end of the first stage of Project Tiger, it was estimated that in the reservation south of Calcutta about a hundred lives a year were lost. Not everyone would agree that such a price should be paid. But even to consider such a price indicates where the balance in our attitude to tigers and other predatory animals lies; we think the world is better for having tigers in it. They have a value in themselves apart from being, along with other predators, necessary for the progress of evolution.

Since the world has a relative independence and was to a large extent free to create itself, God is not directly responsible for predatory animals with their claws and teeth and poison fangs, nor for parasites. But he is indirectly responsible. He did not have to bring into being a world like this one. Yet a world of wonderful beauty with living and self-conscious creatures in

it is a great good. We have seen that the way it was produced
is likely to have been the only way it could have been done. If
that is so it may be judged that the suffering of sentient creatures
was not too great a price to pay.

3. Moral Evil

Moral evil is the suffering that human beings bring about. In the
course of history it has been very extensive. In some ways things
have got better as time has gone on; the treatment of law-breakers,
for example, is more humane than it once was. In other ways
things seem to have got worse and the twentieth century must be
among the worst of all for this kind of evil. There have been
wars, persecutions, genocide, cruelty, torture and indifference to
the suffering of other people. God had created people capable of
acting in this sort of way and indeed liable to do so. If God is
omnipotent why did he not create human beings in such a way
that they would always do right? To say that God is omnipotent
and wholly good while the world is full of evil appears to be
contradictory. This has been presented as a logical argument
against the reality of God. It has also been developed as an
empirical argument against the probability of the existence of
God.

(a) Free Will

What has become known as the Free Will Defense is the most
important way of countering the arguments. Freedom is something
of the highest value. It is part of what gives human life its
greatness. We are free to respond to the call of God or to turn
away; free in any particular situation to align ourselves with the
will of God or not to do so; free to follow ideals. We are
responsible for what we do and for what we leave undone. We
do not do what is right on any occasion because we are
conditioned to do so. We do right, perhaps at considerable cost,
of our own choice. A world which contains free and responsible
creatures we judge to be a better world than one which lacks
them. But it does mean that the free creatures may do evil as
well as good. This is the basis of the Free Will Defense. Following
Plantinga's way of setting it out, the defence centres on the

claim that it is possible that God could not have created a universe containing moral good without creating one that also contained moral evil.[11] It may be that was not possible.

But could God not have created beings who were free yet always did right? If we are created so that we sometimes do right, why should we not be created so that we always did so? That would mean that in this respect our conduct is determined. Is freedom compatible with causal determinism?

To hold that freedom is compatible with determinism depends on taking a particular view of freedom. Freedom on this view means that a person is free to act in accordance with his nature.[12] So long as nothing stands in the way he is free. If there are no external conditions which prevent freedom of action, and there are no internal conditions, such as an obsessional neurosis, which prevent it, the person is free. So on a compatibilist view choice is determined by the nature of the person and yet it is free because there are no constraints on his acting naturally.

The reason for holding that human freedom is compatible with determinism does not come in the first place from a close examination of what people are able to do. It comes from a prior acceptance of determinism. This is accepted chiefly because the description by physiologists of how the brain works is determinist. And there must be a correlation between the working of the brain and the working of the mind. If the one is determined it is not easy to see how the other can be undetermined. In addition one of the consequences of psychoanalysis is to put in doubt whether we can be sure that our choices do not have causes. There are fears and hostilities and defences developed very early in life of which we are quite unaware. Considerations of this kind are a further reason for thinking that complete freedom of the will is an illusion; we do what various factors, including psychological forces, cause us to do. But it must be noted that the case is not proved. From the fact that there are hidden forces and that they sometimes profoundly affect what we do it does not follow that all our choices are determined.

If freedom is held only in the limited sense described above, it means that people could be created free and yet determined so that they always did right. In that case the Free Will Defense fails.

The alternative position on human freedom is that it is incompatible with determinism. Here freedom means very much more. It means that, in the absence of constraints, in any particular situation a person could have chosen to act differently from how he actually did. Or, to put it more briefly, he could have chosen otherwise. This is the libertarian understanding of freedom.

The libertarian can agree that what a person does is the outcome of the kind of person he is. It can readily be admitted that a great deal of our conduct is not dependent on deliberate choice; it springs directly from character—a generous action may be done almost without thinking. It can also be agreed that character may set limits to freedom of choice. There may be actions a person simply cannot bring himself to take. Yet there are occasions when a person may act in a way that is quite contrary to his own character. A person, for example, may be very diffident and this will show itself in his ordinary conduct. But on some occasion he may make a stand against what other people are doing and maintain it in the face of persistent criticism. The libertarian has to draw a distinction between a person's character and the self which is expressed in his decisions. By character we mean a disposition to act in certain kinds of ways. The self which deliberates and decides is something other than this.

The claim that we have real freedom of choice has received very strong reinforcement from existentialist philosophy and the literature based upon it. Existentialists have been criticised for not clearly distinguishing the different kinds of choices that we make. Some are quite ordinary, just deciding what we want to do, for example. But there are other choices which are not ordinary. There are choices between what we want to do and what we ought to do and this may be difficult or dangerous. And there are choices between two different obligations so that there is a conflict of loyalties. Detailed and imaginative descriptions have been given of the kinds of situation in which many people during the twentieth century have found themselves in: military operations, resistance movements, life under political oppression with a constant threat of arrest and torture. There are terrible choices to be made involving the life and well-being of oneself and other people. Individuals who have made them certainly think that different courses of action were open to them, that they chose freely and that they could have chosen otherwise.

The libertarian position is based on careful observation of what people are sometimes able to do. But in maintaining that we sometimes exercise real freedom in deliberation and decision an immense claim is being made. It is that the self can set itself, as it were, above the whole network of causal conditions in which we act, including our own dispositions. Yet it is able to enter into them. It is itself able to initiate chains of cause and effect. In affirming this, and in denying that all action is determined by antecedent causes, something of profound metaphysical significance is being said. But this is not a unique case: it is well known that in the underlying world of sub-atomic physics determinism does not hold. It is not clear whether or not this has any relationship to human freedom of decision.

Freedom in the libertarian sense is incompatible with determinism. If we possess libertarian freedom we cannot be determined so that we only do what is right; we are free to do evil also. Since it is possible that we do have libertarian freedom it cannot be said that God could make free creatures who only did right; it is possible that he could not do so. It is possible, then, that God could not have created a universe containing moral good but no moral evil.

(b) Fundamental Urges

It is not only that we are free to do good or evil; we have a tendency to do evil although we are not bound to do so. In all our conduct we are inclined to follow our own interests. In the common phrase we look after number one. Even our generous actions are often partly motivated by self-interest. This is something deep in human life and operates just as strongly, if not so openly, in the educated as in the uneducated. It is active not only in individuals but also in groups. As groups also we pursue wealth and status and power. And we compete with other groups doing the same. Nation states are even more ruthless in pursuing their interests than are the individuals who make them up. This is because they do not have the element of self-giving which is part of the structure of personal relationships. There is nothing to modify the bias towards self-interest which is present in us all.

This tendency to seek our own interest is partly a legacy of our evolutionary history. Creatures formed by mutation and natural selection are bound to look after themselves. The only way to survive in the struggle for existence is for each individual to seek its own interests. It has to get what it needs to maintain itself—food, water, space to live in, for example—never mind anyone else. As Dawkins puts it, "... selfishness is to be expected in any entity that deserves the title of a basic unit of natural selection".[13] One such unit is the individual creature. Its behaviour is programmed to ensure its own survival and reproduction, not that of others, even of the same species. In the world of living creatures nothing is more basic than self-preservation. God could not have brought into being a living world by means of mutation and natural selection without creatures having a basic urge to self-preservation. This biological requirement of self-preservation leads in human society to the moral problem of selfishness. It is not the only factor making for selfishness, but it is basic.

Self-preservation is not the only deep-seated urge; there is also self-giving. It is the urge to give oneself and give oneself wholly to another.[14] In human beings it may also be directed towards a cause. Life in society could hardly go on and develop without the urge to self-giving so that people were motivated by the urge to self-preservation alone. But if wrongly directed it too can do much harm. When it is directed to limited ends such as a racial group or misconceived ends such as Communism great evil may be done. The urge to self-giving often does not operate alone. It may be combined with self-righteousness and it may lack any concern for people who do not belong to the group or are not associated with the ideology to which it is directed.

(c) Horrendous Evil

There are evils so great in their extent or so appalling in what they do to people as to produce a feeling of horror in those who directly or indirectly come to know about them. A member of Parliament who visited the Belsen death camp not long after its liberation committed suicide shortly after she returned home. This is one example of a horrendous evil. There have been similar horrors in other parts of the world. In our country we read in the newspapers of horrendous evils perpetrated on individuals. These are moral evils. Natural evils can also be horrendous, notably famines and earthquakes. The question here is, can reasons be given as to why God permits such evils?

The issue is more one of providence than of creation. If there are evils threatening why does God not act to stop them happening? God's inaction in the face of evils is discussed in Chapter V. It is maintained that God could not intervene to prevent all serious evils without upsetting the regularities on which human life depended. Nor does he normally act to give a deliverance from evil to some people that is denied to others. And he respects human freedom so that the consequences of these actions, however serious, are allowed to work themselves out. But granting that this may meet the case of ordinary evils, is it adequate to horrendous evils?

The best way of answering this question is probably by looking at particular examples of horrendous evils. The one most frequently discussed is one of the most appalling: the destruction of about five million Jews—the holocaust as it is often termed. It may be mentioned that this was not a unique event, only the worst of a whole series of attacks made on Jews in Europe. But it was unique in its scale and in its systematic planning and execution.

In July 1938 a conference was called by President Roosevelt to save the Jews in Germany. It met at Evian in France. By then it was known that the Jews faced extermination if they did not get out and at that time Germany was willing to let them go. There were in Germany and Austria only 570,000 Jews; the vast majority of those who were later exterminated came from elsewhere in Europe. The conference was attended by thirty two nations. The first speaker was Roosevelt's special ambassador. Since America had called the conference his speech was awaited with the greatest anticipation; perhaps the United States would take all the Jews. The ambassador explained why the United States could not increase its current quota of immigrants, not all of whom were Jews. Then speaker after speaker rose to regret that their countries could not accept Jewish immigrants or only a few. There was a continuation organisation which did manage, with the help of pressure by individuals in the Evian nations, to settle a number of Jews. But the conference itself was indifferent. This was not lost on Hitler. In a speech immediately afterwards he observed that the other world while oozing with sympathy for the Jews, was hard and obdurate when it came to helping them. In the end five million Jews were annihilated because of the fanatical hatred of Hitler; but also because of the indifference of countries which could have acted at the critical time.[15]

The fate of Jews in other countries in Europe who were brought to the camps and exterminated depended on something different. In the twenties the failure of Britain and France to act generously and even reasonably towards the defeated Germany made possible the rise of Hitler. In the thirties the failure was in not responding effectively to aggression or the threat of aggression at a time when Hitler could have been stopped. A key event was the occupation of the demilitarised Rhineland in 1936. The French, to whom the issue was of vital importance could have acted alone; they were quite strong enough at the time to have done so. But they wanted and asked for support from Britain to which they were entitled. This was refused; Britain would do nothing that might lead to war, small as the risk was. So acting against the advice of his generals, Hitler had his first triumph. Had action been taken, so far as we can tell, there would have been no war and no holocaust. A little later first Austria and then Czechoslovakia were threatened. Other countries, notably Britain and France, failed to support them although they had obligations under the Covenant of the League of Nations and although the Soviet Union was ready to join with them. There were reasons for the failure. But it had terrible consequences. Could God be expected to intervene to prevent the consequences of rational and moral failure?

Perhaps he could. But we should look again at our idea of the goodness of God. Paul, writing to the Romans, speaks in another connection of the kindness and severity of God (11.22). In commenting on the verse Barrett remarks that kindness and severity are equally attributes of God.[16]

Many of the words we use of God are metaphors. We borrow words whose meaning is drawn from human experience and clearly they cannot all apply literally to God. Yet we do not use them without reason. There are things we have to say about God which makes it appropriate to use a word even if there are aspects of its meaning which are not appropriate. So in speaking of the severity of God we do not mean everything that we mean when using the word in connection with human beings. But we do mean some things. They come, of course, not from the actions and characters of human beings, but from what we can understand of the actions of God in creation and providence.

It is suggested by Köster that Paul was writing under the influence of the apocryphal book *The Wisdom of Solomon*.[17] For the writer, as for Paul, the kindness and severity of God is one of the things that are to be seen on looking back on the history of Israel and a word related to the one Paul uses for severity occurs there a number of times. In Romans 11.22 Paul is thinking of a severity actively carried out. Writing of the wrath of God, a similar idea, in Romans 1.18ff, Paul uses the repeated phrase "God gave them up" (vv. 24, 26, 28). His severity was shown not in acting but in not acting and allowing the disasters that inevitably follow human sin and folly to take place.

In spite of what has been said the question must arise as to whether God is not indifferent to the lives of human beings. Paul did not think so. In Romans 11.22 he speaks of the kindness as well as of the severity of God. The two attributes are not contrary to one another and both are to be seen in events in the world.

The kindness and severity of God comes out in what seems a very strange way in an incident that occurred in connection with the Shanxi famine of 1876-79 described in Chapter VI. God responded to the prayers of a woman who trusted and obeyed. In great perplexity as to what she ought to do in the face of conflicting claims and conflicting advice she prayed for guidance in a particular way. The guidance came just as she asked. The particularity of the events makes chance unlikely. And yet God did not intervene in the long and terrible famine and left nature to take its course. All that we can say about this strange exemplification of kindness and severity is this: God is creator and director of the world and does not ordinarily intervene for the reasons set out in Chapter V. God is also the Heavenly Father who enters into personal relationships with men and women and reveals himself in acts of providence and answered prayer.

Another way in which we know that God is not indifferent about people is the life and death of Jesus Christ. It was mentioned in Chapter I that from Apostolic times it has always been maintained that God was uniquely present in Jesus Christ. His life therefore manifests under human conditions something of the life of God. Nothing is more evident in it than his care for men, women and children. He had compassion on a crowd because they were harassed and helpless like sheep without a shepherd (Matt. 9.36); and again on a crowd because they had nothing to eat (Matt. 15.32); and on a leper (Mk. 1.41). He wept over Jerusalem when he thought of its future (Lk. 19.41). He carried on his mission although he knew it would end in death. The love he had for people is a reflection of the love of God.

Jesus could be severe too although he was not an austere man. It comes out in his condemnation of the scribes and pharisees, or some of them. For example, he condemned their insistence on people scrupulously carrying out what they took to be the requirements of the law and which were a heavy burden to people in ordinary life although not to them (Matt. 23.4). Jesus made severe demands on his disciples. "So, therefore, whoever of your does not renounce all that he has cannot be my disciple" (Lk. 14.33). "If anyone comes to me and does not hate his own father and mother and wife and children, and brothers and sisters, yes, and even his own life, he cannot become my disciple" (Lk. 14.26). "Do you think that I have come to give peace on earth? No, I tell you, but rather division" (Lk. 12.51). Yet Jesus' most evident characteristic was not his severity but his love.

When Jesus went up to Jerusalem his death was not only the outcome of love and faithfulness on his part, of culpable blindness on the part of the Jewish authorities and of weakness on the part of the Roman governor; always it has been understood as being also an act of the providence of God. As Peter is reported to have put it, "This Jesus, delivered up according to the definite plan and foreknowledge of God, you crucified and killed by the hands of lawless men" (Acts 2.23). The Cross was a horrendous evil. What it reveals is not the indifference of God to these events but his kindness and severity: severity in the condemnation of sin; kindness in the act of redemption.

References

1. Frances Young, Creatio ex Nihilo: a Context for the Emergence of the Christian Doctrine of Creation, *Scottish Journal of Theology*, 44, Edinburgh, 1991, pp. 142ff.

2. Maurice Wiles, *God's Action in the World*, London, 1986, p. 15.

3. T.F. Torrance, *Divine and Contingent Order*, Oxford, 1981, pp. 22f.

4. Eddington Memorial Lecture 1950, *Creative Aspects of Natural Law*, quoted by Alister Hardy, *The Living Stream*, London, 1965, p. 275.

5. G.W. Leibniz, *Theodicy*, 1710, ed. A. Farrer, London, 1952, p. 128.

6. Nelson Pike, Hume on Evil, in *The Problem of Evil*, ed. M.M. and R.M. Adams, Oxford, 1990, p. 46.

7. Murdith McLean, Residual Natural Evil and Anthropic Reasoning, *Religious Studies*, 27, Cambridge, 1991, pp. 180ff.

8. S.W. Hawking, *A Brief History of Time*, London, 1988, 174.

9. F.R. Tennant, *Philosophical Theology*, Vol. II, Cambridge, 1930, pp. 197ff.

10. R. Dawkins, *The Blind Watchmaker*, London, 1986, paperback ed. pp. 178ff.

11. A. Plantinga, *God, Freedom and Evil*, London, 1975, p. 31.

12. J.L. Mackie, *The Miracle of Theism*, Oxford, 1982, p. 166.

13. R. Dawkins, *The Selfish Gene*, new ed. Oxford, 1989, p. 33.

14. M.C. D'Arcy, *The Mind and Heart of Love*, London, 2nd ed., 1954, paperback ed. pp. 286f.

15. Peggy Mann, When the World Passed By on the Other Side, in *The Washington Post*, reprinted *The Guardian* Weekly, 7 May 1978.

16. C.K. Barrett, *The Epistle to the Romans*, London, 1957, p. 218.

17. H. Köster in *Theological Dictionary of the New Testament*, Vol. VIII, ed. G. Friedrich, 1969, E.T. Michigan, 1972, pp. 107f.

Chapter IX
Faith

We have examined the reasons for believing in the reality of God, those drawn from the world and those from providence and miracle. The latter required the detailed study of actual cases; in no other way can the claims to have experience of providence and miracle be assessed. We have also examined the objections to belief based on the evil in the world. It seems to me that these objections can be met. Taken together the case for belief in the reality of God is a strong one. It is strong probability; not certainty, that is given. But to believe on the basis of probability and act accordingly is perfectly reasonable. It is what we have to do in much of life.

There is a question of what part the will plays in belief. It is sometimes suggested that we believe what we want to believe and do not believe what we do not want to. Believing is chiefly a matter of the will. The place of the will in belief was discussed in a celebrated lecture by William James in 1896.[1] He agreed that in all matters where there was enough evidence, belief should be settled on the evidence. If the evidence was not complete it is right to withhold judgment. In all matters of pure knowledge, and in much practical life, it is right not to make a judgment without having full evidence.

But in many aspects of life incompleteness of evidence is characteristic. And it is just in matters which are most important in life that evidence is often inconclusive. In some situations things are too urgent to suspend judgment. In war, for example, a general seldom has complete evidence about the enemy's strength and dispositions. In situations of this kind two things can be done. Decision can be delayed until more information is available; or a decision can be made on the evidence that there is. In the latter case, says James, we take the risk about being wrong in the hope of being right. Unless we deliberately accept the risk of being wrong the chance of being right is gone.

But the fact of the matter is that a decision cannot be avoided. Suppose we prefer not to make a decision on the evidence we have; we will wait for sufficient evidence. That is a decision; it is a decision not to decide. In neither case is the decision based on evidence and logic; it is based on inclination. The decision to wait is no more rational than the decision to go forward on the evidence we have. What it is based on is the fear of being wrong. This is felt to be more important than the hope of being right.

James appears to argue for the right to believe what we like. That is not wholly so. He begins his lecture by making a distinction between hypotheses that are live and those that are dead. A hypothesis which there is no real possibility of believing is not a live option. He also makes a distinction between hypotheses which are of momentous importance to our lives and those which are trivial; it does not make any real difference whether we believe them or not. What he is concerned with is live options, which are of momentous importance, and where not to decide has the same outcome as deciding against. Suppose in such a case the evidence is not in itself sufficient for a decision. Then, because no decision counts as a decision against, James claims that we have the right to believe.

That is a strong case. But, as Bernard Williams insists, belief aims at truth, to believe something is to believe that it is true.[2] That is for the intellect nor for the will to decide. The will in belief does something different. In James' case, where the evidence is insufficient, it is actively to keep the matter open and not just let things slide. That means looking for further evidence and putting oneself in a position to learn of it. It may be that there is evidence but we have not discovered it because we have not been serious enough in trying to find it.

Yet the will does enter more intimately into believing. We have to be willing to believe and be ready for what believing entails. This applies not only to religious belief but is to be seen in other important aspects of life. We speak of refusal to believe. Something may be too painful to face. An attempt is made to interpret the evidence differently or to explain it away. And this may be persisted in until the evidence is overwhelming. Intellect and will cannot wholly be separated; for we are not detached minds but living persons.

Faith is more than belief, even firm belief. It is part of a personal relationship and this has other elements beside belief.

One is personal commitment. It is quite possible to believe in the existence of God and to carry out religious practices but to have little personal commitment. Belief in God and elaborate religious observances while living quite contrary to God's will was what Amos condemned in Israel:

> I hate, I despise your feasts,
>> and I take no delight in your solemn assemblies...
> Take away from me the noise of your songs;
>> to the melody of your harps I will not listen.
> But let justice roll down like waters,
>> and righteousness like an ever-flowing stream (5.21-24).

Personal commitment to God which carries with it the attempt to do his will is part of what is involved in a living relationship with God.

The New Testament also makes clear that faith involves more than belief. James, for example, ridicules the idea that there is any religious value simply in belief. "Thou believest that there is one God; thou doest well: the devils also believe and tremble" (James 2.19 AV). Luther made much the same point. Belief about God "is not faith so much as a sort of knowledge, of taking note of something". But to believe *in* God, he says, is to surrender myself to him, to enter into association with him, to take him as my foundation, even at the risk of life. It is this kind of belief alone which makes a person a Christian and through it all his desires are satisfied by God.[3] Faith in God means something much more than an intellectual belief in his reality; the heart and will enter into it. This must be so if it is faith that brings us into a personal relationship with God; the whole person must be involved.

That faith involves the whole person and not simply the intellect is evident from what happens in conversation. This is the most clear cut way of beginning the life of faith. The person is fully conscious of what he is doing and acts deliberately. It is not the only way of coming to faith and probably not the most usual. What is done explicitly and at a particular time in conversion may be done implicitly and gradually. It is a contention of one of the early psychologists of religion that people who had a definite conversion experience and those who did not, showed a parallel development and reached the same level of spiritual life in the end.[4] But the point here is a different one: both the unbeliever and the nominal believer may be converted. Certainly there is a difference; with the unbeliever there is an important intellectual aspect. Yet the inner experience in the two cases is not very different. This is just because the decision made does involve the whole personality. Beliefs are not held simply as intellectual convictions but are appropriated with a passionate intensity in which the whole being is involved. There is a new outlook and a new attitude to life and this is so whether the beliefs were previously held or not. Conversion means turning round—a change in the direction of life. For this to happen commitment does not have to be completed all at once. There may be a series of occasions when commitment is made more fully, each constituting something of a crisis in the life of the individual. On the other hand a spiritual life may have no crisis because there is no development. Belief remains limited to the intellect.

Decisive commitment is needed not only for the personal appropriation of religion; it is needed also because the objects of faith are unseen. By nature it is the evidence of our eyes we trust most readily; seeing is believing as the phrase goes. So it requires a belief to which we are wholly committed to act on what cannot be seen. That faith is difficult because it means being carried away from the things of sense to the invisible and incomprehensible God is a point which Luther repeatedly makes. It is singularly appropriate, as Rupp observes, that Luther's lectures on Hebrews break off suddenly at 11.27, which speaks of Moses and says, "For he endured as seeing him who is invisible". For now Luther had to leave his students and make a journey alone and on foot, through enemy territory, with his friends turning away from him and unaware of the amount of support that he had.[5] That is faith: amidst doubts and fears, without any perceptual or quasi-perceptual experience of the Divine, to go on. It is staking one's life on the invisible.

The third element in faith is trust. This is the one on which most stress was laid by Luther. Above all it was trust in the God who accepts us as we are. Luther saw us set, each one, in the presence of God. Before him the selfishness of our actions and the distortion of our lives are only too apparent. And God does not only look at the outward activity; he sees the desires and intentions of the heart. Excessive self-love, which is the essence of sin, pervades every aspect of our lives. We cannot get away from it by an effort of will. Nor is there anything we can do that will make amends for what we have done and for what we have failed to do. Our consciences bear witness that we deserve the condemnation of God. No satisfaction that we can make will put to rest an uneasy conscience. There is no escape in vigils and fasts and prayers and other austerities. Luther as a monk had followed them to the limit of his strength. Then he found in the Bible, and especially in Paul's epistles, the liberating message that he needed. God could condemn sin and yet forgive the sinner. He makes us right with himself in spite of our unrighteousness. And his acceptance of us is in no way dependent upon our good works. "He does not first accept our works, and save us. The word of God is prior to all else; faith follows it; then love succeeds faith, and gives rise to every good work".[6] On God's side all is grace; on our side only faith. Luther, in Williams James' phrase, "swept off by a stroke of his hand the very notion of a debt and credit account kept with individuals by the Almighty".[7] God accepts us in spite of our sin and failure; what we have to do is to trust him. This was not all Luther had to say about trust: it covers the whole of life. But trust in God's mercy to sinners is basic.

For Kierkegaard, too, trust was a vital aspect of faith. He, too, trusted God to accept us in spite of our unrighteousness. But especially he was concerned with trust in God in the events of this present life.[8] It had gradually become clear to him that his calling was to be a prophet of inner reformation. Like Jeremiah he took up his work unwillingly and apprehensively. He had to say to the church in Denmark that Christianity no longer existed. You do not become a Christian by being baptised in infancy, although the practice is of value in expressing the concern of the parents and of the Church. You become a Christian by deliberate decision. And it involves following Christ and taking seriously his hard sayings. Membership of the Church, a comfortable state institution, encourages the idea that Christianity is something external and superficial. Not that there is any harm in the state connection in itself, for what finally determines everything is the inner life of the individual with its struggles and decisions; external organisation is of small importance.[9]

Kierkegaard delivered his message in his popular writings. He was able to devote himself to writing because he had been left a considerable amount of money by his father. In expectation of an early death he used up a great deal of his capital. Then he sold his house to raise money. But much of it was lost in the inflation of 1848 caused by war and revolution. So in the last seven years of his life he was in constant anxiety about the future. He wrote in his journal in 1854, "That which takes most out of me in the long run is the thought of what is going to happen, and it is coming closer and closer".

Kierkegaard had been trained for the ministry and he was attracted by the idea of a country pastorate. The question he kept debating in his journal was whether to apply for one; he thought he would be given an appointment if he applied. He went so far on one occasion as to try to meet the Primate and the official concerned but was unable to do so. This he took as "a hint from Providence". The choice was now clear. Either live comfortably in a country parish, doing the work for which he was trained and

using the spare time for continuing his writing. But to have accepted a post in the Church as it was would have meant an accommodation. Or he could be true to his call, continue to attack the Church and trust in God alone for his material well-being. In fear and trembling he chose the latter, continuing his attack on the Church and using up his capital. The day he took the last of his money from the bank he fell paralysed in the street. He was taken to hospital and died there a few weeks later.[10]

In some ways Kierkegaard's situation was a typically modern one. He was not compelled by external events to take the course he did and to trust himself wholly to God; he made his own decision. In the past there have been all sorts of threats to life and well-being. People turned to God because that is all they could do. It may have been in real trust or it may have been as a last resort. Today in many parts of the world such situations have been done away with. Disease can be prevented by good hygiene and inoculations and cured by modern drugs and operations. Anxiety and many mental disorders can be relieved by drugs and psychotherapy. Damage to property can be guarded against by insurance. Unemployment and disability do not lead to starvation. Life is pretty well under our control and that is how it should be. Yet even in ordinary life situations arise that call for obedience and trust. And there are occasions when the call comes to do something out of the ordinary. It may be to go against every consideration of personal safety and well-being in reliance on God alone. In this century there have been many occasions when that is what loyalty and courage demanded. Sometimes it has been to resist the claims of authoritarian governments; sometimes it has been to serve the poor and the politically oppressed. There is no reason to think that such action will be called for less often in future years in this dangerous modern world.

References

1. *The Will to Believe,* 1897, paperback ed. New York, 1956.
2. B. Williams, *Problems of the Self,* Cambridge, 1973, paperback ed. p. 137.

3. A Short Exposition of the Decalogue, the Apostles' Creed and the Lord's Prayer, 1520, in *Reformation Writings of Martin Luther*, ed. B.L. Woolf, Vol. I, London, 1952, p. 83.

4. E.D. Starbuck, *The Psychology of Religion*, London, 1900, pp. 355ff.

5. Gordon Rupp, *The Righteousness of God*, London, 1953, p. 214.

6. The Pagan Servitude of the Church, in *Reformation Writings of Martin Luther*, Vol. I, p. 234.

7. *The Varieties of Religious Experience*, 1902 (1943 ed.) p. 340.

8. *Fear and Trembling*, 1843, E.T. Princeton, 1945, p. 25.

9. G. Malantschuk, in *Armed Neutrality and an Open Letter*, by S. Kierkegaard, ed. H.V. and E.H. Hong, Bloomington, 1968, p. 142.

10. W. Lowrie, *A Short Life of Kierkegaard*, Princeton, 1942, paperback ed. p. 189.